Steve Sturdy

Wellcome Unit for the
History of Medicine.
Manchester University
April 1991

ROCKEFELLER MEDICINE MEN

Rockefeller Medicine Men

Medicine and Capitalism in America

E. Richard Brown

University of California Press, Berkeley, Los Angeles, London

University of California Press
Berkeley and Los Angeles, California

University of California Press, Ltd.
London, England

Copyright © 1979 by
The Regents of the University of California

First Paperback Printing 1980
ISBN 0–520–04269–7
Library of Congress Catalog Card Number: 78–65461
Printed in the United States of America

2 3 4 5 6 7 8 9

To Marianne, Delia, and Adrienne

Contents

Preface

WHEN *Rockefeller Medicine Men* was first published in 1979, it proved to be a controversial work. In reviewing histories of medicine from 1962 to 1982, Ronald L. Numbers called it "the most controversial medical history of the past decade."[1] This reprinting of the book provides an opportunity to respond to some of the book's critics as part of a continuing dialogue about the issues it raises.

Part of the controversy generated by the book comes from its social-historical approach to medicine. The growing body of social histories of health care challenges the "great physician" perspective that for so long has dominated the history of medicine.[2] Some are dismayed by this new approach to health care, particularly when it involves a critical examination of the broader social, economic, and political contexts of medicine and health-related developments.[3] Indeed, "heroic physicians and medical milestones,"[4] whether innovative teachers of clinical practice or breakthrough discoveries by brilliant researchers, do have a profound effect on the development of medicine's technical knowledge and practice. But the history of medicine, like the history of any other social phenomenon, is more than an intellectual history. The actions of men and women, including leaders and the masses of people who follow and participate in professions and social movements, are shaped by economic, political, and social forces as well as by ideas. Ideas themselves develop in a broader context, which they shape but which also shape them.

Perhaps the most substantive and influential criticism has come from Paul Starr, who devoted two pages of his own history of American medicine to critiquing my interpretation of the role of the Rockefeller foundation and the corporate class in the development of American medicine.[5] Starr argues that the character and power of American medicine is a product of its "cultural authority" as well as of the political power it mobilized. He attributes prime importance to American medicine's overcoming its lack of technical credibility with the public, both the well-educated strata and the poorer classes, in the late nineteenth century. He believes that somehow medicine won cultural authority, by which its "definitions of reality and judgments of meaning and value [prevailed] as valid and true," and that this authority permitted the profession to wield sufficient political power to protect and extend its social and economic interests.[6]

It should be noted that Starr's thesis concerning the role of cultural authority is similar to my argument in Chapter 2 concerning the role of scientific medicine in elevating the status and power of the medical profession. I argue that by embracing science the medical profession gained not only more effective techniques, but also technical credibility beyond the actual medical value of contemporary scientific progress in medicine—a credibility that enhanced the profession's legitimacy in a world increasingly dominated by industrialization and technology. Technical credibility and social legitimacy were important weapons in the efforts of the profession's leaders to lift medicine from the ignominious position it occupied throughout most of the nineteenth century. I characterize scientific medicine as providing an ideological tool to leaders of the medical profession in their campaign to elevate medicine. Starr sees the medical profession as gaining cultural authority because of a belief in its broad technical competence that spread among the populace in ill-defined ways. Both accounts give considerable weight to this belief in creating a base of popular support for the profession's increased economic and social power. However, my analysis focuses on the conscious actions of the profession's leaders to take advantage of this spreading legitimacy, while Starr's analysis remains more ambiguous about how this cultural authority was actually translated into the power to elevate the profession.

Starr and I also differ on the role of powerful groups outside the profession in transforming American medicine. In Chapter 3 I argue that, although medicine's newfound credibility was growing in many public sectors, one of the most important sources of support was among leading institutions of the corporate class. Individual philanthropists gave modest sums to build community hospitals, but the foundations created by corporate giants *as* philanthropists provided hefty grants to build medical schools, research laboratories, and teaching hospitals. Although Starr acknowledges their role, he implicitly reduces the importance of their contribution without presenting clear evidence in support of his interpretation. Starr parts company with my analysis on the question of *why* the leaders of these foundations, and of the Rockefeller philanthropies in particular, so generously supported the development of medical science, reform in medical education, and public health.

Let me first describe Starr's account of my views, for therein lies part of the problem with his critique. Despite his eloquent prose, Starr creates a caricature of my argument. He claims I contend that "capitalists personally exercised control over the development of medicine through the foundations they established." [7] Noting that I argue that Rockefeller philanthropy officers saw great value in medicine's cultural role as a subtle purveyor of the dominant ideology, Starr adds sarcastically, that "one must, I suppose, have a deep appreciation of the fragility of capitalism to imagine that it might have been threatened by the persistence of homeopathy." [8] But as the reader of this book will soon observe, Starr misrepresents my position. I show that foundation programs were developed and directed not by John D. Rockefeller, Sr., and Andrew Carnegie, the men of wealth who created the foundations, but rather by foundation officers, acting as managers of philanthropy, rather like the managers of Rockefeller's and Carnegie's industrial empires but with somewhat more authority. It was the Reverend Frederick T. Gates (not Rockefeller, his employer) who, both as a manager of Rockefeller's wealth and as chief architect of the Rockefeller medical philanthropies, articulated the role that medicine might play in shaping society. And it was Gates and other officers who developed the strategies by which the foundations might shape medicine.

Although the Rockefeller philanthropy governing board later did fear for the continued existence of wealth and even capitalism,[9] Gates was motivated by a desire for social improvement—not by fear—at the turn of the century, when he was leading the development of the Rockefeller Institute for Medical Research. As the archival record demonstrates, he was concerned with improving the health of human resources (the workforce) and with extending industrial culture and the ideological perspective of capitalism to those in the United States and abroad who did not share them. For Gates, medicine could improve the health and productivity of workforces and populations if it was scientifically based and emphasized prevention as well as cure. And it was an especially good vehicle for cultural transfer because medicine is "a work which penetrates everywhere." [10]

My interpretation of Gates's views does not rest on "the fragility of capitalism," as Starr suggests. Rather, Gates was an exponent and ardent advocate of the social value of medicine for improving and strengthening corporate capitalism. These views and goals that Gates articulated, often with great passion, shaped the Rockefeller medical philanthropies' early strategies for improving health and well-being in ways described in Chapter 3. And the Rockefeller programmatic strategies were trendsetters for other foundations as well. Although he provides no evidence, Starr attributes the Rockefeller largess to medical research and education in the interest of philanthropists "in legitimating their wealth and power by publicly demonstrating their moral responsibility in ways congruent with the cultural standards of an age that increasingly revered science." [11] This is a popular rationale propounded by authorized Rockefeller biographies and foundation histories, but it has little support in the archival record I found.

In his account of the reform of medical education Starr emphasizes historical developments and the growing cultural authority of the medical profession and downplays the explicit leadership role of the Rockefeller and Carnegie philanthropies. He implicitly takes issue with the weight given by myself and others [12] to the role of the Rockefeller philanthropies in educational reform, although he neither critically examines our evidence nor provides support for his alternative perspective. In my view, Starr even diminishes the importance of specific leaders within the American Medical Association, instead describing institutional changes devoid of the political dynamics that actually bring about these changes. Although acknowledging the role of political power, Starr describes a diffuse political process based on the profession's growing credibility. For example, in his account the AMA's Council on Medical Education appears a natural outgrowth of efforts to improve medical education. This progression begins with the reforms at Harvard by university president Charles W. Eliot in 1870, continues with the founding of the forerunner of the Association of American Medical Colleges in 1890 and the opening of the Johns Hopkins medical school in 1893, and extends to the reforms of the new century. In Starr's narrative, only certain people stand out as doing battle in this process, particularly Eliot, who forced reforms on some of Harvard's reluctant medical faculty, and individual practitioners whose oxen were gored by the reforms.

Starr ignores the role of Arthur Dean Bevan (the combative and wily chair of the AMA's Council on Medical Education), the relationship between Bevan and Henry S. Pritchett (president of the Carnegie Foundation) and Abraham Flexner (author of the famous Carnegie study of medical schools), and the important role of Frederick Gates in directing the Rockefeller involvement in the reform and development of medical education. Bevan was the chief strategist in the AMA's efforts to reform medical education in order to improve the training of physicians *and* to reduce their numbers and raise their social status and income. He consciously sought the legitimacy that the Carnegie Foundation could provide to the profession's efforts (a transfer of cultural authority, if you like), hoping that such legitimacy would then guide the philanthropy of wealthy men and women who might provide the funds needed for medical education reform. Pritchett complied with Bevan's request that the foundation conduct a "no holds barred" critique of American and Canadian medical schools, even keeping secret the foundation's close relationship with the AMA.

Gates hired Flexner to run the Rockefeller philanthropies' medical education program that provided princely sums for the reform of medical education. Gates supported the profession's reform efforts—but with a twist. He insisted that all recipient institutions adopt the strict full-time policy for clinical faculty, making this policy the cornerstone of the Rockefeller philanthropies' prodigious funding of reform. Gates was adamant about this policy because he saw it as a way to bring the medical profession to heel, forcing it to serve the needs of all society rather than the profession's own narrower self-interest. Gates believed that "commercialism" in the medical profession "confines the benefits of the science too largely to the rich, when it is the rightful inheritance of all the people alike, and the public health requires they have it." But, as I show in Chapter 3, Gates's primary concerns were to improve the productivity of workers in the United States and those in other lands and to inculcate acceptance of industrial capitalism and, in particular, the prevailing social order in the first quarter of this century. Gates was a leading member of the corporate class, and he unequivocally believed that he was furthering the interests he shared with other members of that class.

Other foundations have continued up to the present to pursue Gates's goal of rationalizing American medicine so that it might better meet the needs of the larger society rather than being dominated by narrow interest groups within the profession. But unlike many foundation directors in recent years, Gates was willing to go to war with the profession, using the enormous endowment of the Rockefeller philanthropies as his artillery to pound the medical school turf in clinical departments that had been staked out by medical practitioners. As I argue in Chapter 4, Gates ultimately lost this battle, and the foundation has been tamer ever since in its efforts to rationalize medicine.[13]

Because of these omissions and the corresponding emphasis on the profession's cultural authority, Starr's book conveys an impression of a natural progression rather than a series of gains and losses by groups and individual leaders, often involving hard-fought battles over economic and status interests as well as differing ideas. Certainly the spreading and deepening political and social receptivity of the public to developments based on science, or at least associated with science, was an important basis for the reform and elevation of medicine. But these beliefs provided only a necessary base of support. The driving force, in my view, was the political and economic power secured by the medical profession's leaders on behalf of their very conscious campaign. And one of the most important sources of this power was an alliance—at times strong, at other times weak—with some of the wealthiest and most influential agencies of corporate capitalism, the foundations established by the foremost captains of industry and run by occasionally visionary managers.

Foundations today play a less significant role in shaping the health care system in the United States than they did from the turn of the century to the 1930s. In part, this lesser role is due to the growth of the health sector in the economy, the financial role in that sector of private insurance and government programs, and the relatively small resources available to foundations. In 1983, foundation spending accounted for just 0.2 percent of total national health expenditures. Foundations provided $712 million for domestic health-related grants in that year, a substantial decline in real (inflation-adjusted) dollars from the 1975 level.[14]

The approach of major foundations, like the Robert Wood Johnson Foundation, is explicitly cautious. Eli Ginzberg has identified a number of important challenges in health policy and organization that foundations have avoided taking up, preferring instead to shape the system at the margins and to refrain from challenging either government or established interest groups within the health system. For example, although foundations have supported demonstration projects to improve ambulatory care services to middle-class and poor patients, no foundation has critically assessed the dominance and centrality of the hospital in the health care delivery system (despite the fact that hospitals consume 40 percent of total health expenditures); and although some foundations are exploring small-scale approaches to providing coverage for the nearly 40 million Americans who lack any health insurance protection, none has supported assessments of the possible gains that may be realized by revamping our pluralistic health care financing system into a national health insurance program.[15]

Alternative foundation grants and studies along these lines might challenge the medical profession, the hospital industry, the insurance industry, and some government policymakers, resulting in controversy, political conflicts, and public scrutiny—all contrary to the operating principles of philanthropic foundations. Despite the fact that foundations seem to share with Frederick Gates a strong interest in rationalizing health care and supporting the development of biomedical research, they now appear timid compared to Gates's often contentious approach. Nevertheless, these contemporary patterns cannot be fully comprehended without studying their roots in the history of the leading foundations and their leaders who helped shape our present health care system and institutions.

NOTES

1. Ronald L. Numbers, "The History of American Medicine: A Field in Ferment," *Reviews in American History* 10 (1982), 245–63.
2. For a lucid discussion of this conflict, appropriately set in the history of the field, see Susan Reverby and David Rosner, "Beyond 'the Great Doctors,'" in Reverby and Rosner, eds., *Health Care in America: Essays in Social History* (Philadelphia: Temple University Press, 1979), pp. 3–16. Numbers, "History of American Medicine," includes a brief discussion of the subject from a different point of view.
3. See, for example, Lloyd G. Stevenson, "A Second Opinion," *Bulletin of the History of Medicine,* 54 (1980), 134–40, written by the editor because he disagreed with a favorable review.
4. Numbers, "History of American Medicine."
5. Paul Starr, *The Social Transformation of American Medicine* (New York: Basic Books, 1982), pp. 227–29.
6. Starr, *Social Transformation*, pp. 13–24.
7. Starr, *Social Transformation*, p. 227.
8. Ibid.
9. See pp. 130–32 and 167–71 of this book.
10. See p. 122 of this book.
11. Starr, *Social Transformation*, p. 122. Also see his comments about an article by Howard S. Berliner, "A Larger Perspective on the Flexner Report," *International Journal of Health Services,* 5 (1975), 573–92.
12. Howard S. Berliner, *A System of Scientific Medicine: Philanthropic Foundations in the Flexner Era* (New York: Tavistock, 1985).
13. On Bevan and the Carnegie Foundation, see pp. 138–52 of this book; on Gates, the Rockefeller philanthropies, and the full-time plan, see pp. 155–76. For Starr's view, see pp. 112–23 of his book.
14. Betty L. Dooley, "Patterns in Foundation Health Giving," *Health Affairs,* 6 (1987), 144–56.
15. Eli Ginzberg, "Foundations and the Nation's Health Agenda," *Health Affairs,* 6 (1987), 128–40. For additional evidence of Ginzberg's argument, see also Jeffrey C. Merrill and Stephen A. Somers, "The Changing Health Care System: A Challenge for Foundations," *Inquiry,* 23 (1986), 316–21, and Jane Stein, "Health Care Foundations Take Long-Range View, says Aiken," *Business and Health,* 2 (October 1985), 46–49.

Acknowledgments

THE idea for this book grew out of my teaching about the political economy of health care. My students and I asked how the present system came to be. The search for answers led me to histories of medicine, published materials in journals of the period, and the archival files of the Rockefeller and Carnegie philanthropies. The archives provided a rich record of the thoughts, policies, and actions of some of the most influential persons in the history of American medicine.

The search culminated in this book. But the book would not have been possible without the generous help, enthusiastic interest, and personal support of many people. I am especially grateful to Howard Waitzkin, William Kornhauser, Barbara Ehrenreich, Gert Brieger, and Michael Pincus, all of whom gave me detailed and thoughtful criticisms on major portions of the manuscript together with great encouragement. I also received helpful criticism and support from Anne Johnson, Jon Garfield, Charlene Harrington, Barbara Waterman, James O'Connor, Dan Feshbach, Ivan Illich, David Horowitz, June Fisher, Kathryn Johnson, Jack London, Jane Grant, Tom Bodenheimer, Sara McIntire, Joe Selby, Larry Sirott, and Myrna Cozen. Howard Berliner has been an exceptional colleague, sharing ideas and material in a cooperative effort to understand these sparsely studied issues.

Marianne Parker Brown, my wife, gave me continuing encouragement and intellectual criticism and support, even when the burdens of family and household fell disproportionately on her shoulders. My daughters, Delia and Adrienne, were understanding beyond their years while their father was "working on his book."

The staffs of the Rockefeller Foundation Archives and the Rockefeller Family Archives (now combined in the Rockefeller Archive Center) and the Carnegie Foundation for the Advancement of Teaching were very helpful in providing convenient working facilities and making my research in New York excitingly productive. The staffs of the Health Sciences Information Service and the Library Delivery Service at the University of California saved me innumerable hours of retrieving books and journals from the far-flung libraries on the Berkeley campus.

Eva Scipio, Ruth McKeeter, and Sandra Golvin skillfully typed portions of the manuscript in its various phases. Estelle Jelinek carefully and thoughtfully copy edited the final manuscript.

Much of the research for the last chapter was done while I was a consultant to the Childhood and Government Project at the University of California Law School. The Health and Medical Sciences Program, also at Berkeley, helped defray the costs of my research trip to the archives in New York.

The Rockefeller Archive Center and the Carnegie Foundation for the Advancement of Teaching kindly gave me permission to publish excerpts from their files.

Introduction

THE crisis in today's health care system is deeply rooted in the interwoven history of modern medicine and corporate capitalism. The major groups and forces that shaped the medical system sowed the seeds of the crisis we now face. The medical profession and other medical interest groups each tried to make medicine serve their own narrow economic and social interests. Foundations and other corporate class institutions insisted that medicine serve the needs of "their" corporate capitalist society. The dialectic of their common efforts and their clashes, and the economic and political forces set in motion by their actions, shaped the system as it grew. Out of this history emerged a medical system that poorly serves society's health needs.

The system's most obvious problems are the cost, inflation, and inaccessibility of medical care in the United States. Total health expenditures in this country topped $200 billion in 1979, nearly $1,000 for every woman, man, and child. Far more of society's resources now go into medical expenditures than ever before; twice the portion of the Gross National Product was spent on medical care in 1980 than in 1950.

We pay for these costs through our taxes, health insurance premiums, and directly out of our pockets. Public expenditures—four out of every ten dollars spent on personal health services—come out of our taxes. Private health insurance and direct out-of-pocket payments each account for about three out of every ten dollars. No matter what form it takes, the entire $200 billion originates in the labor of men and women in the society. President Carter estimated that the average American worker works one month each year just to pay the costs of the medical system.[1]

Most people feel they should be getting a lot for this money, but instead they find that it is difficult even to get the care they need. Primary care physicians—general practitioners, pediatricians, internists, and gynecologists—are scarce. Doctors and hospitals are clustered in the "better" parts of our cities and largely absent from the poorer sections and rural areas of our country. For the millions of Americans covered by Medicaid (the government subsidy program for the public assistance-linked poor), the coverage has been as sparse and degrading as the demeaning clinics it was supposed to replace. The middle class and the poor share at least long waiting periods for doctors, one of the most common constraints on the accessibility of physicians. Instead of creating a humane and accessible medical care system, Medicare and Medicaid have helped fuel inflation in medical costs by dumping new funds into a privately controlled system ready to absorb every penny into expansion, technology, high salaries, and profits.

A second, somewhat less widely discussed, problem is the relatively small impact medical care makes on the population's health status. Despite a plethora of new diagnostic procedures, drugs, and surgical techniques, we are not as healthy as we believed these medical wonders would make us. Some critics, like social philosopher Ivan Illich,[2] accuse medicine of making us sicker—physically, politically, and culturally—than we would be without it. Many analysts have documented the medical profession's social control functions, medical technology's frequently adverse effects on our health, and medicine's neglect of important physical and social environmental influences on our health.[3] Instead of medicine liberating us from the suffering and dependency of illness, we find that its oppressive elements have grown at least as rapidly as its technical achievements.

Why has medical care grown so costly so rapidly? Why is it so plentiful and yet so inaccessible? How did medicine become technically so sophisticated but remain socially unconcerned and even repressive?

A popular but too facile answer is that such problems are characteristic of technology and industrialized societies. According to this argument, technology and industrialization impose their own limits on forms of social organization and produce similar kinds of problems that call forth similar solutions. Medical sociologist David Mechanic finds problems of cost, organization, and ethical dilemmas in medicine widespread among industrialized countries and concludes that "the demands of medical technology and the growth of the science base of medical activity produce pressures toward common organizational solutions despite strong ideological differences."[4] Illich asserts that "pathogenic medicine is the result of industrial overproduction."[5] In this view, technology has a life of its own, imposing its imperatives on individuals and social organization. By focusing on widespread patterns of industrial organization and technological development, these analysts conclude that technology and industrialization are universal determining forces.

Such technological determinism ignores the particular history in which society and technology interact. In the Marxian view, technology and economic organization constantly shape each other in a dialectical process. Individuals and groups who own the resources and control the organization of production, far from being at the mercy of "neutral" technology, introduce innovations that serve their own ends and oppose those that would serve other interests than their own. These innovations may neglect broader community needs and may hurt the interests of others. Machines and factories undermined the autonomy and even the economic existence of independent craft workers. Hospitals and their expensive equipment may tie many health workers to monotonous jobs and use funds that might otherwise go for more widely distributed community clinics. Those affected by these technological developments may resist them and force their modification. Workers may organize into unions and gain some control over the relations of production. Communities may organize to block hospital expansion and force development of more community-based clinics. In sum, the political-economic organization of society generates certain types of technological innovation and not others, and these innovations generate new social forces that modify technology and political-economic relations.[6]

This book sees scientific, technological medicine not as the determining force in the development of modern health care but as a tool developed by members of the medical profession and the corporate class to serve their perceived needs. Individuals and groups who possess needed resources can apply them to develop certain types of technological innovation in medicine. Those who have the requisite resources can also apply the resulting technological innovation to serve their economic and social needs.

In the United States medicine came of age during the same period that corporations grew to dominate the larger economy. As corporate capitalism developed, it altered many institutions in the society, medicine among them. Its influence was created not simply through cultural assimilation or the demands of industrial organization but by persons who acted in its behalf. This interpretation does not suggest that history is made by dark conspiracies. Rather, it argues that the class that disproportionately owns, directs, and profits from the dominant economic system will disproportionately influence other spheres of social relations as well.

Members of the corporate class, including those who own substantial shares of corporate wealth as well as the top managers of major corporate institutions, naturally try to ensure the survival of capitalist society and their own positions in its social structure. In the case of medicine, members of the corporate class, acting mainly through philanthropic foundations, articulated a strategy for developing a medical system to meet the needs of capitalist society. They believed their goals for medicine would benefit the society as a whole, just as they believed that the private accumulation of wealth and private decisions about how to use that wealth and its income were in the best interests of society. In this book, we will examine the strategies they developed during the Progressive era and the reasons for their actions, leaning heavily on the public and private thoughts of some persons centrally involved in these efforts. We will describe and analyze the interests and strategies of the medical profession and of the corporate class as they developed independently, coalesced, and then clashed. We will also see that the government has increasingly taken over the strategies and struggles begun by the corporate class.

The corporate class influenced medicine, but it could not control it absolutely. The market system in medical care provides special interest groups—today including doctors, hospitals, insurance companies, drug companies, and medical supply and equipment companies—with the opportunity to develop their own bases of economic power, enabling them to carve out and defend their turfs in the marketplace. The larger business class stands "above" these interest groups, trying to tame and coordinate the leviathan but nonetheless committed to private ownership and control and also enjoying medicine's legitimizing and cultural functions. The relationships and the contradictions that emerged among the corporate class and these medical interest groups profoundly influenced the organization and content of today's medical system.

DOCTORS

From our vantage point today it is difficult to believe that in the late nineteenth century the medical profession lacked power, wealth, and status. Medicine at that time was pluralistic in its theories of disease, technically ineffective in preventing or curing sickness, and divided into several warring sects. Existing professional organizations had virtually no control over the entry of new doctors into the field. Physicians as a group were merely scattered members of the lower professional stratum, earning from several hundred to several thousand dollars a year and having no special status within the population.

By the 1930s, however, medicine was firmly in the hands of an organized profession that controlled entry into the field through licensure and accreditation of medical schools and teaching hospitals. The profession also controlled the practice and economics of medicine through local medical societies. "Medicine" had come to mean the field of clinical practice by graduates of schools that followed the scientific, clinical, and research orientations laid down by the American Medical Association (AMA) and by Abraham Flexner in a famous report for the Carnegie Foundation. All other healers were being excluded from practice. Physicians were increasingly drawn only from the middle and upper classes. The median net income for nonsalaried physicians in 1929 was $3,758, above the average for college teachers but below the faculty at Yale University and below the average for mechanical engineers.[7] Overall, doctors were rapidly rising in income, power, and status among all occupational groups.

In the 1970s physicians have continued to climb to the top

rungs of America's class structure. The median net income of office-based physicians—$63,000 in 1976—places them in the top few percentiles of society's income structure. In 1939 the average earnings of doctors were two and a half times as great as those of other full-time workers, but by 1976 the gap had increased to *five* and a half times. Doctors rank with Supreme Court justices at the top of the occupational status hierarchy. And in recent public opinion polls, more Americans said they trusted the medical profession than any other American institution—including higher education, government (of course), and organized religion.[8]

Rising "productivity" has been an important factor in physicians' efforts to raise their incomes, status, and power. The medical profession has drastically controlled the production of new physicians and has delegated to technicians and paraprofessionals below them the tasks they no longer find interesting or profitable. With rapidly expanding medical technology, more and more tasks were shifted down the line to a burgeoning health work force. At the beginning of this century two out of every three health workers were physicians. Of the more than 4.7 million health workers today, only one in twelve is a physician. Thus, doctors have increasingly become the managers of patient care rather than the direct providers of it.[9]

As medical managers, physicians have found themselves drawn out of private practice into employment in hospitals, research, teaching, government, and other institutions. Today four in ten doctors are employed in such institutions, compared with one in ten in 1931. These physicians have had fewer material interests in common with private practitioners and have shown little political support for the AMA.[10]

Physicians entered a struggle to maintain their position at the top of the medical hierarchy soon after that position was won. The challenge has not, for the most part, come from below, except for recent attempts by nurses to increase their authority in patient care. Doctors have found themselves in a struggle with hospitals, insurance companies, medical schools, foundations, government health agencies, and other groups with an interest in a more *rationalized* health system—one in which the parts are more coordinated hierarchically and horizontally and in which more emphasis is given to capital-intensive services. The conflict has emerged between organized practitioners as one interest group, what Robert Alford calls "professional monopolizers," and all the groups seeking to systematize health care according to bureaucratic and business principles of organization, what Alford calls "corporate rationalizers."[11]

OTHER INTEREST GROUPS

In challenging the power of organized medicine to protect its interests, hospitals, particularly through the American Hospital Association (AHA), have tried to appear the "logical center" of any rationalized health system.[12] In their transformation and growth from asylums for the sick and dying poor to their twentieth-century role as the physician's workshop, hospitals developed a powerful position in modern health care as the major locus of medical technology. Because of physicians' growing reliance on technology, hospitals were absorbing an increasing share of dollars spent on medical care. Public and private health insurance (really, medical care insurance) developed as a stable source of income, enabling hospitals to expand their facilities. Collectively, hospitals have become a major force in the medical system, consuming 40 percent of the nation's annual health care expenditures. Blue Cross and Blue Shield (the "Blues"), created in the 1930s and 1940s by hospital associations and medical societies, respectively, together with commercial insurance companies now control 30 percent of medical care expenditures, mostly emphasizing hospital-based technical care. They have developed economic and political clout commensurate with their dominating fiscal role.

While the insurance industry is a new voice in the chorus of corporate rationalizers, medical schools have been in the vanguard for more than half a century. Although run by physicians —for the reproduction of health professionals and as the research and development arm of the medical industry—medical school interests have often conflicted with the interests of practitioner-dominated medical societies. In the nineteenth century, medical schools were generally run by small groups of doctors for their own financial benefit. During most of the twentieth century, medical schools have been university-controlled and responsive to the interests of foundations and, since World War II, government funding sources. For the brief period from about

1900 to World War I, science-oriented medical schools and the AMA joined forces to press for the acceptance of scientific medicine. Since that time they have gone their separate ways—the AMA struggling to preserve the dominance and incomes of private practitioners, and medical schools fostering more rationalized medical care, usually with physicians as top management.

Hospitals, insurance companies, and medical schools all have a relatively greater interest than doctors in promoting capital-intensive, rationalized medical care. While expanding medical technology helped doctors increase their status and incomes, it has been the raison d'être of hospitals, medical schools, and even insurance companies. Medical technology's demands for heavy capital investment also encourage rationalization of medical resources—centralization and coordination of capital, facilities, expenditures, income, and personnel.

FOUNDATIONS AND THE STATE

Besides these interest groups, two other forces—the government and foundations—have exerted a powerful influence in favor of rationalizing medical care. Although the government has been the dominant influence since World War II, foundations were the major external influence on American medicine in its formative period from 1900 to 1930. Their source of power has been the purse, generously but carefully applied to specific programs and policies. Neither foundations nor the government has operated as an interest group in the manner of doctors, hospitals, insurance companies, medical schools, and the drug and hospital supply industries. The enormous sums they expended —from foundations some $300 million from 1910 through the 1930s and from the federal government many billions of dollars since World War II, for medical research and education alone— have not been for their own financial enrichment.

The argument developed and supported in this book suggests that both foundation policy and government policy have served the interests of certain medical groups but only because the interests of these groups coincided with those of the larger corporate class. As evidence from the historical record will show, the programs of foundations earlier in this century were explicitly intended to develop and strengthen institutions that would extend the reach and tighten the grasp of capitalism throughout the society.

In medicine the major objectives of foundations were: to develop a system of medicine that would be supportive of capitalist society; and to rationalize medical care to make it accessible to those whom it was supposed to reach but at the least cost to society's resources. These objectives created their own contradictions. At first, foundations aligned themselves with the aims and strategies of the medical profession, but they soon rejected the narrow interests the profession wished to serve and moved quickly to expand the roles of medical schools and hospitals and to support their dominance over all medical care. By World War II, when the role of the State* in governing the capitalist economy was fully established, the federal government took over the foundations' leading role in medicine, continuing the basic strategy adopted by the foundations more than two decades earlier and opening the floodgates of the treasury to implement it.

In the first chapter, we will see how philanthropic foundations emerged from several parallel developments of capitalist society in the latter nineteenth century. While many members of the new wealthy class were supporting charities to ameliorate the disruptions and deprivations imposed on large numbers of people by capitalist industrialization, others recognized the need for technically trained professionals and managers and supported the development of universities and professional science. Just after the turn of the century men of great wealth, like John D. Rockefeller and Andrew Carnegie, created philanthropic foundations with professional managers in charge of their charitable fortunes. With the Rockefeller philanthropies in the lead, these foundations developed strategic programs to legitimize the fundamental social structure of capitalist society and to provide for its technical needs.

Chapter 2 traces the social and economic role of scientific medicine in the history of the American medical profession.

---

*Throughout this book, capitalized "State" refers to the political institutions and agencies of government which embody society's political authority. Uncapitalized "state" refers to the individual states in the United States.

Modern scientific medicine was not merely a "natural" outcome of combining science and medicine in the nineteenth century. Apart from the concrete scientific developments that permitted the application of scientific thought and investigation to problems of disease, scientific medicine had equally important social and economic origins. It was an essential part of a strategy articulated by reform leaders of the medical profession to enhance the profession's position in society, and it succeeded because it won the support of dominant segments of the American class structure.

Scientific medicine gained the support of the American medical profession in the late nineteenth century because it met the economic and social needs of physicians. By giving doctors greater technical credibility in society, it saved them from the ignominious position to which the profession had sunk. Moreover, scientific medicine became an ideological tool by which the dominant "regular" segment of the profession restricted the production of new doctors, overcame other medical sects, temporarily united leading medical school faculty and practitioners, and otherwise reduced competition.

Despite its appeal for the medical profession, scientific medicine would have accomplished little for doctors if it had not had the support of dominant groups in American society. In Chapter 3 we will see the reasons for this capitalist support, especially through the thinking of Frederick T. Gates, for more than two decades the chief philanthropic and financial lieutenant to John D. Rockefeller and the architect of the major Rockefeller medical philanthropies.

As an explanation of the causes, prevention, and cure of disease that was strikingly similar to the world view of industrial capitalism, scientific medicine won the support of the classes associated with the rise of corporate capitalism in America. Capitalists and corporate managers believed that scientific medicine would improve the health of society's work force and thereby increase productivity. They also embraced scientific medicine as an ideological weapon in their struggle to formulate a new culture appropriate to and supportive of industrial capitalism. They were drawn to the profession's formulation of medical theory and practice that exonerated capitalism's vast inequities and its reckless practices that shortened the lives of members of the working class. Thus, scientific medicine served the interests of both the dominant medical profession and the corporate class in the United States.

Nevertheless, a contradiction emerged between the interests of the medical profession and those of the corporate class. As we will see in Chapter 4, the private practice profession and the corporate class clashed over attempts to reform medical education. The financing of scientific medical schools required tremendous amounts of capital from outside the medical profession. Those who provided the capital had the leverage to impose policy. The lines of the conflict were clearly drawn: Was medical education to be controlled by and to serve the needs of medical practitioners? Or was it to serve the broader needs of capitalist society and be controlled by corporate class institutions?

The Flexner report, sponsored by the Carnegie Foundation, tried to unify these interests by centering its attack on crassly commercial medical schools. However, the Rockefeller philanthropies, substantially directed by Gates, exposed the contradiction by forcing a full-time clinical faculty system on recipient schools against the interests and arguments of private practitioners. Gates made it clear that medicine must serve capitalist society and be controlled—through the medical schools that reproduce its professional personnel and innovate its technique —by capitalist foundations and capitalist universities. By 1929 one Rockefeller foundation, the General Education Board, had itself appropriated more than $78 million to medical schools to implement this strategy, and Gates' perspective was firmly established.

Gates was adamant about keeping his strategy free of involvement with the State by not giving money to state university medical schools. However, within the Rockefeller philanthropies as within the largest industrial and financial corporations generally, most officers and directors had come to see the State as a necessary aid in rationalizing industries, markets, and institutions.

The course that Gates and his contemporaries initiated continued to develop during the next half-century, but with the State assuming the dominant financial and political role in rationalizing medical care and developing medical technology. As we will see in Chapter 5, the State's emphasis on technological medicine ignored some of the most important determinants of disease and death while the economic and political forces of capitalist society assured that rationalization would not eliminate the developing corporate ownership and control over the medical market. How medicine will be contained and rationalized in this private market system is a contradiction that now plagues the State and the corporate class as the demand for national health insurance grows. How medical resources can be transformed into effective instruments for improving the population's health is a contradiction imposed on the entire society. These contradictions and their resulting crises are the legacy of medicine's development in capitalist society.

"Wholesale Philanthropy ": From Charity to Social Transformation

INDUSTRIALIZATION in nineteenth-century America created many problems for those who owned and managed the corporations that came to dominate the economy. Industrial capitalists had to arrange for adequate capital, obtain raw materials, organize production, discipline a reluctant work force, and develop markets and transportation systems. They also had to deal with the political structures and methods intended for older relations of production, centered around agriculture and commerce, that were only slowly adapting to the new industrial, corporate order. Finally, they had to reshape older social institutions or create new ones. Educational, religious, medical, and cultural institutions were some of the glue that held together the *ancien régime*. In sum, the new corporate class had to transform all these economic, political, and social institutions to serve their urbanized, industrialized, and corporate society.

The new economic order created different problems for classes that owned little or nothing of the new system. American society had never been tranquil, but industrialization spread deep disaffection and anger among classes who were dislocated by it and among those who suffered as a result of capitalist accumulation of wealth. The agrarian and merchant rulers of the formerly dominant towns resented the meteoric rise of urban industrialists and bankers. Native craftsmen, foreign immigrants, and dispossessed farmers reluctantly submitted to the factory system. Unionism, populism, and socialism threatened the power and wealth of corporations and even raised doubts about the continued existence of capitalism.

As we will see in this chapter, corporate capitalists turned to philanthropy, the universities, and then to medicine to solve some of the many problems that grew out of capitalist industrialization. For the most part, social transformations were led by the same "unseen hand" that guided the market forces of capitalism; this self-interest provided a limited perspective for social change. Only gradually did leading capitalists and their allies consciously develop broad strategies and supports for the new order they were building. Philanthropic capitalists supported often harsh but hopefully ameliorative charity to control the desperate poorer classes. Others began building universities to meet the new society's needs for trained experts and managers. A new managerial and professional stratum developed to direct corporations, universities, science, medical institutions, and philanthropy itself. After the turn of the century, some philanthropists transformed foundations into a truly corporate philanthropy,* modeled after the dominant economic institutions and fueled with their "surplus" wealth. Representatives of the emerging corporate liberalism made these foundations their chief instruments for transforming social institutions, giving corporate philanthropy an historical role beyond the most visionary dreams of early philanthropic capitalists. This union of corporate philanthropy, the managerial-professional stratum, and the universities and science spawned the Rockefeller medicine men and their new system of medicine.

CREATING PRIVATE FORTUNES AND SOCIAL DISCONTENT

The Civil War was a watershed in American philanthropy, as it was in nearly all aspects of American life. It was a great wrenching experience in American history, spreading death and destruction, stimulating industrial development, and producing

*In this book, "corporate philanthropy" refers to philanthropy characteristic of corporate capitalism, especially foundations that are philanthropic corporations controlled by members of the corporate class.

upheavals within and between all classes of Americans. A new kind of philanthropy, tailored to these new conditions, emerged in the decades following the war.

The Civil War not only freed the black slaves from legal bonds of slavery. It also freed the hand of Northern capital to extend throughout the nation the industrial transformation it had begun mainly north of the Ohio River. As the "underground railroad" was the vehicle and symbol of freedom for ante-bellum slaves, the iron railroad was the vehicle and symbol of industrialization and the ascending capitalist class.

As the railroads were used increasingly to move troops and supplies for the Union armies, they helped extend and integrate the marketplace, making possible a specialized manufacturing and marketing system that could be coordinated across the continent. The railroads pushed into every region of the country. They brought farm produce to new markets and to ports for shipment to distant lands. They carried cotton from Southern fields to New England textile mills. They carried iron ore from Lake Superior to the iron mills and new Bessemer steel furnaces in Pittsburgh, and oil from western Pennsylvania to Cleveland refineries. And they brought the products from the nation's factories to markets in every region. Everywhere, they spread new settlements and development. Despite interruptions during the Civil War, railroad construction added 62,000 miles of new lines in the 1860s and 1870s, tripling the nation's existing track mileage. Railroad construction required iron and later steel rails and bridges. The railroads themselves soon became the biggest customers of America's growing steel industry.

The Civil War and the railroads led some men to their pots of gold. Andrew Carnegie began his rise to fortune as a telegraph clerk for the Pennsylvania Railroad in 1853. By the beginning of the Civil War the ambitious twenty-five-year-old Carnegie was well into railroad management and spent a few months organizing rail transport and telegraph communications for the War Department. But Carnegie quit his exciting and dangerous war front job and returned to the Pennsy and especially to tend his growing investment in iron manufacturing and coal mining. By 1863 his annual income exceeded $40,000.[1]

John Davison Rockefeller's fortunes were also helped by the Civil War. In 1861, as the war consumed the energies and lives of

Northerners and Southerners, the twenty-five-year-old Rockefeller was building a successful merchandising firm in Cleveland. As war orders poured in, commodity prices rose sharply, and Rockefeller's profits soared. Two years later, Rockefeller had saved enough capital to invest in an oil refining business, and by the end of the war he was worth enough to take control of the company. By 1880, led by Rockefeller's determination to "make money and still more money," combined with relentless competition in the marketplace and rebates extracted from the railroads, his Standard Oil Company was refining 95 percent of the country's oil.[2]

While the industrial base had obviously been growing in the decades before the Civil War, it was the changes wrought by the war that cemented the new system's structure. The Southern patrician class, whose position was based on agriculture and slaves, was not crushed, but its subordination to the Northern-controlled capitalist economy was assured. The factory system was extended with the railroad, and an industrial working class was formed out of craftsmen and laborers, native folk and immigrants. Small-town America gradually gave way to industrial and commercial boom, and cities grew faster than their fragile tenements could be built. In the process, the older entrepreneurs and landed gentry were displaced by the new entrepreneurs and their corporations. By the 1870s, for example, only 520, or 5 percent, of the 10,395 businesses in Massachusetts were incorporated. But this 5 percent held 96 percent of the total capital and employed 60 percent of all workers. By 1900 three-fourths of all manufactured goods were produced by corporations. Because of the important logistical role of the railroads, the Civil War has been called the "first railroad war." Yet the war did not rely on an industrial economy. As William Appleman Williams aptly put it, the Civil War "produced an industrial system rather than being fought with one."[3] The ultimate victors of the war were the corporations and the men who, for the most part, ruled the new economy.

Not all was smooth for the new barons of the corporate economy, nor did they make life easy for those under them. The owners of each industry, driven to grab what they could of the available market and accumulate as much capital as possible in the shortest time, pushed wages down in order to lower prices and to get a jump on their competitors. Immigrants were inducted into the growing industrial work force. Some 16 million foreign-born were attracted to the country in the second half of the nineteenth century, totaling 15 percent of the population by 1890 and nearly a quarter of the population of the industrialized northeastern states. Craftsmen saw their skills, the basis of modest security and pride, fall to degradation and unemployment before machines that outproduced them and factories that oppressed them. Migrants from failing farms and immigrants from foreign lands filled the factories and cities of the New World. Working men lost their livelihoods or submitted to the harshest labors. Women were drawn out of more traditional homebound work into factories, shops, and stores. Twenty percent of the nation's women were wage laborers by 1900. Children were sucked into the factories as the cheapest labor. Working-class family and social life were shaken and devastated.

Exploitation of workers, unmitigated by either legal restraints or humanitarianism, led to increased organizing by labor. The depression of the 1870s brought wages in 1875 down to $1.50 for a ten-hour day. Riots were common in cities throughout the country. Labor began to organize, and employers used every available power, from lockouts to Pinkertons, to crush the union movement. In 1877 the first nationwide strike, a spreading walkout against the railroads, was put down with a bloodbath that took the lives of scores of workers, their families, and their supporters in city slums around the country. The labor movement grew and strikes continued to spread in the 1880s and 1890s. The Haymarket Square bomb in 1886, the strike at Carnegie's Homestead steel mills in 1892, and the Pullman strike in 1894 were only the most prominent events that made employers and their allies fear for the continued existence of their society. "The times are strangely out of joint," worried a Kentucky politician. "The rich grow richer, the poor become poorer; the nation trembles."[4]

Town folk and farmers, especially in the Midwest and South, felt their lives and livelihoods increasingly determined by railroad rates and lines of credit from banks directed from distant cities. Semi-feudal sharecropping kept large numbers of Southern farmers in perpetual debt and poverty. Agrarian opposition to capitalist expansion won broad support. In 1896 the growing

Populist party formed a shallow coalition with the Democratic party around the Democrat Bryan for President and the Populist Tom Watson for Vice-President against McKinley, the candidate of big business. The Populist party was decimated by their defeat, but populist resistance to capitalist wealth and control of agriculture continued in the Granges and the Farmers Union well into the new century. To the middle-class professionals who dominated the Progressive movement the society seemed to be breaking up below them because of the greed of those above them. They called for reforms to limit the concentration of power and wealth.

Many members of the richer class felt called upon to justify the great inequality that angered the working class and worried the middle class. Naturally they did not see themselves as "idle" rich. They viewed their efforts to build industrial empires as productive work, and they considered all the people to be the beneficiaries of those empires. No one said it as well as Rockefeller:

> The best philanthropy, the help that does the most good and the least harm, the help that nourishes civilization at its very root, that most widely disseminates health, righteousness, and happiness, is not what is usually called charity. It is, in my judgment, the investment of effort or time or money, carefully considered with relation to the power of employing people at a remunerative wage, to expand and develop the resources at hand, and to give opportunity for progress and healthful labour where it did not exist before. No mere money-giving is comparable to this in its lasting and beneficial results.[5]

The great benefit of such enterprises is *moral,* providing employment to otherwise idle hands, and *material,* "to multiply, to cheapen, and to diffuse as universally as possible the comforts of life."[6] Thus, the building up of private industry is the best method of solving the problems that historically grew with industrialization. "Can there be any doubt that cheapening the cost of necessaries and conveniences of life is the most powerful agent of civilization and progress?" asked Charles Elliott Perkins, president of the Chicago, Burlington, and Quincy Railroad. "The true gospel," Perkins philosophized agreeably, "is to enable men to acquire the comforts and conveniences of life by their own efforts, and then they will be wise and good."[7]

The class of men and women who provided this largess for the rest of society had varied notions about what to do with their money and their power. Mark Hanna, a Cleveland industrialist, showed fellow capitalists that the President and executive branch of the government, as well as the Congress, could be secured "for the protection of our business interests." Fearing the growing ranks of Populists and their increasing political strength, he established an interlocking *political* directorate of corporate leaders to organize their common interests and bring their influence more directly into the federal government. With their first Presidential triumph, electing McKinley in 1896, they inaugurated the modern system of expensive, centrally coordinated national campaigns. Hanna led the formation of a corporate politics that placed the broad class interests of industrialists and financiers ahead of "pork barrel" tactics favoring narrow interests that had dominated state, national, and local political scenes. Hanna and other leaders of this class put together new alliances, like the National Civic Federation, with some labor leaders to create a "harmony of interests" out of the class conflicts that threatened the new economic order. The Progressive movement proved an ideal vehicle for the business class to assert its interests by securing additional, needed capital from the Congress and, through reforms in the federal executive branch, creating and controlling regulatory agencies to bring order and consolidation to a number of industries. The politically wise leaders of this class thus demonstrated that with strategic alliances with social reformers and conservative union officials, the nation's political institutions could be reformed to serve the needs of the corporate order.[8]

Not all capitalists, however, could see farther than their own immediate interests in politics. John D. Rockefeller, whose Standard Oil Trust was accused by Henry Demarest Lloyd of buying out the legislatures and the executive branches of Pennsylvania and Ohio, was unenthusiastic about his friend Hanna's broader political strategy. Hanna's first major success sent John Sherman to the U.S. Senate in 1885, ironically providing the author of the very law under which the Standard empire was eventually broken up. Perhaps Rockefeller suspected such betrayals from politicians who had their own visions of what was good for business, for he customarily reserved his political contributions for candidates closer to the Standard's immediate fields of operations.[9]

Many wealthy men spent their fortunes on ostentatious luxury that left much of the European aristocracy in shadow. The Vanderbilts, Jim Fisk, Jay Gould, and other financiers built palaces along New York's Fifth Avenue, many of them with marble, furnishings, and statuary scooped up from the crumbling baronies of the Old World. Marshall Field and Potter Palmer built their castles on some of Chicago's most prized residential and lakefront land. Mark Hopkins, Charles Crocker, and Leland Stanford transformed San Francisco's Nob Hill with their residences of splendor, using wealth obtained from promoting and governing the westward expansion of the railroads. Carnegie bought himself a castle in his Scottish homeland. And Rockefeller created, not merely a castle, but a royal estate at Pocantico Hills, whose 3,500 acres overlooking the Hudson River was five times the size of Central Park. The spectacle of such living, especially in the midst of tenement-teeming cities, caused considerable agitation. The Massachusetts Board of Education had complained even in 1849, "One gorgeous palace absorbs all the labor and expense that might have made a thousand hovels comfortable." By the end of the century, social scientists cultivated by the wealthy came to their benefactors' defense. A Boston University economics professor retorted to detractors of grandeur, "The notion there is necessarily any causal connection between opulence and poverty is too crude to require serious refutation."[10]

DRIVING THE RELUCTANT POOR FROM POVERTY

Some representatives of the opulent class, both before and after the Civil War, had a broader sense of purpose. They provided luxurious, even princely lives for themselves and their families, but they carefully set aside a share of their wealth for philanthropy. Philanthropy, of course, did not mean giving money directly to the poor. While charity had always implied providing alms for the relief of the poor, the rich and most social reformers in the class immediately below the rich have always been wary of the consequences of giving to the poor. Cotton Mather urged colonial Boston merchants to set a disciplined, moral example and give only to the "poor that can't work." Benjamin Franklin hoped to provide sufficient opportunity in society so there would be no need of poverty, and he tried to develop a strategy for getting the poor to adopt disciplined ways of living. "I think the best way of doing good to the poor," Franklin said, "is not making them easy *in* poverty, but leading them or driving them out of it."[11]

Franklin's maxim and a pitiless Social Darwinist perspective were the heart of the charity organization movement that blossomed in the United States during the last three decades of the century. Patterned after the London Charity Organization Society, founded in 1869, these city and national organizations gave few handouts. Their main purpose was, in the words of a Philadelphia group, to develop "a method by which idleness and begging, now so encouraged, may be suppressed and worthy self-respecting poverty be discovered and relieved at the smallest cost to the benevolent." Even during the vast depression that began in 1873 and lasted until the end of that decade, all takers of charity were suspected of slothfulness and degeneracy.[12]

The poor were a desperate, volatile lot, given to crime, riots, and insolent discontent. Extreme Social Darwinists believed with Herbert Spencer that those who are fit to live do so and those who are not fit die—"and it is best they should die."[13] But the dominant classes of any society need a more positive program than that to deal with oppressed classes' articulated demands for sharing the wealth or even their inarticulate mayhem.

The programs that emerged from charity organization work brought systematic study and the label of "science" to philanthropic work. The annual meetings of the National Conference of Charities and Correction brought together experts from charity organizations, administrators of penal institutions, hospitals and settlement houses, academics from university sociology and economics departments, and clergymen and physicians to coordinate their work and develop strategies for uplifting the poor. The attitudes of these "scientific" charity workers ran from harsh to refined, punitive to ameliorative.[14] Over the years these reformers turned increasingly to the analytic methods of the social sciences and to the political views of the Progressive movement. Edward T. Devine, in his presidential address to the National Conference in 1906, noted that inmates were entering charitable institutions, insane asylums, prisons, and reformatories "faster than all our educational processes, our relief funds, and even our consecrated personal service" have been able to rehabilitate them. The role of "modern philanthropy," Devine continued, is to "seek out and to strike effectively at those organized forces of evil, at those particular causes of dependence and intolerable living conditions which are beyond the control of the individuals whom they injure and whom they too often destroy."[15]

Scientific philanthropy must concern itself with "prevention rather than relief," argued Amos Warner, a Stanford economist active in the movement. Warner compared statistics compiled by charity organizations in the United States and Europe and concluded that nearly three-fourths of all poverty is due to personal or social "misfortune" and less than a fourth to "misconduct" on the part of the individual.[16] "Prevention" involved intervening in the lives of both groups to assist them through their misfortune or change their bad habits and lead them onto the path of righteousness.

Out of this social intervention perspective and the charity organization movement emerged the social work professions. Case workers, settlement house workers, correctional administrators, probation officers, and their academic advisers shared with the middle and upper classes the prevailing Social Darwinist view that dependent poverty, crime, and social deviance in general had biological roots. But this new professional class believed that medical and social intervention could remedy "natural" imperfections.[17]

Given the disintegration of older social relations and the increasing fear of working-class revolt—both products of capitalist industrialization—it is not surprising that wealthy men and women supported the goals and programs of the charity organizations and the social work movement. Charles Hull, who amassed a fortune from Chicago's booming real estate market, gave freely to social rehabilitation programs in the slums and sold cheap land to the poor to give them a stake in the existing society. It was his way of correcting the unequal distribution of land out of which he feared "discontent and revolution will come."[18]

Scorning pity and indiscriminate relief as merely reinforcing the poor in their degraded condition, the charity organization movement, social work professions, and wealthy benefactors in general worked instead to *uplift,* or rehabilitate the poor. They established institutions that would isolate "the poor that can't work" and prevent them from infecting "honest," hard-working poor folk. They also developed programs to give the working poor a loftier vision of life than could otherwise be gotten from the factories and tenements in which they spent their lives. Settlement houses and social workers were established in the slums and ghettos to integrate the foreign-born into American society and to rehabilitate and reintegrate the casualties of an industrial society divided into owners and nonowners. Jane Addams' settlement house, provided by Charles Hull's estate, attempted to fulfill her principal goals to "feed the mind of the worker, to lift it above the monotony of his task, and to connect it with the larger world outside of his immediate surroundings. . . ." Addams opposed the excesses of both capital and labor and worked to bring together these warring classes through programs acceptable to both.[19]

Such programs did not suggest that the capitalist social structure itself should be altered. Rather they were intended to ameliorate the harsh conditions of capitalism by helping individuals escape from its pits and lead both useful and more satisfying lives. While many social workers supported union demands, their work won financial and political support from the wealthy classes because it diverted attention from more militant demands. Social workers held out the hope of ameliorating living conditions with social programs while workers demanded union recognition, higher pay, the eight-hour day, and relief from unemployment. All these programs proved more symbolic and ideological than actually ameliorative. The working poor and the unemployed were being taught to blame their own inadequacies for their conditions and to work and wait patiently for their individual rewards.

Some capitalists, however, both before and after the Civil War, were less concerned with revolt brewing below them or were more thoughtful about the future needs of their social system. They developed another line of philanthropy that centered on creating social institutions whose main functions were not even symbolic amelioration but provided for the training of personnel needed by industrial capitalism if it was to survive and grow. Some of these capitalists, particularly in the first half of the nineteenth century, helped to create compulsory public schooling to socialize working-class and poor children to the rhythms and cooperative needs of factory work and to give them the rudimentary skills—reading, writing, arithmetic, and vocational skills—needed in an industrial society.[20] Other men and women of wealth understood the country's need for more advanced technical skills. They joined forces with foresighted leaders of the nation's traditional colleges, bringing them out of the orbit of the old agricultural and merchant ruling class and into the service of the ascending industrial and financial order.

TRAINING SCIENTIFIC HEADS TO DIRECT AMERICA'S "HARD HANDS"

On the last day of April in 1846 Edward Everett, the new president of Harvard University, stood before his faculty, students, and alumni and inaugurated a new era of cooperation between industrialists and America's colleges and universities. Harvard would no longer be geared mainly to the needs of the agricultural gentry and wealthy merchants, producing educated clergy, lawyers, and assorted gentlemen. Everett laid before his inaugural convocation a proposal, that Harvard found a "school of theoretical and practical science" to teach "its application to the arts of life," to furnish a "supply of skillful engineers" and other persons who would explore and develop the "inexhaustible natural treasures of the country, and to guide its vast industrial energies in their rapid development."[21]

Within a year Abbott Lawrence agreed to underwrite Everett's plans. Lawrence's investments in textile manufacturing and railroad financing had made him a man of wealth and influence in Massachusetts. The industrial revolution in America was in its infancy when he began, but now near midcentury its potential was proven. Lawrence knew first hand the value of the factory system and mechanization in increasing production and profits. He saw that railroad construction brought not only profits on his investment; it also created a demand for iron production and opened up regional and national markets, allowing farmers and factory owners to ship their products to distant markets and increasing America's exports. "Hard hands are ready to work upon our hard materials," he observed. But "where shall sagacious heads be taught to direct those hands?"[22]

To answer his own question and help Harvard realize its self-appointed role, Lawrence gave the university the then princely sum of $50,000 to found a school that would apply chemistry and other sciences to the needs of agriculture, engineering, mining and metallurgy, and the "invention and manufacture of machinery." Thus was the Lawrence Scientific School born. Lawrence was so pleased with the new school that he bequeathed an additional $50,000 for it which Harvard received upon his death in 1855.

Harvard's school was exemplary of the new relationship between science, education, and industrialization. In the nineteenth century, scientists, industrialists, and college presidents developed a profitable alliance. The usefulness of science to industry, the willingness of industrialists to support scientific research, and the opportunity for colleges to train scientists and engineers and do much of the research needed by industry provided a great deal of common ground. It also opened the door for scientists who wanted to make science a full-time occupation and distinguish themselves from others who used the knowledge and methods of the natural sciences in their work.

The great inventors of the early industrial revolution were mostly practical-minded mechanics, craftsmen, and tinkerers, men and women whose lives embraced science through their work. "In contrast with modern practice," observes Harry Braverman, "science did not systematically lead the way for industry, but often lagged behind and grew out of the industrial arts."[23] By the 1830s and 1840s a new group of scientists emerged who wanted to be more than "dilettantes." Like their European counterparts, whose support and status they envied, the upper ranks of American scientists wanted to devote themselves to research, but they lacked the necessary financial resources. Although young men in America's colleges were taught science, there was almost no original research being done in the country. As Joseph Henry, the nation's leading physicist, complained, "every man who can burn phosphorous in oxygen and exhibit a few experiments to a class of young ladies is called a man of science."[24]

In 1844 Alexander Dallas Bache, the superintendent of the U.S. Coast Survey, told an attentive audience at the country's first national scientific congress that America's unoriginal and meager science merely aped European science. America's science, he said, had inadequate institutional support, substituted teaching for scientific research, was overrun with gentleman scientists, and lacked professional scientists. Bache and Henry, together with Harvard mathematician Benjamin Peirce, astronomer Benjamin Gould, chemist Oliver Wolcott Gibbs, zoologist Louis Agassiz, and a few other professional scientists fancied themselves the nation's sole custodians of science and its development. They aggressively sought support for their research and promoted the cause of professional science. In their view, only some men were endowed with scientific talent, and only such an elite should be entrusted with training, facilities for research, and money. As Howard Miller has pointed out, their elitism won them no support from the assertive, democratic populists of Andrew Jackson's era.[25]

These new men of science won increasing support from the entrepreneurial fortunes of the captains of industry. Lawrence was neither the first nor the last capitalist of the nineteenth century to channel his surplus wealth to colleges in order to put science at the service of industry. In 1846, with the financial help of philanthropists, Yale created two new professorships in agricultural and practical chemistry and appointed the eminent Benjamin Silliman, Jr., to one of them to develop and teach the "application of chemistry, and the kindred sciences to the manufacturing arts, to exploration of the resources of the country and to other practical uses." Silliman's prolific accomplishments at Yale included developing the first commercially successful method of refining petroleum. Before the Civil War, Joseph Earl Sheffield, a New Haven man who made his fortune in Southern cotton and in financing Northern railroads and canals, gave the struggling Yale Scientific School a large contribution. The university appreciatively renamed the school in honor of its benefactor, whose contributions to Yale for applied science totaled more than $1 million by the time of his death in 1882.[26]

Perhaps the most symbolic change was the conversion of the Reverend Nathan Lord, president of Dartmouth College. As he assumed the college presidency in 1828, Lord asserted that Dartmouth was *not* designed for men who were to "engage in mercantile, mechanical, or agricultural operations." His strict adherence to the classics and to preparing gentlemen, however, did not survive several large contributions from wealthy advocates of applied sciences and engineering. By the late 1860s Lord eagerly embraced the "necessity now becoming constantly more evident of a higher education in the 'practical and useful arts of life.' "[27]

Some industrialists and finance capitalists, not content with the slow and incomplete transformations of the older colleges, started their own engineering schools. In 1824 Stephen Van Rensselaer, a wealthy landlord farmer who organized and backed the construction of the Erie Canal and thereby experienced for himself the lack of adequately trained engineers, founded the institute that bears his name to teach the "application of experimental chemistry, philosophy and natural history, to agriculture, domestic economy, the arts and manufactures."[28] Other engineering and technical schools were begun around the country from fonts of industrial wealth—Cooper Union in New York City, the Massachusetts Institute of Technology, the Stevens Institute in Hoboken, the Case School of Applied Science in Cleveland, the Pratt Institute in New York, and the California Institute of Technology, to name a few.

Philanthropic capitalists left their marks in American higher education in other areas besides science. Joseph Wharton, a wealthy manufacturer of metals, gave the University of Pennsylvania some $600,000 for a school of finance and commerce that would train the managers, accountants, and leaders of industry who would direct the engineers and applied scientists graduating from technical schools. Entirely new universities were founded in the 1870s and 1880s by some of the wealthiest men and women in the country—Johns Hopkins, Tulane, Clark, Vanderbilt, Stanford, Cornell, and others.

These educational philanthropists were primarily capitalists who disdained the aristocratic pretenses of gentleman farmers and the dabblers' and merchants' ignorance of technique. Remembering their own lack of preparation as they began their careers, they favored practical educations that would promote endeavors like theirs and create a fertile ground from which their new society would grow. They also perceived a need for trained personnel for the growing industrial and corporate economy. As the organizers of factories and other enterprises that employed increasing divisions of labor, they preferred to train technically skilled managers and reduce the skill levels of their laborers; in the words of Abbott Lawrence, let the "hard hands" do the labor and let "sagacious heads" design and direct the labor process. Impressed with the utility of applied science, they subsidized teaching and research in the natural sciences and engineering, and they supported vocational and applied curricula in colleges against the prevailing classical education. By the end of the century they were delighted with the progress that had been made in creating universities and colleges in their own image. And, of course, they were glad to have combined this self-interest with an appearance of generosity and altruism.

The entrepreneurial scientists and college presidents made the philanthropists' job an easy one. The development of modern universities and the founding of professional science in the United States were largely the products of elite college presidents and men of science inviting captains of industry to recognize the importance of their contributions to the nascent industrial and corporate society. They asked for and got money for their work, their institutions, and themselves.

Scientists offered their talents and their services to the capitalists in return for new laboratories and stipends; they gave up to the colleges a degree of autonomy in return for a legitimized base of operations, some financial security, and a protected role in training new basic and applied scientists as well as conducting research. College presidents acted as brokers, eagerly offering their services and institutions to capitalists and scientists alike, in return for new areas of service that would assure the continued relevance and financial security of their institutions under the ascending economic order. Their new buildings and endowments assured them that they were on the right track. By 1872 philanthropy accounted for nearly half the $13 million income received by all the nation's institutions of higher education.[29]

The founding of schools, institutes, and universities was quite a different tack from giving to charity organization societies and creating settlement houses. They were both intended to meet the needs of the developing industrial and corporate society, but in different ways. One was ameliorative: It tried to compensate for the failings of the capitalist social structure. The other was more technical and "preventive": Institutions were developed to meet the needs of the system for technical expertise and industrial and social management. Both were important to the survival and expansion of industry as it was organized in capitalist society.

There were limitations, however, in the resources and strategies of both approaches. The social work approach was ameliorative at a time when most philanthropists were pressing for preventive strategies. The founding of universities and institutes, which had a preventive character, was limited in two ways. First, it often represented an individual action on the part of a particular rich man or woman who founded the institution to reflect a personal perspective of what was needed. While some of them secured the help of visionary university presidents, these institutions often reflected too strongly the personalities and idiosyncratic views of their founders. Only when governance fell to the institution's trustees did it come to reflect a broader perspective within the benefactor's class. Thus, the trustees who implemented Johns Hopkins' bequest for the founding of a university were able to do what they collectively believed worthwhile because their broad charter left them free of detailed instructions from the deceased benefactor while the endowment meant they had "no need of obeying the injunctions of any legislature, the beliefs of any religious body, or the clamors of any press."[30] Most benefactors, especially those who founded their institutions while on this side of their graves, held closer reigns on policies and personnel.

The second limitation on the usefulness of the university movement among the wealthy was one of scale. Most of the founders had fortunes big enough to create only one institution, and those who had the wealth to do more nevertheless concentrated their energies and their money in one place. Thus their direct influence would come from only one place, and their indirect influence would be only as a model. These were often powerful forces. Van Rensselaer's institute claimed, by the middle of the nineteenth century, that it had produced a majority of the country's engineers and naturalists. And the class of wealthy university founders was small and often influenced each other: Ezra Cornell's new university at Ithaca was admired by Leland Stanford, and Stanford's creation in California greatly impressed Jonas Clark and his plans for Massachusetts.[31] These exceptions notwithstanding, the general limitations of individualism and narrowness of resources reduced the utility of university building for corporate capitalism.

The accolades these "good works" generated didn't mean that

philanthropy could not be done better. And certainly the capitalist impulse to believe in perfectability in the organization of any enterprise encouraged many philanthropists to look for errors and seek a better way. The obvious constraints of ameliorative social intervention programs drew most of the criticism. But while the create-a-school movement was not criticized explicitly, a successor was soon seen on the horizon. At best the universities were productive models of capitalist rationality and technical modernness in an untamed, competitive marketplace of seemingly incompetent educational institutions. Not surprisingly, it was the philanthropies created by the kings of oil and steel that started American schooling down the same road to vertical organization and centralized control that they had created in their own industries.

CARNEGIE'S "GOSPEL OF WEALTH"

The growing fortunes of the Carnegies and Rockefellers in this country made them prominent symbols of the success as well as the inequities of industrial capitalism. It was this weighty responsibility that led Andrew Carnegie to explain the problems associated with great wealth and to lay out the responsibilities that came with its possession. In an influential two-part essay entitled "Wealth," published in the *North American Review* in 1889,[32] Carnegie with a flush of confidence set out a plan for assuring continued private accumulation of wealth. "The problem of our age," he boldly began, "is the proper administration of wealth, that the ties of brotherhood may still bind together the rich and poor in harmonious relationship." Speaking to a receptive audience among the "haves" more than to the truculent "have-nots," Carnegie identified the accumulation of wealth as the essential factor in the "progress of the race." Whether it be "for good or ill, it is upon us, beyond our power to alter, and, therefore, to be accepted and made the best of. It is a waste of time to criticize the inevitable," he reassuringly added.

Though capitalism's "law" of competition "may be sometimes hard for the individual, it is best for the race because it insures the survival of the fittest in every department," he observed, paraphrasing the then widely idolized Herbert Spencer. Furthermore, it produced great material wealth so that all people lived better for it. Society must not only accept; it must *welcome* "great inequality of environment," specifically the "concentration of business, industrial and commercial, in the hands of a few." It is not to be regretted that capitalists must "soon be in receipt of more revenues than can be judiciously expended upon themselves." It is simply incumbent upon the wealthy to dispose of their fortunes wisely.

They should not, he warned, leave the bulk of their wealth to their families, for such legacies undermine the moral integrity of the recipients. Nor should the rich man simply bequeath his fortune for public purposes because it is morally reprehensible to accumulate great wealth and not show either the interest or the judgment to spend it wisely. As exciting as Carnegie found his money-making career, it had always seemed to him below the moral and intellectual world to which he aspired. More than two decades before his declarations on wealth, Carnegie had written a memo to himself promising to quit business shortly: "To continue much longer overwhelmed by business cares and with most of my thought wholly upon the way to make more money in the shortest time, must degrade me beyond hope of permanent recovery."[33] Now Carnegie admonished his peers, "The man who dies thus rich dies disgraced."

It is the duty of the wealthy, Carnegie declared in his article, "to consider all surplus revenues which come to him simply as trust funds," to do what, "in his judgment," is best for the community. The wealthy capitalist is thus a "mere trustee and agent for his poorer brethren, bringing to their service his superior wisdom, experience, and ability to administer"—in a word, "doing for them better than they would or could do for themselves."

He then recommended to men and women of substantial means seven uses for their surplus wealth, declaring the priorities that he followed in the years to come. Topping the list were universities, to which Carnegie gave more than $20 million in his lifetime. Next were free public libraries, which, to Carnegie's mind, squared with his goal "to stimulate the best and most aspiring poor of the community to further efforts for their own improvement." Carnegie contributed 2,811 libraries to communities that promised to support them; this most famous of his philanthropies consumed more than $60 million of his wealth. Carnegie also recommended giving money for medical institutions, public parks and city beautification, halls for "concerts of elevating music" and enlightening lectures, swimming baths, and—last—church buildings.[34]

Carnegie's round face glowed and his eyes sparkled as he received the adulation of wealthy admirers and fawning supplicants. Gladstone sanctified Carnegie's proposals with a review of his article in the prestigious British magazine *Nineteenth Century,* criticizing only Carnegie's condemnation of inherited wealth. From his celebrated position, Carnegie dismissed the critical reviews of his article. The Reverend Hugh Price Hughes, a prominent Methodist minister and Christian populist, condemned this new "Gospel of Wealth," as it had come to be called. "Mr. Carnegie's 'progress' is accompanied by the growing 'poverty' of his less fortunate fellow-countrymen," he wrote. William Jewett Tucker, a liberal theologian and later president of Dartmouth College, pointed out that the assumption "that wealth is the inevitable possession of the few, and is best administered by them for the many, begs the whole question of economic justice now before society." "I can conceive of no greater mistake," Tucker protested, "than that of trying to make charity do the work of justice."[35]

Carnegie's giving never aimed at justice; his goal was "to lead people upward." Like his politics, Carnegie's philanthropy was a mixture of moralistic programs to civilize the masses, impulsive decisions, and sentimentality. Libraries, institutes, concert halls, and church organs—7,689 organs costing more than $6 million—were given to uplift the poor and working classes. In 1904 he provided more than $10 million for the Carnegie Hero Fund to honor men and women who are injured or killed while trying to save their fellows; medals were presented to the hero, or his or her surviving family, and occasionally monetary grants, to encourage the masses to follow examples set by "the heroes of civilization." Carnegie also provided his birthplace of Dunfermline, Scotland, with a $3.75 million fund for parks, recreation, and general beautification.[36]

REVEREND GATES INTRODUCES ROCKEFELLER TO "WHOLESALE PHILANTHROPY"

Like Carnegie, John Davison Rockefeller's interest in financial benevolence antedates his most famous philanthropies. From the time of his youth, Rockefeller's life consisted of work, family, and the Baptist church. More like his pious mother than his genial and impulsive father, Rockefeller lived a disciplined life, forever pinching pennies but mindful of his Christian duties. Even in 1855, when he was earning $3.50 a week as a clerk accountant in Cleveland, Rockefeller carefully apportioned about 10 percent of his income to charities and church work. His philanthropy grew with his riches; by 1881 he was giving away more than $60,000 a year.[37] By the end of the century, he and Carnegie were competing in their philanthropy—with Carnegie ahead.

Rockefeller was diligent in giving to charity but ungenerous in spirit. Like other men of his day climbing the ladders of business success and those who had reached the top, Rockefeller saw no excuse for poverty. Having gone into business for himself at the age of twenty, the oil king "knew" that hard work and disciplined living were the means to escape poverty. In 1887 Rockefeller answered a poor young man's plea for fifty dollars with a check, a request for an I.O.U., and a warning: "It will be injurious for him to receive from others what he can in any way secure for himself by his own efforts." And after a visit to a "house of industry" in New York's incomparable slum of Five Points, he complained that although the institution gave free meals to the area's "tramps" only on Thanksgiving Day, he "would give them work and make them earn their food."[38]

Whereas Carnegie's secular views led him to Social Darwinism as a biological and social explanation for the maldistribution of wealth, Rockefeller's religion exorcised all self-doubts. Particularly as he grew older and more comfortable with his fortune and his role as philanthropist, Rockefeller came to believe that "God gave me my money." When he uttered these words in 1905, "Rockefeller" was not the most revered name in North America. He thus felt called upon to explain: "I believe the power to make money is a gift from God . . . to be developed and used to the best of our ability for the good of mankind. I believe it is my duty to make money and still more money and to use the money I make for the good of my fellow man according to the dictates of my conscience."[39]

Rockefeller's conscience led him to heap great benevolence on a wide range of socially uplifting charities. Andrew Carnegie put churches last on his list of recommended philanthropies, but for Rockefeller the Baptist church and its numerous charities and missions were the highest priority. Hospitals and other public welfare charities were also favorites. He hoped his contributions would enable the denomination to lead all people to live with rectitude and to aid the fallen poor to gain the proper path. In 1890 Rockefeller's contributions to charities and colleges topped $300,000, and the next year half a million dollars.

But in May 1889, one month before Carnegie published the first of his two-part "Gospel of Wealth," Rockefeller committed himself to a particularly ambitious philanthropic project and a relationship with a man who was to write a new chapter in philanthropy. For several years a group of Baptists in the East and another group in the West had been trying to develop a new seminary and university for the denomination. The eastern group wanted the institution to be located in New York while the other group desperately hoped to develop it in Chicago, the rapidly growing metropolis of the nation's westward expansion. Both groups were pressing Rockefeller, the richest Baptist in the world, to contribute the millions needed to endow a first-rate institution. While interested in such a project, Rockefeller was not swayed by the emotionalism of either group's appeal.[40]

The struggling academies, seminaries, and colleges of the denomination met in Washington in May 1888 to form the American Baptist Education Society, to raise money for Baptist education, and to coordinate its development. They named the fast-rising Reverend Frederick T. Gates executive secretary, a position from which he leaped to the pinnacle of both philanthropic and corporate power.

Gates immediately conducted a survey of Baptist educational needs throughout the country. Armed with his data, he wrote a detailed and eloquent report. Gates demonstrated that nearly half the country's Baptists lived west of Pennsylvania and north of the Ohio River but that the denomination's educational facilities in this region were practically worthless. He concluded that a new Baptist university should be built "on the ruins of the old University of Chicago," a weak and by then bankrupt denominational institution. While the new university should bring together the most capable specialists in both its classical and scientific departments, it must be "an institution wholly under Baptist control as a chartered right, loyal to Christ and His church, employing none but Christians in any department of instruction, a school not only evangelical but evangelistic."[41]

Gates' report was the turning point in the denomination's

campaign for a university. As he himself put it, "The brothers were 'all torn up' over it." The Chicago proponents coalesced around the report, and the dwindling supporters of a New York location became even more emotional in their desperate appeals to Rockefeller. The Education Society executive board unanimously approved the proposal at the December 1888 meeting. Within six months Gates won Rockefeller's approval and an initial gift of $600,000 that soon became a torrent of support, totaling $35 million in the next twenty-one years. Rockefeller was so impressed with Gates that he wrote University of Chicago president Harper in 1889, "I have made up my mind to act in my educational benefactions through the American Baptist Education Society."[42]

Rockefeller, worn out by his total immersion in business since the age of twenty, was a physical wreck as he entered his fifties in 1889. He suffered increasingly from nervous fatigue and stomach ailments. He soon lost all his hair, including his eyebrows, because of a nervous disease, generalized alopecia. His doctors had warned him to reduce his activities as much as possible, but his responsibilities were mounting. Although Standard Oil was now in the hands of experienced and trusted lieutenants, there was an increasing flow of requests for large and small portions of his wealth from churches, missionary societies, hospitals, colleges, charity organizations, and individuals—once running as high as 50,000 requests in a single month.[43]

In March 1891 Rockefeller sat Gates down and laid out his problem.

> I am in trouble, Mr. Gates. The pressure of these appeals for gifts has become too great for endurance. I haven't the time or strength, with all my heavy business responsibilities, to deal with these demands properly. I am so constituted as to be unable to give away money with any satisfaction until I have made the most careful inquiry as to the worthiness of the cause. These investigations are now taking more of my time and energy than the Standard Oil itself. Either I must shift part of the burden, or stop giving entirely. And I cannot do the latter.[44]

"Indeed you cannot, Mr. Rockefeller," replied Gates, listening with great care and at the same time anticipating the benefactor's point.

"Well, I must have a helper," Rockefeller continued. "I have been watching you. I think you are the man. I want you to come to New York and open an office here. You can aid me in my benefactions by taking interviews and inquiries, and reporting the results for action. What do you say?"

Fervently aware of the wealth and power that would rest in his hands to use on behalf of all the things he believed important, Gates accepted without the slightest hesitation. He thus began a relationship with Rockefeller that transformed the world's largest fortune into the most strategically applied philanthropy, establishing principles, methods, and directions that were soon emulated by other philanthropists and continued through the next two generations of the Rockefeller dynasty. The numerous medical and public health programs would become the central part of Gates' strategy.

In September 1891, Gates took an office in the Temple Court Building in New York City, not far from Rockefeller's Standard Oil offices at 26 Broadway. He continued his work for the Education Society even while he took charge of Rockefeller's philanthropy. The supplicants who hounded Rockefeller "almost like a wild animal" were sent to Gates' office. "I did my best to soothe ruffled feelings, to listen fully to every plea, and to weigh fairly the merits of every cause," Gates recalled of his days at Temple Court.[45]

With the same systematic thoroughness that marked his report for the Education Society, Gates investigated each request that came his way. "I found not a few of Mr. Rockefeller's habitual charities to be worthless and practically fraudulent. But on the other hand I gradually developed and introduced into all his charities the principle of scientific giving, and he found himself in no long time laying aside retail giving almost wholly, and entering safely and pleasurably into the field of wholesale philanthropy."[46]

Gates' first act on behalf of "wholesale philanthropy" was to increase Rockefeller's contributions to state and regional Baptist agencies and cut off contributions to individual churches, missions, and charity organizations. By forcing every church and mission to get their aid from centralized denominational boards, Gates increased the latter's power over the far-flung flock.[47]

Not long after he moved to New York, Gates took charge of

Rockefeller's many investments outside the Standard companies. As with his charities, Rockefeller always intended to check on his investments thoroughly before buying into them. Often he was persuaded by acquaintances to invest in a project or industry they assured him would pay off handsomely. Most of the immense "surplus" wealth that Rockefeller was taking out of oil he was putting, not into charity, but into "a good many different industries." By 1893 he had accumulated, besides the Standard, sixty-seven major investments, valued at $23 million, in railroads, mining, manufacturing, and banks. "It occurred to me," Rockefeller later recalled, "that Mr. Gates, who had a great store of common sense, though no especial technical information about factories and mills, might aid me in securing some first-hand information as to how these concerns were actually prospering." He asked Gates to investigate some of these investments when he happened to be in the area on Education Society business.[48]

Gates checked on several of Rockefeller's distant stakes: an immense land speculation scheme in the Pacific Northwest that two fellow parishioners of Rockefeller's Fifth Avenue Baptist church had persuaded the oil baron to invest in; a $600,000 investment in a West Superior, Wisconsin, steel mill and land speculation fraud, recommended by the same brethren; and a smaller iron furnace in Alabama. Gates demonstrated his varied abilities and singular value to his employer. "His report was a model of what such a report should be," Rockefeller remarked with uncharacteristic praise. "It stated the facts, and in this case they were almost all unfavourable." One investment that Rockefeller thought was earning $1,000 a day was instead losing that amount.[49]

One more investigation by Gates, of some reputedly rich gold mines in Colorado that turned out to be a complete fraud, settled the matter for Rockefeller. His income was now upwards of $10 million a year, he was physically and emotionally coming apart at the seams, and he desperately needed a lieutenant in whom he could place complete confidence. He asked Gates to drop his office in the Temple Court Building and share his private offices at 26 Broadway. "That," wrote Gates, "is how I came to be a businessman."[50]

THE REVEREND FREDERICK T. GATES:
THE MAKING OF A ROCKEFELLER MEDICINE MAN

It is not surprising that Gates should be such an appealing assistant in both philanthropy and finance. Although he graduated from the Baptist-controlled Rochester University and the Baptist seminary in Rochester and then spent eight years in the ministry, Gates was at heart a businessman in spiritual clothing. As he himself said in his autobiography,

> Much of my life has been in fact an unconscious preparation for successful business. My interesting experience in selling harrows, my months as a clerk in a country store, and as cashier of a country bank, my interest in my father's financial affairs and the ways and means of paying our debts, my studies of political economy under Doctor Anderson [at Rochester], my close study of the finances of our church building in Minneapolis, a habit of looking at things in their financial tendencies and relations, my study of denominational finances at home and abroad, all these things had given me a business experience and my mind a financial turn.[51]

Gates was nearly thirty-eight years old when he went to work for Rockefeller. His early years were spent in rural poverty. His father had studied medicine but turned to the Baptist ministry for his life's work. The elder Gates' successive congregations were mainly poor farmers in rural New York; his family shared that poverty which bred at least part of Frederick's determination to leave it behind in his own life. When the family moved to Forest City, Kansas, Frederick began but had to quit high school and then taught school to earn money to help his family pay off the accumulating debt on their farm.[52] Through high school and college jobs Gates worked with his characteristic diligence and energy and discovered how much he pleased his employers. His shrewd salesmanship earned him $1,500 for selling harrows. Gates was developing a sense of where his ambition might eventually take him.

Young Gates' experiences with religion were as important in shaping his future life as were his experiences with poverty. "The best that religion had to offer me as a boy," he wrote near the end of his life, "was death and heaven, the very things I most dreaded—being a normal, healthy boy." With his teaching job

Gates developed a strong attraction to the intellectual and personal elements of religion, though his conversion was not an emotional one. He found Christ's social and moral teachings very attractive: "I was drawn to his person and character, and felt that throughout my life I wanted to side with him and his friends against the world and his enemies. Such, frankly, was the only 'conversion' I ever had."

He found his seminary training so academic as to leave him poorly prepared for ministerial work. He dispensed with the philosophical idealism the seminary had cultivated, and from his own reading, his life experiences, and examination of the economic and social issues affecting his congregation, Gates took up a pragmatic philosophy that was more in keeping with his personality and his ambition. His fund-raising work for his poor parish in Minneapolis and his less solemn, more modern sermons attracted a bigger congregation and with it, more wealth.

One day George Pillsbury, whose flour fortune made him the wealthiest Baptist in the Northwest, asked Gates' advice in making up his will and especially in leaving $200,000 to a Baptist school. Pillsbury was very pleased with Gates' suggestion that he immediately give $50,000 to the school on the condition that the denomination in Minnesota raise an equal amount—to assure their committed interest in it—and that he bequeath another $150,000 to the school in his will. Baptist leaders were also pleased and commissioned Gates to raise their $50,000 share of the funds. Gates resigned his pastorate and took up the challenge. So effective were his methods of button-holing Baptists in the state that he had soon raised $60,000.[53] Gates knew he had found his calling!

He developed a number of rules for fund raising which he learned "mostly on the pastorate" and a couple of years later wrote them down at the request of his admirers in the trade. Dress well, act in a dignified manner, pretend the visit will be a short one, be good-natured, and "keep your victim also good-natured. . . . Let him feel that *he* is *giving* it, not that it is being taken from him with violence." Rule number 7 he followed unswervingly through his nearly four decades of service to Rockefeller: "Appeal only to the noblest motives. His own mind will suggest to him the lower and selfish ones. But he will not wish you to suppose that he has thought of them. He wishes you to believe him to be giving only from the highest motives."[54] In a few years Gates rose from pastor of an average Baptist congregation in Minneapolis, to a statewide position with the denomination in Minnesota, to chief officer of the Baptists' national Education Society, to the side of Mr. Rockefeller himself, administering a panoply of investments and an immense philanthropy.

As soon as he joined Rockefeller's private office to manage his finances, Gates began a meticulous evaluation of all Rockefeller's holdings outside the Standard Trust. He was given a free hand in reorganizing investments and corporations alike and was provided with assistants, credit, and confidential information. "I had every needed tool," Gates remembered, "and the machinery was well oiled and without the least friction. No man of serious business responsibilities ever had a happier business life than I. No man was ever furnished with more of the external elements of success, or given better opportunities." In some companies Gates bought enough stock to take control and put in management acceptable to him and Rockefeller. Other investments were sold off completely. In the end, Gates was made president of thirteen corporations in which Rockefeller now had a controlling interest. He added sizeable chunks to Rockefeller's geometrically increasing fortune, the grandest chunk being the $55 million profit Gates made on selling the Mesabi iron ore range and associated industries that he had developed.[55]

Although Gates came to Rockefeller's employment a poor man, he soon remedied this unfortunate condition. While executive secretary of the Baptist Education Society, Gates was paid a then-respectable income of $2,500 a year. When he moved East and opened an office in the Temple Court Building, Rockefeller added $1,500 to his income. His added responsibilities led to annual increases in salary "always paid by the corporations which I managed," until after ten years with Rockefeller he was getting a salary of $30,000, a very good income in the first decade of this century. Out of his earnings Gates and his wife had saved enough to pay for their Montclair, N.J., home and had invested some $60,000 in the companies he had organized and managed for Rockefeller. That small investment brought him more than $500,000 when he sold his shares in 1902. "Prudent investments with few losses gradually increased this sum." In 1916 Gates began converting all his investments into then-rising and profitable bank stocks and encouraged Rockefeller to do the same, recommending especially the Chase National Bank, which was paying dividends of 20 percent on invested capital. By the time of his death in 1929 Gates was a wealthy man though, needless to say, his fortune fell far short of his employer's.[56]

Though Rockefeller never paid direct compliments to any person, he more than once recorded his appreciation of Gates' "phenomenal business ability." In response to a reporter's question, "Who is the greatest of all the business men you have known?" Rockefeller heaped warm praise on Gates. "He combines business skill and philanthropic aptitude to a higher degree than any other man I have ever known."[57] Though Gates was involved with Rockefeller's finances in important ways, his organization of Rockefeller's philanthropies, and especially the medical programs, makes him historically significant.

In 1897, John D. Rockefeller, Jr., graduated from Brown University and was cautiously trying to find a place for himself in a world preempted by his father. His hereditary position in the world of industry and finance left him little room for any achievement that he could call his own. His own name was inseparable from his father's, who was perhaps the most vilified of all the great robber barons. The one area in which he might stake out new ground and at the same time help clear the family name was philanthropy. And thus he entered his father's private offices at 26 Broadway, an imperium presided over by the Reverend Gates.[58]

With difficulty Gates and "Mr. Rockefeller, Junior" developed a working relationship. Junior was then twenty-three years old, inexperienced, and reserved to the point of shyness. Gates, twenty years his senior, did not hide his self-confidence derived from varied experience and personal achievement; he was ebullient. Nevertheless, Junior learned from Gates and from his own successes and failures and built an independent role for himself in both philanthropy and finance. For his part, Gates learned to tolerate this scion of the man he worked for and truly respected. Gates considered Junior "diligent" but unimaginative. "He was home-made and hand-trained," he recalled disdainfully. Rockefeller, Sr., had found, as his biographer Allan Nevins observed, "just the combination of qualities he needed: Gates endowed primarily with imagination, fire, and vision, the son endowed primarily with hard sense, caution, public spirit, and conscientiousness."[59]

Gates and Junior investigated new lines of philanthropy and the value of Senior's investments, bringing major proposals for action on both to the financier for final decisions. Gates wrote his views in eloquent reports; Junior relied on oral persuasion. "Gates was the brilliant dreamer and creator," Junior recalled years later. "I was the salesman—the go-between with Father at the opportune moment." Senior seldom jumped into any new venture. "I'll let the idea simmer," he often told his son and Gates. Then weeks, months, or even years later, moved by considerations inscrutable to his assistants, he was ready to act.[60]

Gates was also quite a contrast to his employer. As Raymond Fosdick, president of the Rockefeller Foundation for more than a decade, revealed:

> Mr. Gates was a vivid, outspoken, self-revealing personality who brought an immense gusto to his work; Mr. Rockefeller was quiet, cool, taciturn about his thoughts and purposes, almost stoic in his repression. Mr. Gates had an eloquence which could be passionate when he was aroused; Mr. Rockefeller, when he spoke at all, spoke in a slow measured fashion, lucidly and penetratingly, but without raising his voice and without gestures. Mr. Gates was overwhelming and sometimes overbearing in argument; Mr. Rockefeller was a man of infinite patience who never showed irritation or spoke chidingly about anybody.[61]

From this triumvirate came the influential philanthropies that asserted extraordinary leadership in shaping the social, economic, and political order of the twentieth century. Rockefeller, the individualistic captain of industry from the rough-and-tumble old order that was being transformed at the turn of the century, supplied the money but left the directing to his lieutenants. Gates, the transition figure from unbridled individualism to the discipline of the corporation, provided systematic methods and a rudimentary strategy for asserting corporate capitalism's needs for supportive social institutions. Junior, emerging gradually as the nation's foremost representative of modernism in corporate relations with labor and the public, brought a refinement and sensitivity to the philanthropic work being developed by Gates.

The programs and strategies that emerged from this center of financial power had an enormous impact, especially on medical care and health systems in the United States and throughout the world.[62]

THE GENERAL EDUCATION BOARD: $129 MILLION FOR STRATEGIC PHILANTHROPY

Gates shared Carnegie's fears that excessive hereditary wealth diminishes individual initiative and achievement, that it saps the participation of its bearer in the social and economic processes that make society strong. "Your fortune is rolling up, rolling up like an avalanche!" he warned Rockefeller. "You must keep up with it! You must distribute it faster than it grows! If you do not, it will crush you, and your children, and your children's children!"[63]

Having acquired the fortune, it fell to Rockefeller and his associates to maintain it as a trust for the people, just as Carnegie had advocated. "It is the duty of men of means," Rockefeller wrote early in this century, "to maintain the title to their property and to administer their funds until some man, or body of men, shall rise up capable of administering for the general good the capital of the country better than they can." In his view, neither experiences with state and national legislatures nor "schemes of socialism" offered any promise that "wealth would be more wisely administered for the general good" than it was by its private owners.[64]

Since the owners of capital were mortal men, it was incumbent on them to provide some ongoing trust to see that their wealth would be used wisely even after they passed from the scene. There was nothing new in this concept as understood by the Rockefellers as they launched their first grant-giving foundation, the General Education Board, to aid Southern education. Charitable trusts independent of the state and the church have had legal status in Anglo-Saxon law since the "statute of charitable uses" was enacted by Queen Elizabeth in 1601. Most of these, however, had been narrowly prescribed uses—endowing a particular hospital, giving relief to wayward girls in Brooklyn, and providing scholarships for young men entering mechanical engineering at a particular college.[65]

However, there were a few precedents that greatly influenced the creation of the General Education Board, providing the first of its strategic philanthropic programs aimed at transforming major social institutions. At the close of the Civil War, merchant-banker George Peabody provided $2 million for a Southern education fund. The war had left the South in ruins and its schools destroyed or otherwise defunct; a generation of Southerners was growing up uneducated and essentially illiterate. The Peabody Education Fund hired Barnas Sears, the president of Brown University, to set up a grant program to help schools that were run and generally supported by Southerners. Sears was succeeded by Jabez L. M. Curry, a Confederate politician and planter from Alabama, who had saved his land from confiscation after the Civil War by swearing allegiance to the United States.[66]

The Peabody Fund set an example for John F. Slater, a textile manufacturer from Connecticut, who endowed a $1 million fund in 1882 to educate Southern blacks. By the end of the nineteenth century increasing numbers of Northern businessmen and Southern reformers were coalescing around the need to develop Southern schools in general and educate Southern blacks in particular. The South was not only economically and educationally undeveloped; it was the section of the country from which militant populism still received its widest political support, threatening the ambitions of Southern liberal reformers and Northern conservative businessmen who wanted to "modernize" and industrialize the region. In 1899 these leaders organized the first of several Conferences for Southern Education.[67]

John D. Rockefeller, Jr., was a guest at the third conference in 1901. Robert C. Ogden, a partner of John Wanamaker and general manager of their New York department store, chartered a special train, dubbed the "millionaires' special" by hostile Southern newspapers, to bring Northern businessmen on a tour of Southern black schools and then to a conference with Southern activists in the cause. Junior and the other guests visited the Hampton and Tuskegee institutes and other schools and ended their tour with a meeting in Winston-Salem. This conference established a permanent organization called the Southern Education Board (SEB) to raise money among Northerners, assume formal leadership of the campaign to develop Southern schools, and conduct propaganda on its behalf. Though the board's budget was low—not more than $40,000 a year—and they never gave grants as the Peabody and Slater funds were doing, the SEB hired agents to carry their campaign to influential Southerners and state legislatures.[68]

Like the Peabody and Slater funds, essentially combined under the leadership of their chief agent J. L. M. Curry, the Southern Education Board unanimously supported only "industrial education" for blacks. Schools organized around this model taught the rudiments of literacy and emphasized industrial and agricultural skills, disciplined work, thrift, and right living. Hampton Institute, whose chief trustee was Ogden and whose principal was fellow SEB member Hollis Frissell, was the prototype of industrial schools for blacks. Booker T. Washington, an early graduate of Hampton, founded a similar school at Tuskegee, Alabama, and became the country's chief black proponent of the gradualist strategy of racial progress. For half a century this model of education guided the work of the movement for compulsory schooling, and now it was the centerpiece of the progressive education movement, sweeping educators and businessmen alike into a national educational reform campaign.[69]

Northern and Southern businessmen were enthusiastic. "Every element for success exists in the South," the *Manufacturers' Record* declared in support,

> in raw material, in climate, in the forces of Nature, and above all, in an abundant supply of labor, which when properly trained and disciplined will be the main reliance of the South in the future for its prosperity. It only remains for the South to do its duty to its black population by way of training and educating in the simple manual trades.[70]

With the support of Northern money, the industrial schools flourished and the few genuine colleges for blacks struggled under their less than benign neglect. The Southern Education Board and its allies won grudging acceptance of schools for blacks from Southern white supremacist political leaders, and in return Northern members of the SEB campaigned in the North for acceptance of black disfranchisement and Jim Crow laws as the best way to progress for blacks. "The white people are to be the leaders, to take the initiative, to have the directive control of all matters pertaining to civilization and the highest interests of our beloved land," Curry, former Confederate officer and now chief of staff of the Southern campaign, brazenly proclaimed. "This white supremacy does not mean hostility to the Negro, but friendship for him."[71]

For John D. Rockefeller, Jr., his 1901 tour and conference in the South were "one of the outstanding events in my life." Filled with a sense of mission, Junior discussed the new Southern Education Board and its program with his father, Gates, his friend Morris K. Jessup, and Dr. Wallace Buttrick, the portly and jovial secretary of the Baptist Home Mission Society, who also attended the conference and was now a member of the SEB. A small group was formed to develop an ambitious project in support of the Southern work. In January 1902, they outlined a munificent philanthropic enterprise. In February an expanded group met for dinner at Junior's house and worked through the evening. Junior announced a pledge he had secured from his father for $1 million to spend over the next ten years, the first and smallest of many gifts to come. They formed a board of trustees to oversee the expenditures and appointed Buttrick executive secretary.[72] "The South with its varied resources and products," their memorandum of agreement observed, "has immense industrial potentialities, and its prosperous future will be assured with the right kind of education and training for its children of both races."[73]

The General Education Board was announced to the press. "The object of this association," they explained, "is to provide a vehicle through which capitalists of the North who sincerely desire to assist in the great work of Southern education may act with assurance that their money will be wisely used."[74]

The General Education Board (GEB), with its large resources, quickly became the locus of leadership in the Southern campaign. At its first meeting in 1901 the Southern Education Board had arranged a "community of interest" with the Peabody and Slater funds. By 1903, according to Southern board member Frissell, "the Peabody and Slater boards are now acting very largely through the General Education Board." In fact a more interlocking directorate could not be found, even among the Standard Oil companies. Several trustees of the Slater and Peabody boards were trustees of the GEB. Curry was a member or agent of all four funds. Buttrick was a member of the Southern board, executive secretary of the GEB, and from 1903 to 1910 he was an agent of the Slater Fund—and so on.[75]

While the General Education Board developed other programs over the next several decades, medical ones prominently among them, their work in the South remained important and never deviated substantially from their original perspective. Over the years the GEB worked to make all schools "more responsive to our social, economic, and professional needs." The black population's role in society was clear. The board believed "the Negro must be educated and trained . . . that he may be more sober, more industrious, more competent." When the GEB finally came to support full-fledged colleges for blacks, it was not because their general outlook on race relations had changed. College training would be "provided for carefully selected Negroes" who will "lead the race in its efforts to educate and improve itself." The black's leaders "must be trained, so that, looking to them for guidance as he does, he may be as well guided as possible."[76]

The GEB was not concerned only with education of blacks. It worked to build up high schools for whites and for blacks throughout the South. Always with an eye to creating "local responsibility for self-help"—what Gates called the "foundation of character and social life itself"—the board's strategy was to stimulate and organize community support for school taxes. The GEB got each state university to create a professorship for secondary education. Then with the university's approval, the board defined the duties of the position and named the person to be hired and, in return, paid the person's salary and all his expenses. The main function of this professor was not to teach but to organize. He would visit the towns of his state—"as an officer of the university, laden with its wisdom and its moral authority"—and develop and channel local support for high schools and taxes to support them. At the end of two decades of work, the GEB had spent a little over $3 million promoting public schools in the rural and urban South. They considered the plan effective "beyond our most sanguine anticipations" and took considerable credit for the 2,000 new high schools built in that period at a cost of $60 million, for which annual appropriations in the Southern states increased from $1.7 million in 1905 to $15 million in 1922—"all raised by local taxation."[77]

The public schools program of the GEB led to a farm demonstration program run for the board by Seaman Knapp and then to the first of a long tradition of public health programs conducted by the Rockefeller foundations. Rooted in the same concern for Southern economic and social development that guided the public schools program, the public health programs, at first in the Southern states and then exported around the world, became important supports for the growing domination by U.S. capital, trade, and military power.[78] Gates, a charter member of the GEB and its chairman from 1907 to 1917, was the eloquent orator and, in Junior's words, "the brilliant dreamer and creator" of most of these programs.

The permanence of the General Education Board was assured with a broad congressional charter, dedicating the new foundation to "the promotion of education within the United States." Senator Nelson Aldrich, Junior's father-in-law and a powerful representative of business in Washington, "took the bill into his own hands and put it through in record time." It was officially chartered in January 1903, a year after it began its first Southern program, yet the most influential work of the GEB was yet to come.[79]

Gates took into his own bosom the worries about Rockefeller's still-growing fortune. "I have lived with this great fortune of yours daily for fifteen years," he wrote his employer in 1905. "To it, its increase and its uses, I have given every thought, until it has become a part of myself, almost as if it were my own."[80]

Recognizing the mortality that all persons must face, Gates laid out the alternatives to Rockefeller. "One is that you and your children, while living, shall make final and complete disposition of this great trust, for the good of mankind. The other is that you shall not do this, but shall hand it down to unborn generations, for them to decide how this trust shall finally be discharged for humanity."

For Gates, embracing Carnegie's "Gospel" and fearing the "powerful tendencies to social demoralization" of inherited wealth, the first alternative was the only moral one. He proposed that Rockefeller decide what major lines of work for "human progress" he wanted to serve and who should administer the funds and then create an endowment "to provide funds in perpetuity, under competent management, with proper provision for succession."

Gates then suggested several funds for different areas of work—"a great fund for the promotion of a system of higher education in the United States, . . . a fund for the promotion of medical research throughout the world, . . . a fund for the promotion of the fine arts," and more. "These funds should be so large that to become a trustee of one of them is to make a man at once a public character." The work of these enterprises should employ "the best talent of the entire human race."

Junior followed this letter with his own enthusiastic endorsement of Gates' proposal. Within two weeks Rockefeller, Sr., gave the General Education Board $10 million and followed that a year and a half later with another $32 million. By 1921 Rockefeller's gifts to the GEB totaled more than $129 million. Larger and more numerous endowments began to flow to the Rockefeller Institute for Medical Research, fathered by Gates from his employer's fortune in 1901, and soon discussions began that led from Gates' 1905 letter to the creation of a much larger and broader fund, the Rockefeller Foundation, to which Senior gave more than $182 million.

It is not so clear that Gates' only concern in recommending that Rockefeller himself dispose of his fortune was the danger of inherited wealth to its possessors. The notoriety that accrued to Rockefeller and other robber barons along with their profits cast a long shadow on the future of wealth, and the Rockefellers felt the chill as much as anyone. Henry Demarest Lloyd, in *Wealth Against Commonwealth* published in 1894, and Ida Tarbell, in a magazine series ending in 1904, had tarred and feathered the Standard Oil Trust. The Socialist movement was winning the support of working people throughout the country for its program to do away with private capital altogether. And perhaps most frightening of all, upstanding middle-class Americans, professionals and businessmen with values very much like the Rockefellers themselves, were joining the call for Progressive reforms. The Progressive movement, while firmly supporting capitalism, was calling for constraints on the accumulation and concentration of private wealth. Roosevelt was elected in 1904 on a platform that at least threatened to break up monopolies.

"I trembled," Gates later recalled, "as I witnessed the unreasoning popular resentment at Mr. Rockefeller's riches, to the mass of the people a national menace." Gates might believe that Rockefeller "used his wealth always and only in the public interest," that his fortune had been created by economies rather than by theft, that his wide investments in industry and finance constituted "vast permanent contributions to the wealth and well-being of the American people." But few people in the country not connected with 26 Broadway agreed with him.[81]

In the fall of 1906 the federal government launched a major suit to break up the Standard Oil Trust, and that litigation began its five-year journey through the courts. After Rockefeller gave the GEB $32 million in 1907 to finance Gates' plan to create "a system of higher education in the United States," many respectable newspapers and magazines suggested that "the purpose of Mr. Rockefeller's large gift is to head off, if possible, the teaching of socialism, which is on the increase . . . in a number of universities." Also in 1907 federal Judge Kenesaw Mountain Landis hit the Indiana Standard company with a $29 million fine for obtaining rebates on its railroad shipments, one of the "economies" in which Gates and Rockefeller took pride. "No oriental despot . . . has committed such arbitrary acts of confiscation as the present administration is responsible for under the forms of law," Gates railed.[82]

The Landis fine was quashed on appeal, but the spectre of dissolution and ultimately of confiscation pursued the Rockefellers and many of their class. The Rockefeller philanthropies created new programs and with them new images for the benefactors. The programs appealed to their perceptions of social needs, but in their perceptions, society's needs were indistinguishable from their own. Colleges were expanded and organized into a system of higher education to produce the professionals and managers the corporate society badly needed, but the GEB for two decades consciously followed Gates' directive to strengthen private rather than state universities because private institutions, controlled by men and women like themselves, would be more likely to "direct popular opinion into right channels."[83] The medical philanthropies, outwardly appearing only to fill an obvious social need, helped to develop a medical care system peculiarly suited to the needs of corporate capitalism, as we will see in subsequent chapters.

SOCIAL MANAGERS FOR A CORPORATE SOCIETY

It is clear that John D. Rockefeller, Sr., was neither the initiator nor the strategist in his philanthropies. In the early years it was Gates and then Gates and Junior whose ideas and strategies shaped the elder Rockefeller's fortune into purposeful programs. In part the insight they showed concerning the needs of capitalist society may be attributed to their individual personalities, shaped by their own life experiences. But they were also representative of the new class of men (and very few women at that time) who provided the managerial skills needed by corporate industry and finance. Unlike the individualistic entrepreneurs who built the enormous industrial and financial empires around themselves in the latter nineteenth century, these new managers were more sensitive to the smooth workings of their enterprises.

In industry, management's role was to rationalize production, to divide the productive process into "efficient" units, and simultaneously to coordinate each with the other to produce a unified organization, linked in a similarly coordinated fashion with disparate sources of investment capital and raw materials at one end of the production line and with a system of distribution and marketing at the other end. Analogous managerial roles were also developed in government bureaus and departments, then in colleges and the emerging universities. The last major area to which skilled management was directed were the social services—charity and social welfare programs, philanthropic foundations, and medicine.

The foundations were key instruments in early efforts to rationalize social services, public health, and medical care under the control of specially trained managers in those fields, and the foundations themselves became the turf of this same management class. It made little difference whether one owned a substantial share of the country's corporate wealth or whether one simply ran the factories and institutions owned by the wealthy. The actions of each group were essentially the same, and their values were quite similar. They both accepted the prevailing economic, social, and political system as given, and they sought to make the system work smoothly.

Some of these system managers used charity to try to make capitalist society, whose ideal model is a purely competitive marketplace, a less "rigid and heartless" one, as a recent proponent of this view put it. He believes that philanthropy should "provide at least some softening of the corners and relaxation of the rigid rule of self-interest."[84]

Others like Gates and John D. Rockefeller, Jr., conceived of a more strategic role for philanthropy—the transformation of social institutions. They worked to make the nation's colleges and universities into a system that would more efficiently yield technically trained and properly socialized professionals and managers for the system. They developed new roles for professionals as managers, and they helped rationalize the institutions in which these professionals worked.

Men like the Senior Rockefeller and Andrew Carnegie knew little of this work. They had understood its relevance to industry where they had been the first ones in oil and steel, respectively, to create vertically integrated corporations, owning or controlling the entire process from oil wells and iron ore mines, to transportation, refining and manufacturing, distribution, and marketing. But running a corporation is different from running a corporate society, and though they understood the need to take more control over social institutions, they did not understand how.

Carnegie, egotistical and individualistic, *thought* he understood. Until Andrew Carnegie began giving away libraries in the 1880s, the world had never seen such a vast fortune applied to private philanthropy. This remarkable innovation in magnitude of philanthropic wealth—due, of course, to his insatiable ambition in industry rather than to any strategic genius in philanthropy—gave him a social power so vast that it proved truly befuddling. Armed with a crude social philosophy, he set forth to civilize the lower classes and set a model of responsibility for the upper echelons of society. The society he hoped to preserve was one based explicitly on enormous disparities of wealth. And he attempted to preserve the individualism he and other Social Darwinists revered with a largely individualistic approach to social transformation. His programs represented his own personalized views, shared in varying degrees by contemporary capitalists. But Carnegie's vision was a limited one and his programs often stepped over the edge into absurdity. When Carnegie retired from the steel business in 1901, his philanthropic plans were vague and scattered. In the words of his biographer Joseph F. Wall, "For someone who had written so extensively and preached so eloquently as he on the duties of the man of wealth, it is rather surprising that he faced this task better armed with platitudes than with any concrete program of action."[85]

After several years of massive spending without a real plan, Carnegie set up his foundations, and his hired managers began accomplishing what he had not. In 1905 Carnegie began to move from his individualistic method of dispersing money to a more rationalized, systematic model. Appalled by the pitiful incomes of college professors—usually not more than $400 per year—Carnegie had meant to do something about them for some time. But it was Henry S. Pritchett, the president of the Massachusetts Institute of Technology, who moved him to action. While visiting Carnegie at his ancient castle in the Scottish Highlands in the summer of 1904, Pritchett lamented the difficulties he had in attracting young scientists and engineers to teach at MIT. Academic salaries could not compare with those offered by private industry, and few colleges even had pension systems to provide a minimum of financial security for professors. There were more discussions the following winter, and in April 1905 Carnegie announced the creation of his college teachers pension fund with an initial endowment of $10 million in U.S. Steel bonds. A board of trustees was selected consisting mainly of the presidents of the most elite universities and colleges in the country. Pritchett was appointed president of the new Carnegie Foundation for the Advancement of Teaching.[86]

Under Pritchett's guidance the new foundation set out to recast American higher education. The free pensions became the carrot-at-the-end-of-the-stick that colleges would follow down the path of reform. An applicant college or university had to have a minimum of $200,000 endowment to qualify for the pension program. Neither state colleges nor those controlled by religious denominations were eligible. Finally, to be eligible a school had to require of its students a prescribed minimum of high school preparation prior to admission. This last requirement proved a successful attempt by the foundation to "throw its influence" in favor of a "differentiation between the secondary school and the college" in order to create "a system of schools intelligently related to each other and to the ambitions and needs of a democracy." Although only fifty-two of the original 421 applicants were eligible for the pension plan, other schools soon modeled themselves on the Carnegie system to make themselves eligible. Denominational colleges cut loose from their controlling churches to take advantage of the plan, and the foundation's rules were changed to include state institutions. Soon virtually every high school and college in the country measured student progress in "Carnegie units." A national system of education was taking shape with the prodding of Carnegie pensions and the Carnegie Foundation as the unofficial accrediting body.[87]

Almost immediately after opening the offices of the Carnegie Foundation, Pritchett began consulting with the General Education Board. His only regret, he told GEB executive secretary Wallace Buttrick, was that "I did not come to you before renting my office for it would be of great benefit to us to be located near you." Pritchett admired Gates, often asked for his advice, and tried to get Carnegie to mend his philanthropic ways. In fact the record left behind suggests that Pritchett's ideas on systematizing higher education were derived from Gates.[88]

The leadership that attracted this following was Gates' vision of how wealth could rationalize higher education. He described a picture of the GEB, through its "moral influence" as well as its money, fostering cooperation among colleges and universities and securing economies "in administration, in teaching force and in the use of men." He hoped that such a philanthropic board, properly endowed, would "select" and "direct" the resources of higher education, much as the Standard Oil Company had transformed the "universal competitive system" that characterized the oil industry in 1870.[89]

Rockefeller was fortunate to find a man like Gates to develop "wholesale philanthropy" for him. As Junior and other officers of the Rockefeller foundations readily admitted, Gates was the source of most strategic ideas, major programs, and important policies in the foundations' first decade and a half, with Junior developing an increasingly important role. In that time there was no serious challenge raised to Gates' dominance. The board of trustees was the final authority, but other staff members knew that if they had Gates' or Junior's support, "we were on safe ground" and would have little problem winning approval from the board.[90]

Gradually, however, Gates' influence declined. While the times changed and the much younger Junior became a leader of the growing image of corporate responsibility and concern, Gates' limitations became apparent. Following the 1914 massacre of striking miners and their wives and children in a Ludlow,

Colorado, mining company controlled by the Rockefellers, Junior was held largely responsible by public opinion throughout the nation. But the posture he developed afterward, formulated by consultant W. L. Mackenzie King, made him the leading representative of the new, more benign face of industrial relations that was winning support from many corporate executives. When Junior, who had been called before a Presidential commission created to investigate such problems, claimed he thought it perfectly proper for "labor to associate itself into organized groups for the advancement of its legitimate interests," Gates criticized him for adopting a "spirit of conciliation toward those who came to him in the spirit of these Unionists." Yet it was Junior's support of company unions that was assuaging public opinion and winning the respect of other corporate leaders. Gates did not adapt himself to the changing times.[91]

With Gates' leadership passing from the scene, especially following his resignation from the GEB executive committee in 1917, problems of accountability began to be raised. Trustees who had willingly followed Gates now found the foundations without comparable leadership. Other foundation officers had never demonstrated the broad and clear perspective that Gates had shown, and with Gates gone from daily participation in foundation activities, a vacuum was created. Trustees wanted to fill it by increasing their participation. Foundation officers quarreled with one another. The foundations drifted.[92]

With Gates these problems did not arise because his carefully developed and forcefully presented proposals won immediate support. Gates never expected the trustees to play an important role in social innovation. When a trustee suggested that GEB members were appointed to throw new light on "the great problem of education in this country," Gates impatiently explained that he and Rockefeller gave an "overwhelming preponderance to business men" in composing the board "to fix the policies of this Board along the lines of successful experience." They knew, he said, that "successful business men would steer the ship along traditional lines and would not be carried out of their course by any temporary breeze or even by hurricanes of sentiment."[93] The trustees were there to assure in perpetuity that Rockefeller's money would be judiciously applied to preserving the system and strengthening it, letting professional educators promote innovative ideas while the trustees supported only those directions which seemed desirable and whose consequences were more certain.

Though Gates ran the GEB with firm leadership and a fiery tongue during his tenure as chairman, he and Junior both wanted the other trustees to take an active interest in the foundation. Without involvement, their interest and sense of responsibility for the fortune would decrease—the very thing to be avoided. "In the remote future," Junior advised his father, "you must of necessity trust to the character and integrity of the men who come after you."[94]

It was clearly just as important to encourage local communities to take "responsibility for self-help." Gates' reasons for this guiding principle were moral, tactical, and strategic. He believed in the moral precepts of self-reliance and self-discipline. He also wanted to enlist the active participation of property owners in community institutions. Although they were not as reliable as the men appointed to the Rockefeller foundations, the local ruling classes recognized, as did he, that "the right to earn and hold surplus wealth marks the dawn of civilization."[95] Gates, Junior, and Rockefeller all understood that to fund a local institution without requiring contributions and participation from local men and women of wealth would be to lessen these people's sense of responsibility for what goes on in the institution. They had a genuine concern for the preservation of their society, and its preservation required the active involvement of all those who had a stake in it.

Rockefeller's involvement with the University of Chicago is a good example of this principle in action. Rockefeller contributed $35 million to the university during its first two decades compared with $7 million from all other donors. He was consulted about appointments to the board of trustees and approved the initial list before it was finalized. But thereafter Rockefeller did not desire to control the university, as many people charged. "He prefers to rest the whole weight of the management on the shoulders of the proper officers," Gates wrote the university president on behalf of his boss in 1892. "Donors can be certain that their gifts will be preserved and made continuously and largely useful, after their own voices can no longer be heard, only in so far as they see wisdom and skill in the management, quite independently of themselves, now." Rockefeller's trust in the management was well founded. There is no evidence that he ever tried directly to influence the university administration to fire teachers who expressed radical views. It was University of Chicago president Harper who took the initiative to drop Professor Edward Bemis after he made a speech, following the 1894 Pullman strike, critical of the railroads. Rockefeller and Gates had merely appointed the "right" men to manage their philanthropic and financial enterprises, men who were led by values and considerations similar to their own and who could be counted on to do what was expected. In many ways, local authorities in whom Rockefeller placed his trust proved the correctness of this rule.[96]

One final and important tactical reason for securing local involvement was to multiply the impact of each grant. The Rockefeller foundations required virtually all recipients to raise an amount equal to, or as much as four times greater than, the grant being given by the foundation. Besides being chosen for their stabilizing influence, foundation trustees were also chosen for "the prestige and authority of their names." Andrew Carnegie, Long Island Railroad president William H. Baldwin, Harvard president Charles W. Eliot, Johns Hopkins president Daniel Coit Gilman, publisher Walter Hines Page, banker George Foster Peabody, and other prestigious individuals were appointed to the GEB to "secure general public approval and active and powerful public cooperation" for GEB programs. In gaining public support and in requiring matching contributions from others, the foundation was able to multiply the impact of the grant programs. By 1925 the GEB had given $60 million to the endowments of colleges and universities in the United States for certain reforms they deemed desirable, and they had, by their matching-grant policy, required the institutions to raise an additional $140 million to support these GEB-required changes. By 1928 the General Education Board had contributed some $50 million to medical schools for very specific reforms,* generating total resources estimated at ten times that amount for those same reforms.[97]

Thus the Rockefeller philanthropies, under the guidance of skilled managers, developed self-consciously strategic programs

---

*This program is described in detail in Chapter 4.

to transform higher education and medical care, among other social institutions. The thrust of their programs was to systematize and rationalize these institutions to make them better serve the needs of corporate capitalism.

The rise of industrial capitalism brought with it many new needs that provided opportunities for groups besides the capitalist class. The work process was reshaped to reduce the costs and increase management's control of production. Scientists developed the basic understandings on which technological innovation was based. Engineers adapted scientific knowledge to production, designing new methods and machines that reduced the need for skilled workers, increased productivity, and generally gave management more complete control of the entire production process.

A new stratum of managers and professionals emerged in the society's class structure to design and organize production and the institutions that reproduce and control capitalist society's social relations. Colleges and universities became the training and research agencies, producing knowledge and reproducing engineers, scientists, lawyers, teachers, and other technicians and social managers. Managers were well paid for their efforts, and some, like Gates, were incorporated into the highest circles of the owning class. But despite their separation from predominant ownership, managers of corporations and institutions alike "still *think* and *act* as though the firm belonged to them," as William Appleman Williams put it.[98] Their commitments to the prevailing economic system are complete.

Out of an earlier mercantilist philanthropy grew a new corporate philanthropy, intended not to ameliorate the lot of industrial capitalism's victims but to shape and guide social institutions. Foundations were, and still are, important ramparts through which private wealth, acting through creative and loyal managers, influences and often controls universities, medical schools, and other "public" institutions. The Rockefeller foundations established directions and strategies that other foundations followed. Gates led the Rockefeller philanthropies with his "imagination, daring, and an intuitive sense of educational strategy."[99] Pritchett, following Gates' leadership, made Carnegie's foundation an engine of social transformation. In many ways, Gates, Pritchett, and other managers understood the workings and needs of capitalism better than the ostensible owners of the system did.

Broad social transformations, however, require the participation of more than the ruling class. While the working class suffered greatly from the capitalist reorganization of production, some groups attached themselves to the ascending corporate class and benefited greatly. New occupations, like engineering and social work, and old ones, like law and medicine, gained elevated professional status in return for becoming the new order's managers of production or social relations. Medicine's almost fantastic transformation from rank ignominy to Olympian heights of status exemplifies the powerful consequences of an interest group adapting itself to the needs of the dominant class.

2 CHAPTER

Scientific Medicine I:
Ideology of
Professional Uplift

THROUGHOUT the nineteenth century the medical profession was almost constantly frustrated in its attempts to gain public confidence and raise professional incomes and status. Despite varied attempts to alter the competitive market economy for medical services, the dominant portion of the profession continued to be plagued by competition within its own ranks and from those beyond the pale of orthodoxy.

In this chapter we will see how the rise of science in the latter part of the century provided the solution that medical reformers had previously sought in vain. Physicians and biological researchers consciously applied the methods and principles of scientific research to problems of disease, though even in the 1860s their work had little support and played a very minor role within the medical profession. At about midcentury, however, leading reformers among elite medical practitioners took up "scientific medicine" as the ideology of professional reform and uplift. Medical science gradually provided practitioners with a somewhat more effective medical practice, enabling them to increase their credibility with the public and reduce economic competition within the profession. "Scientific medicine" was adopted as the unifying theory that enabled the dominant profession to develop strong political organization and to win political and financial support from wealthy people in society. Perhaps most fundamental, the association of medicine with science won support from the new technical, professional, and managerial groups associated with the growth of corporate capitalism.

AMERICAN MEDICINE IN THE 1800s

In 1800, nearly all American physicians received their training as apprentices at the side of a practicing physician, assisting with simple techniques and mixing medications. In the eighteenth century, medical lectures had not been widely available in this country, so young men from the upper class went abroad for their medical education, especially to Scotland. The handful of Edinburgh-trained physicians in America developed very successful practices, with the wealthiest citydwellers for their clients and lucrative consulting practices besides. By 1800 only about a hundred American physicians had attended medical courses at Edinburgh, and only three American medical programs—at Pennsylvania, Harvard, and Dartmouth—were offering lectures to supplement the apprenticeship. The graduates of these institutions formed a medical elite, and together with the rank-and-file apprentice-trained physicians they formed the self-styled "regular" profession.[1]

But most Americans were probably not getting their medical care from "regular" physicians. Whereas most of the populace lived in the countryside or small towns, most apprentice-trained doctors and the few medical school graduates lived in the large towns and cities. In Virginia, by 1800 the eleven largest towns had only 3 percent of the state's population, yet 25 percent of all physicians known to have practiced in Virginia during the eighteenth century lived in those eleven towns.[2]

Most Americans, when they were sick, consulted herbal practitioners. These empirical healers had no formal training but apprenticed mainly with other herbalists. Some of the herbalists were midwives, and others were men and women who had experimented with herbs and were known for their abilities to heal the sick. Lay healers were distributed throughout the countryside. They seldom relied on healing for their entire support and charged little for their services.[3] Regular physicians were increasingly plying their art on a full-time basis and charging substantially higher fees, often supported by medical societies' publishing "fee bills" to place a floor under competing doctors' charges.

The maldistribution of regular physicians and their higher fees were only two reasons why the regular profession was widely unpopular in the first half of the nineteenth century. Very much related to their social, economic, and geographic separation from the populace, the orthodox profession's clinical practice was greatly feared by much of the population. Not only did medicine offer little hope for curing disease, but the heroic methods used by regular doctors were unpleasant and often lethal. The lancet was the physician's indispensable tool for nearly every ailment. Benjamin Rush, the most prominent physician in America from the Revolution through Jefferson's time, urged bleeding for yellow fever "not only in cases where the pulse was full and quick, but where it was slow and tense."[4] When bleeding was not recommended, and even when it was, calomel (chloride of mercury), jalap, or another purgative was administered. The violent vomiting and purging that resulted were more detested than even the pus-filled blisters induced as another form of therapy. After attacking the body as well as the disease with bleeding, blistering, and purging, the physician administered an arsenic tonic to restore the weakened patient's vigor.

Against this distasteful and frequently disastrous treatment by regular physicians, the empirical herbalists' mild treatments were pleasanter and at the very least did not interfere with natural rates of recovery. Their mild emetics and stimulants seemed closer to nature than the regulars' profuse blood-letting and harsh purges.[5]

Still experiencing competition from the empirically grounded herbalists, regular physicians resorted to ever larger doses of their therapies through the first half of the nineteenth century. Believing that any desired change in a patient's gross symptoms was to the good and seeking to distinguish their art from lay practice, regular doctors bled their patients more profusely and doubled and tripled their doses of calomel and jalap. The profession's heroic therapy became the focus of increasingly bitter and widespread attacks. Thomas Jefferson called them an "inexperienced and presumptuous band of medical tyros let loose upon the world." By the middle of the century cholera victims were given an even chance of being done in by the disease or by the doctor. The profession's fearsome and futile methods reduced public confidence in regular doctors to an all-time low.[6]

Leading local and regional members of the profession tried many methods of increasing public confidence in doctors and reducing competition. At various times during the nineteenth century, they sought licensing laws, formed new medical sects, started medical schools and issued diplomas, organized state and national medical societies, demanded medical school reforms, and adopted codes of ethics, all with little or no improvement in technical effectiveness, credibility with the public, or their own status and fortunes.

LICENSING

Despite the antipathy of much of the populace, regular doctors at the end of the eighteenth century persuaded fellow gentlemen in the state legislatures to pass medical licensing laws to restrict or prohibit practice by herbal healers. Licensure bestowed exclusively on regular physicians the right to sue for fees. The legally sanctioned economic privilege did not provide the regular profession with an economic monopoly, but it did set them apart from and above lay healers and most other Americans.

In addition to the public's lack of confidence in regular physicians' clinical methods, populists in the Jacksonian era articulated their opposition to any form of class privilege. By 1850 medical licensing laws were repealed in nearly every state through the efforts of the Popular Health Movement, a loose populist movement of lay healers, herbal practitioners, artisans, farmers, and working people who fought to remove the legal sanctions that protected the privileged position of physicians.[7]

MEDICAL SECTS AND MEDICAL SCHOOLS

The humiliated profession was badly divided. Many physicians, critical of heroic medicine, were attracted to the pleasanter new professional sects, such as homeopathy and eclecticism, that were growing in popularity. These sects built their materia medica around herbal drugs or some distinctive technology or procedure, each adding elements that enabled them to claim the necessity of extended study in their field.

Homeopathy, as formulated by its founder Samuel Hahnemann (a German physician), was based on the widely accepted medical view that the symptoms of a disease constitute the disease itself and, a corollary, that eliminating the symptoms constitutes a cure. Hahnemann found that some drugs produced the same symptoms in a healthy person (that is, caused the "illness") that they eliminated in a sick person (whom they "cured"). For example, he found that cinchona bark, at the time used to relieve the symptoms of malaria, produced malarial symptoms in a healthy person. From these observations he developed what he called the law of *similia similibus curantur*—or "like cures like." Hahnemann also maintained that diluting the dosage of a drug down to one ten-thousandth or one-millionth of its original strength *increased* the drug's potency.[8]

Competition between the sects and the lack of decisive public support for any one of them, left none of the sects in a position to establish control through licensing. The orthodox profession and the other sects turned to medical education and degrees as a method of recruiting and certifying new physicians in their ranks and uplifting the profession. Medical schools proliferated throughout the country, and some 400 were founded between 1800 and 1900.[9] Local physicians organized schools to supplement their practices with lecture fees paid by medical students and, through their graduates, to fatten their incomes with increased consultations. At a time when physicians considered $1,000 to $2,000 a year a good income, the average part-time medical school faculty member earned more than $5,000 annually from student fees and private practice while more enterprising and popular colleagues earned at least $10,000.[10] Like hundreds of general colleges started before the Civil War by rival Protestant sects and political groups, many medical schools were started by rival medical sects to improve their competitive position vis-à-vis other sects. The orthodox profession controlled by far the largest number of schools.[11]

The proliferation of medical schools in the 1800s assured the dominance of diploma-carrying regular doctors over lay healers and physicians of other sects. By 1860 regular physicians outnumbered other sectarian doctors ten to one.[12] The inexpensive and widely dispersed medical colleges encouraged large numbers of young men and some women to attempt careers in medicine.

Graduates, many of them from yeoman farming and working-class families, filled the cities, towns, and countryside of America. Elite* regular physicians resented the competition within the dominant sect, but they saved their most venomous denunciations for competing sects. The sectarian doctor was "the greatest foe to the medical profession," argued the dean of the Tulane University medical department, because he was "an obstacle to the financial success of the respectable medical practitioner."[13]

As the number of physicians increased, organized doctors became increasingly worried. It was clear to all physicians that producing a lot of doctors would lower rather than raise the status and incomes of the profession as a whole. Lacking the public support necessary for effective medical licensing laws and still smarting from the humiliating defeat of medical licensing earlier in the century, the reformers turned to medical school reform. Raising medical school standards and thereby reducing their enrollment, medical reformers believed, would simultaneously win public confidence in medical practice and reduce the output of doctors. The problem they faced was how to control the independent, proprietary medical schools.

MEDICAL SOCIETIES

Local and state medical societies, representing the practitioners, fought with medical schools in their areas. In 1847 the societies banded together to form the American Medical Association (AMA). At the founding convention, leading practitioners passed resolutions that sought to raise requirements for preliminary education prior to admission to medical school. So few Americans had the requisite education at the time that enforcement of these standards, according to historian William Rothstein, "would have closed down practically every medical school in the country, and would have depleted the ranks of formally educated physicians in a few years."[14]

From its founding onward, the AMA was hostile to the interests of proprietary medical colleges and their faculties. The practitioners wanted to reduce the output of medical schools in

*The term "elite" refers somewhat loosely to physicians who, by their reputations for clinical or research techniques, by income, and/or by organizational leadership positions, had achieved prominence within the profession.

order to reduce competition within the profession, while the medical faculties opposed any attempted reforms because of their interests in maximizing their lecture fees and future consulting fees. Unfortunately for the practitioners, the reform leadership mistakenly thought that including medical schools in the new national organization would allow the medical societies to control them. This strategic mistake immobilized the AMA as the vanguard of practitioners' interests until 1874 when medical college voting rights in the association were abolished.

CODES OF ETHICS

The AMA's attacks on medical education and especially on other medical sects were supported by a "code of ethics" adopted at their first convention. With the code the AMA hoped to deny the ability of patients to judge their physicians or disagreements between physicians, to encourage attacks on "irregular" doctors and "quacks," and generally to reduce competition among regular physicians. At the same time that the AMA complained about the low standards of medical education, the association commanded patients to trust their doctors. "The obedience of a patient to the prescriptions of his doctor should be prompt and implicit," the code of ethics instructed. The patient "should never permit his own crude opinions as to their fitness to influence his attention to them."[15]

These efforts to bolster the profession's falling economic status and power were legitimized on moral and ethical grounds by the medical societies. Since the colonial period, violation of "ethical codes" had been grounds for ostracizing nonconforming physicians. Codes were used not only against other sects and lay healers but against members of the regular profession who consulted with homeopaths and eclectics and even against the developing medical specialties which offered competition to the general practitioners. The AMA code failed to win public support or stamp out competition although the medical societies' attacks on members for code violations intimidated some doctors and increased intraprofessional antagonisms.[16]

In short, conflicts between practitioners and medical faculties, generalists and specialists, and "regular" physicians and other sects kept the profession badly divided throughout the nineteenth century. The incoherent strategy of the regular profession's

leadership and the weak structure of their organization, the
AMA, left the field with no sect able to secure undisputed control
over the competitive marketplace.

Medical school output continued unabated. By the end of the
nineteenth century, the United States averaged one physician to
every 568 people.[17] Compared with prevailing ratios in European
countries (Germany, with one doctor to 2,000 population, was
the favorite example), the United States was "overcrowded" with
physicians. Physicians' incomes ran the gamut from poor ($200 a
year) to wealthy (as much as $30,000 a year for a small number of
elite doctors). The chief complaints of the most prominent
professional spokesmen by the end of the century were the
"surplus" of doctors, "low" incomes, and the low social status of
the profession.

Three underlying problems plagued medical reformers who
tried to heal these wounds. First, physicians lacked an agreed
upon *technical* basis for settling among themselves disputes
between the sects. Without public consensus on technical criteria
of effectiveness and validity, all sects competed for business in the
medical market. But without sufficient public confidence in the
validity of any one sect, no sect could win a monopoly of medical
practice and thereby eliminate the competition.

Second, their lack of a technical basis for establishing public
support put them all in a weak position to establish *political*
control over entry into medical practice. Earlier efforts to use
licensing ended in humiliating defeat for the regular profession
because of organized opposition from other sects and a distrustful
public.

Third, within at least the dominant sect different economic
interests divided those who practiced medicine from those who
trained future practitioners. Practitioners wanted to restrict the
supply of physicians, and part-time faculty wanted to preserve
institutions that were lucrative additions to their own practices.

INCOMPLETE PROFESSIONALIZATION

Without actually having public confidence in their technical
ability, physicians throughout the nineteenth century and earlier
had nevertheless proclaimed norms to support their authority
over the lay public. Demands for recognition of the regular
profession's technical competence (in which they undoubtedly

believed) were the means of legitimating their claims to professional authority. The recognition of that authority, however, was seen as necessary to the profession's controlling the economic conditions of its work. By proclaiming a set of norms and values associated with their work, regular physicians hoped to end the competitive market for medical services and to win a regulated market for themselves.

The basis of professional status and power is still debated by sociologists, who traditionally have posed a set of essential features that are supposed to distinguish professions from the general run of occupations. In 1928, A. M. Carr-Saunders, the father of the sociology of professions, defined a profession as an occupation: (1) based on specialized intellectual training or study, (2) providing a skilled service to others, and (3) in return for a fee or salary.[18] Thirty years later, William Goode stressed prolonged specialized training in a body of abstract knowledge and a collectivity or service orientation as the "core characteristics" of professions.[19] The list of formal characteristics of professions has been extended by other sociologists to include a systematic body of theory, acceptance of the authority of the professional by all who come to him or her as clients, protection of the professional's authority by the political community, a code of ethics to regulate professional relations, and a set of values, norms and symbols that build solidarity among the profession's members.[20]

However, lists of formal characteristics turn out to be fairly useless in the real world in distinguishing professions from other occupations. Even worse, they tend to gloss over the political and economic dynamics that are essential to the process of professionalization, making professional status and power appear an inevitable and desirable feature of modern societies. In reality, as Eliot Freidson has observed, any occupation wishing professional status creates a systematic body of theory, claims exclusive authority of its practitioners, adopts a code of ethics, tries to build solidarity among its practitioners around formal values, norms, and symbols, and otherwise cloaks itself with the well-known medallions of professions to support its claims. "If there is no systematic body of theory," Freidson argues, "it is created for the purpose of being able to say there is."[21]

The commitment to service, argues Harold Wilensky, is "the pivot around which the moral claim to professional status revolves."[22] Like many such professional norms, there remains no clear evidence that a service orientation is *in fact* strong and widespread among professionals. In reviewing the sociological literature that makes such claims, Freidson has concluded: "the blunt fact is that discussions of professions assume or assert *by definition* and without supporting empirical evidence that 'service orientation' is especially common among professionals."[23]

Indeed, many academic social scientists have been beguiled by their own (usually self-serving) beliefs in "science" and "expertise" into confusing professional norms with the reality of professional practice and motivation. Codes of ethics were accepted by some sociologists as genuine efforts by the profession to guarantee competence and honor. Carr-Saunders believed that "if the foundations of the codes were better understood, they would not be generally regarded with hostility."[24]

More recently, some sociologists have approached professional norms more critically. Everett Hughes, for example, argues that the widespread acceptance of norms, like the professional "should have almost complete control over what he does for the client" and "only the professional can say when his colleague makes a mistake," have been used by professionals to hide mistakes.[25]

What much of the sociological literature ignores in examining the process of professionalization is how essential political power is in gaining and maintaining professional status. As the history of the medical profession in the nineteenth century demonstrates, without sufficient political power the profession remained unable to control its economic and working conditions. Initial efforts at licensure were defeated by a popular movement of lay healers and other Jacksonian-era populists. Attempts to use medical education as a strategy of reform were thwarted by the organized profession's lack of control over medical schools. The leading reformers organized a national professional association, but the medical school faculties were beyond the reach of the American Medical Association. Ethical codes, articulating prevailing professional norms, failed to win public support for the profession and could not overcome intraprofessional competition. What the medical reformers sought was the power to enforce the instruments of professionalism that assure high incomes, social status, and continued prosperity for the profession.

Freidson is adamant in this interpretation of professionalization. "Not training as such, but *only the issue of autonomy and control over training granted the occupation by an elite or public persuaded of its importance* seems to be able to distinguish clearly among occupations," he argues. "And the process determining the outcome is essentially political and social rather than technical in character—a process in which power and persuasive rhetoric are of greater importance than the objective character of knowledge, training, and work." The nature of training, as well as the service ideal, ethical code, and body of abstract theory constitute a profession's "ideology, a deliberate rhetoric in a political process of lobbying, public relations, and other forms of persuasion to attain a desirable end—full control over its work."[26]

The history of medicine, from this perspective, can be understood as a political process in which the specific reforms—however much they may increase the technical effectiveness of physicians—are also instruments of persuasion and symbols of legitimacy. The goals of reform leaders were to gain collective control for the profession over its working conditions and economics in order to establish a hierarchy of authority and power among healing occupations, to assure that physicians reign firmly at the top of the hierarchy, and to assure them as high incomes as possible in any given historical period.

Support for such interests would have to come from outside the profession. While efforts were made to win the credibility of "the public," leaders of the profession did not see their struggle as a grassroots campaign. Seeking a social and economic position above the majority of the population, they could at best hope for the acquiescence of the people. Active support would have to come from the already higher social classes. In the eighteenth century, practitioners had turned to gentlemen farmers and wealthy merchants in the state legislatures to protect their interests. In the nineteenth century a political rebellion from below demonstrated the insufficiency of merely legislated sanctions. Furthermore, political power increasingly rested in a new class in society—those capitalists who controlled great manufacturing and marketing enterprises. These were the men who, for good or bad, were changing the face of the nation. Around their enterprises grew the great cities. From their factories came the steel and machines that enabled the same men to unify the country commercially with railroads, products, and even armies. From their corporations came the demand for foreign resources and the products for foreign markets that were rapidly making America a world power. This was the ascending class in America at the end of the nineteenth century. Those groups in society who connected with their enterprises or their interests could rise with them.

It became clear to increasing numbers of physicians that the complete professionalization of medicine could come only when they developed an ideology and a practice that was consistent with the ideas and interests of socially and politically dominant groups in the society. It was *desirable* that everyone in society recognize their technical effectiveness, but it was *essential* that the classes and groups associated with the ascending social order believe in their efficacy. The development and increasing dominance of scientific medicine within the profession provided the virtually perfect material and ideological basis for an alliance of the medical profession with other professionals (mainly engineers and lawyers), corporate managers, and all ranks of the capitalist class. The medical profession discovered an ideology that was compatible with the world view of, and politically and economically useful to, the capitalist class and the emerging managerial and professional stratum.

MEDICINE AS SCIENCE

Medical research was flourishing in Germany and France during the nineteenth century, and even in the United States biologists and physicians made their contributions. In 1818 Valentine Mott, a New York physician, was among the first to attempt major arterial surgery near the heart. Other Americans also attempted new surgical procedures while some physicians contributed new understandings to internal medicine. The New York Academy of Medicine, founded in 1847, and the Pathological Society in Philadelphia promoted discussion of medical research and science.[27]

Few of the findings and developments in medical research were directly useful in improving medical practice. It is doubtful that many patients survived the new surgical techniques in the absence of aseptic practices. While the differentiation of diseases made observation more precise, the usual heroic treatments were just as likely to do the patient in as before.

Beginning in midcentury, medical research in Europe started producing more applicable findings. In 1858 Rudolf Virchow unveiled a general concept of disease based on the cellular structure of the body. From the findings of cell physiology, anatomy, and pathology, Pasteur, Koch, and other medical researchers developed new concepts and applications of bacteriology.[28] In the last quarter of the century specialized German laboratories began to replace the more generalist botanists, biologists, and physicians. Their findings gave medical science a more reductionist and technically more effective turn.

Changes in American medical practice reflected the gradual acceptance of recent developments in Europe. Starting in the 1870s, American physicians flocked to the famous laboratories of German and Austrian universities for a year or more of study—if they were ambitious and could afford the expense of travel and living abroad without income. Between 1870 and the outbreak of World War I in 1914, about 15,000 American physicians studied medicine in Germany alone.[29]

While most American doctors who studied in Europe returned to develop lucrative private practices, a few put their main energies into developing laboratory medical sciences in the United States. Carl Ludwig's physiology institute in Leipzig produced several luminaries of America's infant medical science. Henry Pickering Bowditch, one of Ludwig's pupils, founded the country's first experimental physiology department at Harvard University in 1871. William Henry Welch, another of Ludwig's pupils, started America's first pathology laboratory at Bellevue Hospital medical school in 1878.[30]

Fifteen years later American medical science came of age with the opening of the Johns Hopkins medical school, modeled after the German university medical schools with a heavy emphasis on research in the basic medical sciences. At Hopkins, for the first time in the United States, the laboratory science faculty were to be full-time teachers and researchers, supported by salaries adequate to live on and unencumbered by the distractions of private practice. Virtually the entire Hopkins faculty was trained in Germany. Hopkins, and then Harvard, Yale, and Pennsylvania, became the indigenous producers of scientific medical faculty. As scientific medicine gained increasing acceptance, medical schools throughout the country vied for Hopkins graduates to add gleam to their lackluster local faculties.

Medical practice likewise began to change with the increased acceptance of medical science. Physicians began introducing into their work those scientific medical practices that were uncomplicated and acceptable to their patients and at least *seemed* effective in reducing suffering and ameliorating the symptoms of disease.[31] The use of bleeding and calomel began falling off in the 1870s though many physicians continued to use them on a more limited basis as late at the 1920s.

Physicians who had the money to take an extra year's study in Europe were able to build more prestigious practices than the ordinary American-trained doctor. Usually they would take themselves out of direct competition with the majority of physicians by specializing in gynecology, surgery, opthalmology, or one of the other new branches of medicine. They quickly formed a new elite in the profession, with reputations that brought the middle and wealthy classes to their doors.[32]

As the base of scientific medicine spread out to include more practitioners, the peaks of elite physicians rose even higher. They quickly found that "scientific medicine" not only seemed more effective than the heroics of old, it was also far more profitable.

Professional leaders had tried numerous ways of uplifting the profession during the nineteenth century, but none of them had succeeded. It was medical science that provided the key to professional reform. Medical research yielded new tools of understanding and held out the hope of more effective techniques of prevention and treatment than orthodox medicine offered. But scientific medicine was utilized by professional leaders beyond merely increasing the technical effectiveness of their practice. It became as well the *ideology of professionalization,* used to gain support from the dominant groups associated with industrial capitalism, to cement the complete dominance of health care by the medical profession, and to raise the incomes and status of physicians as a group.

The obvious advantages to the profession notwithstanding, scientific medicine contained within it the seeds of ultimate destruction for the profession. The remainder of this chapter and the rest of this study will examine how this dialectic played itself out—the benefits the profession derived from the adoption of scientific medicine, the contradictions inherent in this historical process that began to undermine the position of the medical profession, and the new forces and contradictions that are now emerging.

GAINING PUBLIC CONFIDENCE

Scientific medicine solved two broad problems the medical profession faced in the late nineteenth century: lack of public confidence in the effectiveness of their service and competition within the medical profession.

Rather than inspiring awe and confidence, the regular medical profession had won the public's fear and ridicule. To win public support and patronage was the major task set by professional leaders during the nineteenth century. The AMA's code of ethics sought to assure the lay public that doctors were ethical and competent and attempted to command the public to place their confidence in regular physicians. But no claims or commands were effective in the absence of convincing personal experience or persuasive propaganda that could substitute for personal experience.

While homeopathy, eclecticism, and osteopathy did not have as much public patronage as the regular profession, they had a strong base of support. They had a following, including many wealthy and influential people, who believed in their absolute effectiveness. Their practitioners were widely believed to be, relatively at least, as effective as and certainly less dangerous than most regular doctors. And they did not demand a monopoly of practice, a wise and practical political course given the disreputable condition of the profession and the almost universal reliance on home remedies for most minor acute and chronic ailments.

For the regular profession to win in their competition with the other medical sects, they needed first of all to gain absolutely and relatively in public confidence. Scientific medicine provided the basis for a concerted and successful campaign to win this public support. The effort never depended on the common folk of America. The campaign for acceptance of scientific medicine was aimed at the wealthy and powerful in society and the new "middle" classes. Both of these groups owed their privileged positions to the intensive industrialization that began with the Civil War. They were particularly attracted to a kind of medicine that shared their industrial culture, their values, their world outlook, and their ideologies. "Scientific management" analyzed the labor process in production into its constituent elements and reorganized them under management's control and for management's profits.[33] In a similar vein, "scientific medicine" analyzed the body into its parts, subjected the parts to the control of scientific doctors, and thereby kept the bodies healthier and more efficient.

The germ theory of disease was especially attractive to both the regular profession and these new industrial and corporate elites. The germ theory emphasized discrete, specific, and external causal agents of disease. It gave encouragement to the idea of specific therapies to cure specific pathological conditions.[34] The payoff for the medical practitioners would be increased technical effectiveness and improved standing in the eyes of the public. That was not the foremost concern of either influential capitalists or medical researchers. These men (there were hardly any women in their ranks) saw in scientific medicine the possibility of preventing diseases through technological intervention that identified the offending organism and its means of contagion, and attacked the organism at the source or used it to create an immune response within the body. Disease was thus seen as an engineering problem, surmountable with sufficient talent and resources. To the medical researchers the germ theory and discoveries in bacteriology confirmed the value of their craft and assured increased support for their work. For capitalists, bacteriological investigations and the application of the findings opened the possibility of reducing the toll that disease took of society's resources.

The forerunners of scientific medicine, along with practitioners in other medical sects, had already greatly improved the classification of diseases. European physicians had long dominated the field of medical discovery although now and then an American made a contribution. In 1836 William Gerhardt, a physician at Philadelphia Hospital, clinically differentiated typhoid from typhus. But there was little practical benefit from such classifications when no therapy was forthcoming to cure the condition. Bleeding, purging, blistering, and tonics were the standard bag of tricks available to regular physicians. Homeopaths and eclectics, along with lay healers, used a wide assortment of herbs, and many claimed high rates of cures. By the 1880s the regular profession still had only a few drugs that were widely recognized to be curative: Quinine could save the victim of malaria, mercury could cure syphilis, and digitalis was often successful in treating heart disorders.[35]

The field of disease prevention was somewhat more successful. In the eighteenth century wealthy Europeans and Americans adopted the practice of variolation, a somewhat dangerous inoculation against smallpox used in the East for centuries. In 1798 Edward Jenner introduced inoculation with cowpox that was effective and somewhat safer than variolation.[36]

By the time of the third major cholera epidemic in the United States in 1866, the notion that cholera was a specific and contagious disease had finally won near-unanimous support from the medical profession, joining the already strong popular belief in its contagion. Medical support for cleaning up the accumulated filth in American cities won the backing of the business class and helped prevent the spread of cholera and the high death rates that had characterized the previous epidemics. The success of this preventive effort was credited to sanitary engineering and brought increased support for sanitation programs.[37]

Despite the scant results, leading practitioners and the new class of medical researchers sustained their faith in the eventual success of medical science. The major breakthroughs came from Europe in the 1880s and 1890s. In 1883 and 1884 Edwin Klebs and Friedrich Loeffler isolated the germ involved in diphtheria, a major killer in the nineteenth century. Emil von Behring and his coworkers produced a diphtheria antitoxin in the early 1890s, which although of little significance in reducing the death toll from diphtheria, supported the belief that deadly epidemics that were borne with resignation could in fact be prevented by understanding their causes.[38]

These and other discoveries in the 1880s and 1890s were lauded around the world. Medical science benefited with new respect and political and financial support. Success indeed paved the road to fortune. The German government provided laboratories for Robert Koch and Paul Ehrlich. In France popular contributions supplied a research institute for Louis Pasteur. In England and Japan private philanthropy paid for new medical research institutes.

In the United States private and government support for medical research lagged behind these other countries. Veterinary medicine received help from the Department of Agriculture to stem epidemics that were wiping out livestock investments. Government officials and philanthropists saw little value in researching human disease, as Richard Shryock notes, "partly because of the nature of medical science prior to 1885 and partly because human welfare brought no direct financial return. Hogs did."[39] Discoveries of the 1880s and 1890s, however, held out the promise that as science uncovered the germs that caused the great pestilences, further investigation would provide not only cures but methods for guarding against infection and for preventing the spread of epidemics. These expectations guided the lives of medical researchers, but they were also spreading rapidly among the middle classes and those who owned and managed America's new industrial empires.

Medical science rescued the medical profession, in particular the practitioners, from the widespread lack of confidence in their effectiveness. These few but significant discoveries, mostly in bacteriology, increased the belief in the technical effectiveness of the profession as a whole. The actual impact of progress against infectious disease was not nearly so great as its proponents claimed. The arsenal of effective weapons against diseases did not increase spectacularly, but its limited advances did provide the basis for persuading the public that scientific medicine reflected on all members of the profession—practitioners as well as researchers—who had been trained in the theory and methods of scientific medical research.

The slight increase in the effectiveness of the new medicine was embellished in propaganda by the profession and the media. From the 1890s on, popular magazines and newspapers joined the leading medical journals in praising the accomplishments and prophesying the future success of medical science. Articles ridiculing "Popular Medical Fallacies" and extolling the "Triumphs of Modern Medicine" and the "War Against Disease" appeared in many popular magazines as well as professional journals. They portrayed medicine as an "exact science" and the physician as an inquiring and skeptical scientist who avoids "hasty jumping at conclusions or too-ready dependence upon formulae."[40]

The increased credibility of medicine was important in convincing the public that doctors with scientific medical training had an expertise worth paying for. If doctors could do little more for a patient than an herbal healer or a patent medicine, there was not much point in people wasting their money on expensive doctors' fees. Scientific medicine wrapped the modern doctor in an aura of therapeutic effectiveness, and the limited improvements gave support to that aura. Furthermore, the technical expertise associated with scientific medicine helped to mystify the role and work of the physician more effectively than did older notions of the etiology of disease, unpleasant remedies, and transparent codes of "ethics." Scientific medicine thereby supported the claims of the profession for a monopoly of control over all healing methods. These benefits provided the basis for other gains and were effective in undermining sectarian medicine, midwifery, and other forms of competition.

In seeking to destroy its competitors' hold on the medical marketplace, the regular profession proffered scientific medicine as more effective than "medicine as art" and "sectarian medicine" and "quacks." Not only was it *more* effective, it was, as each sect before it had claimed, the *only* truly valid medicine. Scientific medicine was held up as *the* nonsectarian medical theory and practice—the only one based not on dogma but on verifiable truths.[41] As the only valid medicine, it should be granted a monopoly of practice; "none but men and women who have an interest in scientific medicine" should be allowed to join any county medical society.[42] But making the claim was not equivalent to having it accepted.

Folk medicine was still widely used in the United States, particularly in the countryside but also in the cities. Every family had its traditional remedies that were part of the family lore, believed in and passed down from generation to generation. Generally, the young woman's own family's remedies prevailed in her new family.[43] Some of the remedies undoubtedly acted as placebos, but many were certainly effective in providing relief and even cures. Such traditions were effective obstacles to the acceptance of scientific medicine.

Most practitioners were also very pragmatic, developing a repertoire of skills and utilizing some new techniques that seemed effective and readily accepted by their patients. These country and city doctors were not much impressed by medical science. They saw it as a tool enabling them to heal more effectively when its claims worked and when its techniques did not require a whole new method of practice.

Robert Pusey, a Kentucky country doctor who practiced in the 1870s and 1880s, used the clinical thermometer, assorted specula, and a syringe. Occasionally, he used the stethoscope although he preferred to place his ear to the patient's chest. With this simple method he could hear and distinguish most conditions as well as his scientifically trained son could with a stethoscope. He used judgments based on practice, read up on cases in the more concrete and concise medical texts, and distrusted journal articles. The older Dr. Pusey vaguely accepted bacteriology, especially as an explanation for infections causing pus but not generally for infectious diseases. He sometimes used calomel, made and sold his own drugs, did not use patent medicines, and often prescribed strichnine and arsenic as tonics. He practiced surgery in which he used chloroform as an anesthetic and asepsis when the knowledge and techniques became available to him.[44]

The propaganda for scientific medicine was sure to be effective, but it would take time. John Shaw Billings, a leading medical reformer in the late nineteenth century, observed that doctors whose practices were not interfered with by quacks were indifferent to reforms while those in need of larger practices were more indignant about such competitors. Many quacks had effected cures where science had failed, Billings admitted. But rather than giving him pause in his rejection of any but scientific medical methods, Billings saw it as a tactical problem of persuading the American public that it is in their interests to suppress quackery. The remarkable achievements of medical science were being brought to the public, but, Billings cautioned, "it is necessary to go slowly and allow such evidence to accumulate."[45]

The reformers believed scientific medicine would increase the technical effectiveness of the medical profession, and they promoted it as the *only* effective therapeutic method. Through propaganda they hoped to undermine public resistance to its use, increase the public demand for it, and thereby force practitioners to join the new "nonsectarian" medicine.

REDUCING COMPETITION

As scientific medicine won public and professional credibility, it also solved the second and fundamentally more serious problem facing the profession in the nineteenth century: competition.

Plagued by competition among numerous medical sects, between practitioners and medical school faculty, and within the "crowded" ranks of regular practitioners themselves, the profession was saved from its own internal competitive struggles by the triumph of scientific medicine. First, the technical requirements of teaching scientific medicine provided several advantages for the profession's elite. Second, scientific medicine forged new unity in the interests of elite practitioners and medical school faculty. Third, as it gained increasingly widespread legitimacy, scientific medicine undermined the major medical sects. It thereby imposed unity among those sects in their subordination to the dominant forces in the profession. And, finally, medical science made possible specialization which was largely a response to competition within medicine. The overall impact of scientific medicine within the profession was to legitimize control by elite practitioners and medical school faculty.

TECHNICAL REQUIREMENTS OF SCIENTIFIC MEDICAL EDUCATION

THE NEW ACADEMICIANS

Making the doctor the purveyor of a broad range of skills within a context of mystified knowledge required extensive and esoteric training. Nineteenth-century medical reformers envisioned the physician as a bedside scientist. Medical practitioners must think and talk like scientists. They must be trained in anatomy, physiology, bacteriology, pathology, pharmacology, and the physical sciences. They must think of health and disease, not holistically as general relationships between bodily systems or between the person and the environment, but in terms of the micro-concepts of physiology and anatomy, bacteriology and cell pathology. These sciences and their reductionist concepts were gradually recognized in the late nineteenth century as the foundations of medical education.

The medical schools of the last century were staffed by practitioners, often very talented men who were heavy on the "art" but less expert on the "science." Increasingly, laboratory science courses were taken away from the local practitioner and given to physicians with special training in the laboratory sciences. The new academic physicians who preferred these laboratory sciences over medical practice prospered with the increased demand for more faculty with training in these fields. Those who could afford to spend a year or two studying in Germany or Austria after medical school had secure, if not lucrative, academic careers awaiting them on their return.

In 1893 Johns Hopkins became the first medical school in the United States to employ these laboratory men full time and to pay them salaries that enabled them to devote all their time and energy to research and teaching. The new full-time organization of the laboratory science faculty was hailed as a great advance for American medical education. It was quickly adopted by other elite schools and gradually became the norm emulated by the average institution. Although the laboratory science faculty gave up private practice incomes of $10,000 a year and more in return for salaries of $3,000 or $4,000, there were more than enough people to fill the demand.[46]

Some of the giants of medical reform, like William H. Welch, loathed medical practice, feared the insecurity of competition among private practitioners, and longed for the opportunity to pursue medical research without the diversions of maintaining a private clientele. Before going off to Europe in 1876 to advance his medical science skills, Welch confided to his sister his fears of trying to set up "by hook or by crook a patronage of some kind." Echoing the pipe dreams of most medical graduates, Welch observed, "it is much finer to hold a chair in a medical college, and to have a salary . . . and to be sought by patients instead of seeking them." His studies abroad would give him a jump on his competitors: "If by absorbing a little German lore I can get a little start of a few thousand rivals and thereby reduce my competitors to a few hundred more or less, it is a good point to tally."[47]

The emphasis on scientific medicine thus created unprecedented job opportunities for physicians qua medical scientists. As positions expanded, a core of professionals developed who were more dedicated than ever to seeing medicine as science completely displace medicine as art. These medical scientists' interests and identification were bound up solely with medical schools and not with private practice. As the vanguard of the profession's successful strategy and the recipients of millions of dollars in capital investments in medical research and education, the new medical academicians became the symbol of the new profession. In the 1890s, for the first time in the United States, the medical profession came to exalt the scientist over the practitioner.[48] Despite their more modest, middle-class incomes, the scientists were the new elite in the profession.

The faculty at the most prestigious schools won their professional reputations on the basis of their research contributions to their fields. The best reputations attracted the best students and the wealthiest patients. In 1903 William Halsted, a famous surgeon on the Johns Hopkins faculty, got $10,000 for an appendectomy, and his colleague, Howard Kelly, charged $20,000 for a major operation.[49] Unlike the old-time medical faculties, whose material interests were enhanced by student fees and referrals from their many former students, the new academicians' material interests were tied to the promotion of medical science. It was in their interests to raise the standards of medical schools and to make scientific medicine the only acceptable theory and practice.

The predominant type of medical school, owned by the faculty and existing on student fees, prospered as long as enrollments could be kept high and costs low. However, practitioners would prosper only if the production of physicians was decreased, reducing competition within the profession. This conflict of economic interests had divided elite practitioners from medical school faculty throughout the nineteenth century. The ascendancy of scientific medicine transformed the old conflict into the basis for an alliance between the scientific medical faculties and elite practitioners.

The interests of the new medical scientists in medical education were thus tied to the dominance of scientific medicine and *not* to large numbers of students or even large numbers of medical schools. They joined the elite practitioners as the leaders of reform in the profession. Together they gained control of the AMA at the turn of the century and completely reorganized it to make the AMA the profession's instrument of political action as we know it today and to use it and the leading medical schools to alter completely the technical, economic, and social forces within the medical profession.

The technical requirements of developing and teaching scientific medicine sharpened the distinction between laboratory science faculty and practitioners, provided new and expanding job opportunities for medical scientists, and hoisted them to elite and influential positions within the profession. At the same time these developments provided the basis for the alliance between these new elite faculty and the elite practitioners, giving them sufficient power to take control of the profession and transform it.

"FEWER AND BETTER"

As a professional consensus developed around scientific medicine, the scientific medical faculty and elite practitioners agreed upon "objective" criteria for judging medical schools. The needs of scientific medical education were pretty clear cut. If students are to be trained as medical scientists, they need to be taught the biological and physical sciences, and they need to be taught how to apply the principles they learn in those sciences to the diseases of real people. Experience as well as common sense argued for laboratory courses in the sciences and hospital experience for the clinical application of those sciences: Learning *how* is at least as important as learning *about*.

The technical requirements of teaching scientific medicine suggest fairly clear criteria for judging medical schools. If the premise of training scientists is accepted, then any worthy medical program must have adequate laboratory facilities, clinical teaching facilities, and well-trained laboratory and clinical faculty.

While the criteria of what is "adequate" might be (and were) argued, the standards were set by those who secured positions of power. The AMA became the vehicle for political action within the profession and the larger society. The reformers used the technical requirements of training medical scientists to set standards and then evaluate medical schools according to those standards. With a few exceptions—Johns Hopkins the shining example among them—virtually all nineteenth-century medical colleges were weak when judged by these standards.

Unquestionably, scientific medical education was and is an expensive affair. The capital outlays for laboratories and hospital facilities were beyond the resources of most nineteenth-century and early twentieth-century medical schools. Student lecture fees could not cover the larger salaries for faculty who devoted substantial time to research and teaching, let alone the increasingly widespread full-time salaries for laboratory science faculty. No medical school could exist on student fees and at the same time provide these increasingly necessary medical science programs for their students.

In some states, students who graduated from medical colleges that did not have these programs, facilities, and personnel were barred from taking licensing examinations. Increasingly, state exams were geared to the information and perspectives provided in scientifically oriented schools, and graduates of inadequately equipped schools failed their licensing exams with increasing frequency.[50] Since the schools were supported by students' fees and students had little incentive to attend a school that did not prepare them to pass state board exams, inadequate schools lost out in the competitive market for enrollees and their money. AMA president Charles Reed observed in 1901, "Under the pressure of legal requirements the weight falls with almost fatal force upon the small, private and poorly equipped institutions."[51] The technical requirements of scientific medical education thus brought about the conditions of collapse of proprietary medical schools. As Abraham Flexner later noted, "Nothing has perhaps done more to complete the discredit of commercialism than the fact that it has ceased to pay. It is but a short step from an annual deficit to the conclusion that the whole thing is wrong anyway."[52]

In Chapter 4 we will see how these conditions provided an opportunity for the AMA and capitalist foundations to transform medical education in the United States. For the moment it is enough to note that without sufficient capital and endowments, no medical school could survive in the era of scientific medicine. Schools collapsed and consolidated all over the country beginning in 1905, coinciding with the first year of serious activity by the AMA's new Council on Medical Education. Between 1905 and 1910, thirty schools merged and twenty-one closed down altogether.[53] The number of medical schools declined from a high of 166 in 1904 to 133 in 1910, 104 in 1915, and hit a low of seventy-six in 1929. In the reorganization of medical schools the number of students was reduced at many institutions in order to intensify the teaching and research resources within each school. Thus the technical requirements of scientific medical education were used to close schools and decrease the production of new physicians, easing the competition within the profession and raising doctors' incomes.

Furthermore, scientific medical education "required" greater preliminary education. Students must come to medical school, it was argued, having had a full year each of college chemistry, physics, and biology.

The demands for stringent requirements of preliminary education were not new to the era of scientific medicine. In eighteenth-century and nineteenth-century England, where "physicians" were a tiny elite above surgeons and apothecaries, it was essential for physicians to be regarded as gentlemen. Because they practiced only among the wealthy, it was important to their pocketbooks to be able to mingle with the upper class. As professions developed, a liberal education became the mark of upper-class origins. "It might not make you a gentleman," W. J. Reader has observed, "but without it a gentleman you could hardly hope to be."[54] In the United States as well, a college education was the mark of a gentleman. For those who were not born into a privileged class, a college education—if it could be gotten—"rubbed the raw edge off many a country boy," giving them sufficiently proper appearances to make their way to a higher social class.[55]

It is not surprising then that substantial educational requirements had been declared an imperative in the mid-nineteenth century because it would assure that doctors would be gentlemen. Daniel Drake, probably the most illustrious American physician of the midcentury, criticized his colleagues' ignorance of Latin and Greek without which, "whatever may be his genius and professional skill," a physician would still necessarily "appear defective and uncultivated."[56] This persistent concern was echoed by Johns Hopkins' famous Dr. Welch who wrote in 1906, "The social position of the medical man and his influence on the community depend to a considerable extent upon his preliminary education and general culture."[57]

Elite physicians frequently complained of the "coarse and common fiber" of much of the profession.[58] Even a minority of the profession lacking upper-class polish cheapened the status of all doctors. The proliferation of inexpensive proprietary schools enabled a young man to live at home while attending medical school and thereby made medicine a ladder that some farm boys, artisans, and shop clerks could climb to middle-class status and income. It was not only the inadequacies in the training provided in commercial colleges that angered the elite reformers; it was also whom they brought into the profession. Frank Billings, in his presidential address to the AMA in 1903, disdained "these sundown institutions" that provided evening classes and enabled "the clerk, the streetcar conductor, the janitor and others employed during the day to earn a degree."[59]

Prior to the acceptance of scientific medicine, attempts to lengthen the medical school term of instruction and raise preliminary education requirements were met with charges of elitism. "There is an aristocratic feature in this movement" by medical societies, Martyn Paine, a faculty member in the New York University medical department, asserted in 1846. "It is oppression towards the poor, for the sake of crippling the medical colleges."[60]

Even after the turn of the century some education leaders warned against excluding the poor from medicine. In 1908, W. L. Bryan, president of Indiana University, criticized the Association of American Medical Colleges' proposed requirement of two years attendance at a liberal arts college prior to admission. Raising the entrance requirement would "shut out of the medical schools thousands of men who are not ignorant nor incompetent" but who would be excluded because "poverty and other hard conditions" have kept them from the colleges.[61] The profession's objective was exactly that—to exclude the poorer classes from their ranks.

Scientific medicine provided an "objective" basis for requiring a lengthy preliminary education. If students had to come prepared with college courses in physics, chemistry, and biology, then there could be no argument against lengthening the requirements. The standard-setting schools raised their requirements from completion of high school to two years of liberal arts college and finally to a bachelor's degree. From the moment it opened its doors in 1893, Johns Hopkins medical school led the way by requiring a bachelor's degree for admission and four years of instruction for its prestigious M.D. degree. When Harvard instituted the baccalaureate requirement in 1901, its entering medical class dropped from an all-time high of 198 students the previous year to sixty-seven.[62] The preliminary education requirements were several steps ahead of the great majority of American youth and enabled the profession to draw its recruits from the "better" classes.

Was this an unintended outcome of the technical "requirements" of medical education, or was it the desired outcome for which scientific medicine provided the mere rationale? Given the goals of professional leaders throughout the nineteenth century —to reduce the numbers of physicians and to raise the social-class standing of the profession—it seems that scientific medicine provided the credible rationale that all previous generations of medical elites had sought in vain. The preliminary requirement would weed out the economically and socially "unfit." Some reformers justified this selectivity by the cost of scientific medical education. "It does not pay to give a $5,000 education to a $5 boy," intoned John Shaw Billings in 1886 while helping to organize Johns Hopkins medical training.[63] But most elite physicians simply desired to eliminate "professional degeneracy," as Dr. Inez Philbrick put it at the turn of the century. Philbrick, a successful practitioner in Lincoln, Nebraska, rallied his colleagues to "Let fewer and better be our motto."[64]

In sum, the technical requirements of scientific medical education gave new career opportunities to physicians as medical scientists, creating a whole new position of full-time researcher and teacher and a new group of elite medical school faculty who combined a material interest in medical schools with a commitment to promoting scientific medicine. At the same time these technical requirements of the new medical education provided the standards and the rationale for reducing the output of medical schools and raising the social class base of the entire profession.

"NONSECTARIAN" MEDICINE
UNDERMINES THE SECTS

As scientific medicine gained increasingly wide acceptance, it undermined the other medical sects. Scientific medicine thereby forged unity within the profession by enabling the AMA to subordinate the sects to its own standards of medical education and practice. Overwhelmed by the increased claims of technical effectiveness for scientific medicine, the major sects began incorporating scientific medicine into their own doctrines and practice.

Homeopathy, the most formidable competitor of the regular professions in the nineteenth century, gradually dropped its unique features. Most homeopathic physicians in America broke with pure homeopathic theory in the mid-nineteenth century, taking what they believed valid from regular medicine and discarding especially heroic therapies. They purged the purists from their ranks by founding homeopathic medical colleges, previously believed unnecessary, and requiring training in general medical skills, including surgery.[65] Most midcentury American homeopaths were regular physicians unhappy with the ineffectiveness of regular medicine and with its growing unpopularity. In 1849, 1,000 Ohio physicians and lay people, disaffected by the orthodox profession's inability to relieve suffering during the cholera epidemic, organized a homeopathic society in Cincinnati.[66]

The direct competition that homeopathy posed to regular physicians led to campaigns to exclude them from medical societies and hospital privileges. The Massachusetts Medical Society began excluding homeopaths in 1860. By the 1870s there was a general attack, led by the AMA, on homeopathy and other "exclusive systems of medicine." Physicians violated the AMA code of ethics if they consulted with sectarian physicians or female or black doctors. In the 1870s the restrictions against female physicians were rescinded under pressure from the growing women's rights movement, and the exclusion of blacks was relaxed though local medical societies and hospitals openly continued their racist practices. But the attacks on "irregular" doctors continued throughout the century.[67]

By the end of the nineteenth century, nearly all homeopaths were using both regular and homeopathic drugs. Leading homeopaths announced that the great majority of homeopathic doctors did not believe in infinitesimal doses, rejected the universality of the law of "like cures like," and generally used drugs like regular physicians. Homeopaths also became interested in clinical specialties. In 1899 the American Institute of Homeopathy redefined a homeopathic physician as "one who *adds* to his knowledge of medicine a special knowledge of homeopathic therapeutics."[68] Homeopathy, as well as other sects, were being overcome by the competition from scientific medicine.

Nonetheless, the continued popularity of homeopathy and eclectic medicine and the incomplete acceptance of scientific medicine made it difficult for regular professional leaders to win exclusive licensing privileges in the states. With the convergence in practice and education of homeopaths, eclectics, and regular physicians, it was possible to assure the dominance of scientific training and politically necessary to ignore, for the moment, the sectarian separations. Only through the combined efforts of the regular and "irregular" profession could laws be secured to restrict medical practice to scientifically trained physicians. The profession's leaders around the country agreed with William Osler, the most eminent American physician of his day, who advised the Maryland state medical society in 1891, "if we wish legislation for the protection of the public, we have got to ask for it together, not singly."[69] And together they asked.

Beginning in the 1870s, state legislatures established medical licensing examination boards. In 1873 Texas passed the first modern medical practice act, a morale-boosting victory to the profession that offset the bitter memories of the Jacksonian era's repeal of licensure. The Illinois Board of Health, the state's licensing agency, was a model for the nation. Beginning in 1880, it began to list American and Canadian medical schools according to qualitative criteria set by the Association of American Medical Colleges, an organization of elite, scientifically oriented institutions.[70]

Nonregular doctors participated in some way in medical licensing in at least thirty-three of the forty-five states that had enacted licensing laws by 1900. Physicians from at least two sects served on the same licensing boards in twenty states.[71] By cooperating in licensure, the nonregular profession won inclusion among the respectable. With scientific medicine gaining ground every year, it appeared to the leaders of homeopathy that they had nothing to lose and everything to gain from their association with the regular profession. The president of the AMA even acknowledged in 1901 that "with broadened and increasingly uniform curricula" it made little sense to argue that competing sects did not share the profession's competence.[72]

The reform leaders in the regular profession won the biggest rewards. By cooperating with the nonregular sects, they won licensing laws that recognized scientifically oriented reforms as the only valid basis of medical education. In a short time they secured complete control of licensing and the resources for medical education reform. Whether these elite professionals foresaw their ultimate gain from cooperating with the homeopaths and eclectics or they were guided by expedience undiluted by strategy, the cooperative licensing efforts hastened the elimination of sectarianism amid the growing chorus of support for scientific medicine.

By 1903 the AMA adopted the strategy explicitly. At its annual convention the delegates voted to eliminate the decades-old exclusion of physicians who were trained as homeopaths or eclectics but chose not to "designate" themselves as such.[73] Two years earlier AMA president Charles Reed had drawn attention to the good effects of allowing all licensed physicians into state medical societies. By ending its exclusionary policy, he said, the New York society had reduced the registration of sectarian physicians by "nearly ninety percent."[74]

Scientific medicine was perhaps more effective than homeopathy and eclecticism in treating some diseases for which it had developed cures, but it was not, particularly at the turn of the century, the panacea it was believed to be. The reformers' overly optimistic assessment is shared by many contemporary medical historians. William Rothstein, for example, maintains that "sects could survive in medicine only so long as medically valid therapies constituted a small part of the therapies used by physicians. Once medically valid therapies became the dominant part of medical practice, medical sectarianism declined markedly."[75]

In reality the number of medically *effective* therapies had not increased significantly in the first few years of this century, the period when sectarianism declined in medicine.[76] Rather the campaign to win acceptance for scientific medicine struck a responsive cultural chord among the new technical and managerial groups associated with industrial capitalism and with the media they controlled. The campaign established a popular belief in the broad effectiveness of scientific medicine and, together with political action by elite medical reformers, undermined the medical sects that competed with the regular profession.

SPECIALIZATION: LESS COMPETITION FOR THE ELITE

Advances in medical science during the late nineteenth century rapidly developed the technical basis for some physicians to offer highly specialized expertise not available from the ordinary practitioner. Medical advances were presumably usable by any physician, but in reality only those who studied a particular area developed the expertise to apply techniques and inventions. The ophthalmoscope, invented by Helmholz in 1851, required considerable study and practice to know what to look for on the other side of the cornea. Anesthetics, antisepsis, and asepsis made surgery a relatively safer procedure, but the masters of surgical techniques were those who devoted their entire practice to it.

The very existence of medical specialization rested upon a reductionist analysis of the body and disease. Its concrete development was made possible by advances in medical science. Nevertheless, specialization among practitioners was encouraged by economic competition within the profession and grew to take advantage of the new market for more technical, seemingly, more scientific medical services.

With dissatisfaction rampant among more ambitious members of the profession, some 15,000 American physicians studied medicine in Germany alone. They returned to reap the benefits of their advanced training and confidence to specialize in some branch of clinical medicine.[77] Successful specialists soon earned more than twice as much as the better-off general practitioners.[78] Elite, scientifically oriented physicians saw specialization as a solution for themselves in the competitive medical market.

The demand for specialists grew with the urban upper middle class. Patients whose own social position was based on the growth of technology and industrialization sought out physicians whose practice suggested the same world view. Gynecological theory viewed most female disease as being rooted in or associated with uterine problems. As Barbara Ehrenreich and Deirdre English have amply demonstrated, Victorian femininity itself was associated with invalidism and physical and emotional frailty. Women of the "better" classes were defined as sick in order to support their role as social ornamentation, demonstrating the financial and social success of their husbands and distinguishing them from lower-class women who were expected to work and were considered sickening.[79]

Gynecological surgeons preyed upon the supposedly delicate nature of upper middle-class women and the terrible consequences of having a "tipped" uterus or sexual appetite. Hysterectomies, ovariotomies, and cliteridectomies were prescribed for these and other female maladies. Some gynecologists, like Horatio Bigelow writing in the AMA *Journal* in 1885, favored a "conservative" approach over too rash use of the knife or mechanical devices. He believed that better results could be obtained "by attention to every detail of life, even the most insignificant, for the aggregation of the little things go to the making of the big ones, and also, by attention to psychical conditions and reactions."[80] Such attention, of course, required daily visits from the doctor.

Gynecologists tailored their medical theories to the prevailing notions of the place of women in society and thereby developed a new and lucrative medical market. Upper-class women became the objects of knife-wielding gynecological surgeons or the invalided captives of overly "attentive" gynecological practitioners. From the early 1890s abdominal and pelvic surgery seemed the profession's own Gold Rush, and surgeons were, in the words of the AMA *Journal,* "as restless and ambitious a throng as ever fought for fame upon the battlefield."[81]

General practitioners obviously suffered to the extent that their patients went to specialists with complaints the GPs formerly treated. From the 1850s onward, the GP-dominated medical societies attacked what they viewed as unfair competition. In 1874 the AMA's judicial council ruled that specialists could advertise only that their practices were *"limited* to diseases peculiar to women" or "diseases of the eye and ear." Such restrictions on specialists denied the claims of scientific leaders that specialism was based on greater expertise not available to the general practitioner. Moreover, few physicians at that time could completely limit their practices to specialties since specialization was not yet widely enough accepted.[82]

Conditions soon changed, at least in large and medium-size cities. Specialists promoted the medical sciences through their own societies. Following a rebuff by the AMA, which named a committee of medically conservative professionals instead of distinguished medical scientists to host the 1887 International Medical Congress, specialists and other medical scientists formed the Association of American Physicians. In 1888 all national specialty societies formed an alliance outside the AMA in the American Congress of Physicians and Surgeons. In the last years of the nineteenth century, as scientific medicine increased and the economic base of specialism grew more secure, membership in scientific societies increased—particularly in Eastern cities where medical centers were beginning to dominate medicine—while membership in the AMA languished.[83]

Medical specialty societies were intended not only to promote development of the specialty but also to gain acceptance of the specialists by general practitioners. Even though they were competitors, specialists relied heavily on referrals from other physicians for much of their practice. Generalists had to be induced to refer their difficult cases to other physicians. To encourage referrals, many, if not most specialists, gave a portion of their fee to the doctor who made the referral.[84] Fee-splitting became a widespread practice to control competition and gain acceptance of specialists by GPs.

Fee-splitting, however, was a private tool of individuals used to soften competitive relations among themselves. For fee-splitting to be used collectively by the organized profession would require an open admission of its existence and legitimacy within the profession. That would have been worse than the competition that fee-splitting was attempting to regulate because it was a

purely commercial arrangement that undercut professional claims
of expertise and privilege. It thereby reduced public confidence in
physicians and further weakened the social and political position
of the profession. Fee-splitting could not resolve conflicting
interests between specialists and GPs at the national level.

Ultimately, the development of specialties and subspecialties
has indeed reduced overall competition within the medical profession. The ratio of primary care physicians has fallen from more
than 170 per 100,000 population in 1900 to less than sixty per
100,000 today.[85] But the division of physician labor into specialties created intraprofessional problems, pitting general practitioner against specialist. The decline in primary care physicians
has eased the problem somewhat, but it was still a serious split
in the ranks at the turn of the century and an obstacle to the
efforts of the scientifically oriented elite practitioners and medical
faculty who led the reform movement.

New levels of accreditation of specialists emerged in the
twentieth century. The American College of Surgeons was
charged with being elitist and un-American for its efforts to
restrict surgery to specially licensed physicians and to accredited
hospitals. In 1912 Franklin Martin's public relations tour for the
College of Surgeons was interrupted with heckling by hostile
GPs. The college fellows were accused either of degrading the
profession by forming "a glorified surgical union, along labor
lines" or of establishing a new oligarchy, "an exclusive Four
Hundred in the profession."[86]

The reform leadership gathering in the wings of the AMA
included many leading specialists, but they saw the importance of
putting the interests of the profession as a whole at the forefront
of their campaign. After failing in 1898, they succeeded in 1901
and 1902 in their efforts to reorganize the AMA into a more
effective national organization. Their strategy included the
delicate issue of unifying the competing specialists and general
practitioners and bringing the specialists into the profession's
main political arm—the AMA.

GAINS AND LOSSES

Scientific medicine was clearly an effective doctrine for the
reform and uplift of the medical profession. It increased the

technical effectiveness of doctors, providing a basis for increasing public confidence in the profession. The need for research and the teaching of medical sciences created a whole new category of academic medicine. It united the interests of these academic physicians, who sought total victory for scientific medical schools over less adequate ones, with the interests of elite practitioners, who wanted to reduce production of and competition among doctors in order to raise their incomes and status. The requirements of scientific medical education strained the resources of "commercial" medical education to the breaking point, closing down many medical schools and reducing the production of physicians. It also provided the rationale for requiring extensive preliminary education of medical school applicants, forcing the poorer classes out of medicine and thereby raising the social class base of the profession. Furthermore, scientific medicine undermined sectarian medicine, uniting most of the divided profession under the banner of "nonsectarian" scientific medicine. Finally, it provided a basis for further decreasing competition within the profession through the development of specialization. Thus, scientific medicine helped complete the professionalization of medicine.

These gains to the medical profession were accompanied by some losses. Some of the losses were borne by less powerful members of the profession. The gains of specialists, the new elite among practitioners, were the losses of the general practitioners. Scientific medicine provided the profession's scientific elite with the means of securing its position and taking complete control.

While society benefited from more effective techniques against infectious diseases, people lost the benefits of traditional techniques and became dependent on technological medicine. The propaganda of the reform-minded elite sold scientific medicine as the last word on matters of health and disease. Through their campaign, the medical profession excluded herbal methods of prevention and therapy that are only now regaining popularity. They also narrowed the scope of medical inquiry to reductionist concepts, all but ignoring the social and economic contexts of health and disease.

The doctor was portrayed as omniscient and his skill as all-powerful. Patients, accepting the profession's claims and wanting something for their money, began to expect their doctors to provide remedies for their suffering. Not wanting to discourage this profitable attitude, most physicians believed that, in the words of a late nineteenth-century physician, "he fails of his duty and his privilege who neglects to do something for the patient."[87] However, even this lucrative attribution of physician omniscience was a double-edged sword. Armed with assurances of the near-infallibility of medical science, patients demanded compensation when they were maimed by the therapies or mistakes of scientific doctors. The number of malpractice suits from 1900 to 1915 exceeded the number of suits during the entire nineteenth century.[88]

Naturally, the most oppressed groups in society suffered the most from the complete professionalization of medicine made possible by scientific medicine. The poorer classes in general and ethnic and racial minorities in particular have suffered doubly—by being excluded from entering the profession and by losing medical care that was indigenous to their communities and accessible to them. By the early 1900s people who could afford specialists increasingly relied on them, often by-passing the general practitioner altogether. The poor filled the waiting rooms and examining tables of teaching hospitals to become the teaching and research material for interns, residents, and specialists. The nation's wage earners, excluded from charity clinics by means tests and often unable to afford private specialists' fees, became the bread-and-butter clients of the nonelite general practitioners.[89] Following the largely successful doctors' campaigns to rid the country of midwives, working-class and rural women and men lost the services that helped maintain the integrity of their families during the disruption of childbirth and found themselves having to pay the higher fees of physicians and the cost of a hospital bed.[90] Women suffered from unnecessary surgery and suffocating attention from gynecologists. They, like the working class and racial minorities in general, were also excluded from becoming doctors.

The fewer physicians competing for consumers' dollars, the higher physicians' incomes rose and the fewer doctors who practiced in working-class and poor sections of the cities and in the countryside. The middle class became the main source of income for the majority of the profession. As Morris Fishbein, editor of the AMA *Journal,* complacently observed in 1927, "The physician of the future will deal largely with this group. From them most of the physicians, who are themselves of the middle class, will derive their incomes."[91]

The dynamics that lifted white middle-class and upper-class male physicians to the top of a hierarchy were not based on conspiracies or conscious deceptions. Physicians acted in their collective self-interest. While the different interest groups within the profession often clashed, their conflicts were gradually overwhelmed by the growing belief that all who embraced scientific medicine would benefit. Old-time homeopaths and eclectics, of course, fell by the wayside, and proprietors of crassly commercial medical schools lost their lucrative businesses. But most physicians could relate to the purposes of the reform campaign—more respect for their skills, higher social status, more money—and to the necessary means of achieving them. Undoubtedly conspiracies and conscious deceptions occured along the way (we will see some examples in Chapter 4), but even the reform leaders believed their mission would benefit society as well as the medical profession. Nevertheless, it strains the imagination to conclude that the complete professionalization of medicine served the interests of more than a small minority of the population.

The technical limitations of nineteenth-century medicine were replaced by technical narrowness in the twentieth century; the professional pluralism, by professional monopoly controlled by elite specialists and medical academicians; the culturally diverse and widely distributed group of healers, by a more fully stratified and, for many, inaccessible professional class. These were some of society's losses that accompanied the profession's gains. The consolidation of a scientific medical profession, however, also provided important gains for the corporate class in America.

Scientific Medicine II:
The Preservation of Capital

SCIENTIFIC medicine, while providing well for the medical profession, also posed a major and unresolvable contradiction for doctors. Medical science, as it developed in capitalist countries, was built up around technology. The higher the level of technology, it was believed, the more effective or, at least, salable were the services of practitioners and researchers. But the higher the level of technology, the more capital was required for medical practice as well as for research. Investments in hospital and laboratory facilities and tremendous expenses for highly specialized faculty and researchers were beyond the resources of physicians themselves.[1] Doctors had to turn outside the profession for capital, and in 1900 there was only one class who had such money. Wealthy capitalists were in a position to dictate terms to the profession—policies that served their own interests as much as or even more than those of the profession itself. In this chapter we will see how medical science opened the door to capitalist intervention and the ways scientific medicine served not only the needs of the medical profession but the interests of capitalism as well.

MEDICAL TECHNOLOGY AND CAPITAL

The nineteenth-century family doctor owned a few instruments—specula, a thermometer, and a stethoscope for examinations, saws for amputations, a chest of medicines to be sold to their patients—a small investment indeed. But twentieth-century medicine required greater technology than any single physician could afford. Hospitals, once the institutions to which the poor were taken to die, became the workshop for the doctor. Not only did the hospital provide the doctor with fully equipped operating rooms, x-ray machines, and other diagnostic and therapeutic instruments. It also provided auxiliary personnel who would isolate patients from their families, place them under the control of technical experts, and insure that the doctor's orders were carried out. Just as the buggy carrying the doctor to the patient's house symbolized the nineteenth-century doctor-patient relationship, the patient in the doctor's moderately equipped office and then the doctor and patient in the hospital symbolized the modernized counterparts.

Large-scale development of hospitals in the 1890s followed the development of surgery as a specialized skill. The renowned surgical skills of Halsted at Johns Hopkins and of others at the Mayo Clinic provided popular support for the profession's pleas that hospitals with modern surgical facilities be built. Rosemary Stevens notes, "Most of the hospitals now in existence were founded between 1880 and 1920, and the middle class for the first time entered hospitals on a large scale." In 1873 there were only 178 hospitals in the United States. By 1909 there were 4,359 hospitals with a total bed capacity of 421,000.[2]

Physicians grew increasingly dependent on hospitals. By 1929, seven out of ten physicians had some kind of hospital affiliation. In New York and Chicago, the average physician, whether generalist or specialist, spent as much as 30 percent of his or her time in hospitals and clinics.[3] Even by the turn of the century the medical profession was growing dependent on expensive, institutionalized technology.

The capital needed for hospitals, medical education, and research was beyond the means of the profession itself. A fully equipped, medium-sized hospital was an expensive building project. Then, too, room and service charges could not reasonably be expected to pay for the annual costs of running the hospital, especially when hospitals were free-of-charge workshops for the doctor. Patients could be expected to pay a certain amount for their hospital care, but beyond a very vaguely determined limit, any additional hospital charges would reduce utilization and cut into the revenues of both hospital and physician. Thus, each year hospitals accumulated deficits that had to be paid off.

Deficit financing reflected the social role of hospitals as charitable institutions. Historically, from their development as medieval refuges for the diseased poor to their more recent role of providing for the sick of all classes, hospitals have consistently reflected the class structure of the society. Fitting their position in the class structure, the rich have been expected to pay the complete costs of their own private space and attentive care. The middle classes, with less commodious facilities and fewer staff to attend to their wants, have been expected to pay their own costs but not necessarily to support all aspects of the hospital. The poor, until recently, have been expected to pay in accord with their means, and that has been very little. Their care has been categorized as charity, and, consistent with widespread notions of the importance of work and of the slothfulness of the poor, the facilities and care provided for them have been austere at their best and humiliating at their worst. Furthermore, with the association of increasing numbers of hospitals with medical schools, the poor have become the profession's research and teaching material. To complete the differentiation of class relations reflected within the hospital as well as to balance the hospital's books, the rich have been called upon to give money to the hospital to pay the costs of care given to the poor. The charitable nature of hospitals gives wealthy people an almost perfect opportunity to demonstrate their noblesse oblige within an institution that publicly reflects and thus reinforces the class structure of society.

The organization and financing of hospitals clearly provides physicians with the facilities to practice their profession and make money, and it benefits the upper-middle and upper classes by providing them with facilities consistent with their social status and opportunities to demonstrate their superior class positions through charity to the hospital. The dependence of the medical profession on the wealthy could create antagonism, but with their compatible interests in the hospital, their relationship has been symbiotic. Local wealthy men and women opened their hearts and loosened their purse strings to hospital fund raisers.

Medical research and medical education were different issues. Hospitals appealed to a local constituency whereas the new scientific medical schools drew their students and faculty from at least the state and more often a whole region or even the nation. Medical research was a long-term investment in developing new knowledge and technology that would serve the country as a whole rather than provide a subordinating service to the poor. Medical faculty and researchers were no longer the local physicians of distinction; their reputations were made nationally within their own ranks, or not at all. Local rich men and women could be cajoled into providing a laboratory at their nearby medical school through appeals to local pride, but these objects of charity lacked the drama of hospitals serving the poor and providing facilities for physicians known throughout the local community. Medical education and medical research involved much larger sums of money than hospital construction, and the endowments to support faculty and researchers required still larger investments out of the wealth of the local upper class.

The combination of the larger sums required, the less directly charitable and less visible functions of medical research and education, the long-term investments they represented, and the more national character of their appeal made medical education and medical research the philanthropic objects of a *national* wealthy class more than of those whose wealth was local in its character or size. By the 1890s a new national capitalist class overshadowed the local business and aristocratic elites.[4] Their wealth was derived from investments in national corporations, and their visions of what was good and necessary for society were broader than their local and lesser counterparts. Many of them gave without strategy in their benefactions, except the courting of good will, but some had strategies and interests of their own.

Just as well-connected local physicians appealed to the local pride and charitable obligations of the local upper-middle class to build a modern hospital for their community, so did academic physicians and medical scientists turn to men and women of broader wealth with appeals to the needs of society. A few illustrious centers of medical education and research were relatively well off. Charles Eliot clearly saw that the way to attract large gifts and endowments was to reform Harvard's medical school. Johns Hopkins willed a hospital and medical school as well as a general university from his Baltimore and Ohio railroad fortune; yet more was needed and gotten from wealthy individuals to open the medical school. These cases were the exceptions.

"Not half a dozen institutions have received any considerable sums, and very few anything at all," the AMA *Journal* complained in 1900. The endowments necessary to "advancing medical education and medical science" must come from outside the profession.[5] As some reform leaders foresaw and feared, there was danger in dependence on philanthropy for that capital.

WELCH: A ROCKEFELLER MEDICINE MAN

William H. Welch's personal plight and eventual success are indicative of the rising star of medical research. Returning in 1878 from his pathology studies in Germany, Welch found little support in New York for devoting himself to laboratory research. Although he received mild encouragement from Francis Delafield at the prestigious College of Physicians and Surgeons, he could not find any space in which to set up a laboratory. Finally, he turned to the lesser-rated Bellevue Hospital medical college and negotiated the use of three rooms, some kitchen tables, and twenty-five dollars in equipment. With frogs gathered from the marshes of his sister's upstate New York home, Welch began the first laboratory course in pathology given in an American medical school. He got by with fees from his six students, a partnership with another doctor preparing medical students for competitive examinations, and assisting Dr. Austin Flint, a rich and socially prominent professor of medical practice at Bellevue.[6]

Welch's European studies and original work brought him immediate recognition. Within a year the alumni of the College of Physicians and Surgeons contributed enough money to offer Welch a modest pathology laboratory at their alma mater, but Welch felt a commitment to Bellevue and also wanted to hold out for the security and completeness of the chair in pathology at the new Johns Hopkins medical school. Drawn by the "more academic" environment at Hopkins, relief from "the drudgery of teaching," an endowed $4,000 a year salary and paid assistants, Welch shocked the New York medical profession and friends by giving up a future income of "at least $20,000" for provincial Baltimore.[7]

Welch took the position at Hopkins in 1884. Before going to Baltimore, he spent most of a year studying bacteriology in Leipzig and in Berlin with Koch. He studied bacteriology largely because he feared he would be left behind in the growing competition for medical discoveries.[8] Welch's singular devotion to his career brought him success. Despite the adulation and social popularity he received, he isolated himself from personal intimacy with any other person, male or female.[9]

Welch's reputation as a researcher and organizer of research grew even before the Johns Hopkins medical school opened its doors in 1893 with Welch as its first dean. By the turn of the century, Welch's professional reputation began spilling over into lay circles. In 1901 he came to the attention of Frederick T. Gates, the grand master of the Rockefeller philanthropies. Welch was asked to help organize the Rockefeller Institute for Medical Research. He soon became chief adviser to the Rockefeller foundations on medical projects, assisting in important ways in funding medical education in the United States and China, in developing public health programs in the United States and around the world, in organizing and heading this country's first school of public health, and more. In 1930 his eightieth birthday was honored around the world with a live radio broadcast throughout the United States and Europe presided over by President Hoover and simultaneous celebrations in major cities in Europe and Japan.

William H. Welch was indeed a man whose life and career spanned the fortunes of medical science, from its struggling infancy to its prodigious material success. His life combined the perfect mix of ambition, talent, single-minded dedication, and opportunity to make him the ideal of academic medicine in the United States. His gregariousness and wit kept him from being the recluse that his rejection of intimate relationships might have otherwise encouraged. His considerable talent combined with his initially almost frantic ambition to give him a competitive edge in medicine.

Nevertheless, these qualities would have yielded few rewards had the opportunities not come at the right moments. If Welch had not been born a white male into a prosperous class, he would never have had the material support he needed. If Welch had been born fifty years earlier, there would have been no support for scientific medicine. If he had been born fifty years later, he might well have been just another competent medical researcher. If Johns Hopkins medical school had not been filling its faculty slots when he was an ascending star in New York medical science, he might have been forced to divert energy into a lucrative private practice and lost his singular immersion in medical academia. If the Rockefeller philanthropies had not sought to develop scientific medical research, to reform medical education, and to develop public health programs, he might not have had a sufficient vehicle for his talents and might not have achieved his reputation as a world statesman and celebrity. While Welch was the right person in the right place at the right time, his spectacular career depended upon more than luck. His sex, race, and social class were crucial conditions for his success. But the development of corporate capitalism was perhaps the most important condition because it provided the ideological and cultural support for scientific medicine and the material support for his research.

It is likely that Welch would have fared well even without the Rockefellers since his reputation would have enabled him to skim off the best positions in medical science. Medical research and education as a whole, however, were helped immensely by the wealth of the Rockefeller fortune. Under the skillful direction of foundation officers, the Rockefeller wealth became the *largest single source of capital* for the development of *medical science* in the United States, the conversion of *medical education* to a scientific research basis, and the development of *public health* programs in the United States and abroad.

For the first quarter of the twentieth century the Rockefeller officers developed a definite strategy for their capital investment in medicine. That strategy sometimes supported and often opposed different interests in medicine, but such alliances and conflicts were never accidents on the part of the foundation. They were anticipated and necessary consequences of the role of modern medicine in the society, as desired and articulated from the very pinnacles of the American class structure.

Why was so much Rockefeller money—$65 million by 1928— lavished on a single institution devoted to scientific medical research? What motivated the men at the Rockefeller philanthropy to spend so much of their energy and money on medicine? How important were their humanitarian feelings for their fellow human beings? Did they envision material benefits from their work? As capitalists and corporate managers, did they believe it would further their personal interests or their class interests? The self-consciousness of their pioneering effort made accessible the concerns and thinking behind the façades constructed in foundation-funded histories and authorized biographies.

ROCKEFELLER MONEY AND MEDICAL SCIENCE: A SOCIAL INVESTMENT

On June 2, 1901, New York's newspapers hailed the founding of the Rockefeller Institute for Medical Research. The most celebrated example of private philanthropy supporting medical research, the institute began a new epoch in the United States. More than its predecessors abroad, the Rockefeller Institute would attack a broad range of diseases, seeking understandings of their biological and chemical causes, developing methods of prevention and cure, and training hundreds of researchers for medical science.

The institute began modestly with a commitment of $20,000 a year for research grants and soon after an outright gift of $1 million from John Davison Rockefeller. By 1928 Rockefeller gifts to the institute totaled $65 million, an enormous sum for the period. Although the elder Rockefeller and his son are most widely known for the benefactions, it was Frederick T. Gates who formulated the strategies and initiated the investments in medical research, medical education, and public health.

In 1915 Gates set down his memories of the origins of the institute. His anecdotal recollection stands as the widely quoted history of the origins of Rockefeller medical philanthropy.[10] As folklore, it conveys the process and motivations the creator of the Rockefeller Institute wished us to believe about the germination of his interest.

In his retrospective story, Gates describes how the idea for the institute came to him. As minister of the Central Baptist church in Minneapolis from 1880 to 1888, Gates had countless experiences with regular and homeopathic doctors. His visits to "hundreds of sick rooms" and his close relations with several physicians confirmed "a profound scepticism about medicine of both schools as it was currently practiced." As for homeopathic medicine, he concluded that Samuel Hahnemann, the founder, was "little less than a lunatic." He had little more confidence in the regular, or orthodox, school.

Then in 1897, six years after joining Rockefeller's staff, he befriended a former member of his Minneapolis congregation who was a medical student in New York. He asked the young man to suggest a readable medical text used in the best medical schools. On his young friend's recommendation, Gates bought himself a copy of William Osler's *Principles and Practice of Medicine,* first published in 1892, and a pocket medical dictionary.

Gates took Osler's book with him to join his family vacationing in the Catskills and read through its approximately 1,000 pages of revelations about the state of medicine. Osler laid bare the limitations of current medical knowledge and practice. Gates learned that many diseases were caused by germs, only a very few of which had been identified and isolated but many of which "we might reasonably hope to discover."

> When I laid down this book, I had begun to realize how woefully neglected in all civilized countries and perhaps most of all in this country, had been the scientific study of medicine. I saw very clearly also why this was true. In the first place, the instruments for investigation, the microscope, the science of chemistry, had not until recently been developed. Pasteur's germ theory of disease was very recent. Moreover, while other departments of science, astronomy, chemistry, physics, etc., had been endowed very generously in colleges and universities throughout the whole civilized world, medicine, owing to the peculiar commercial organization of medical colleges, had rarely if ever, been anywhere endowed, and research and instruction alike had been left to shift for itself dependent altogether on such chance as the active practitioner might steal from his practice. It became clear to me that medicine could hardly hope to become a science until medicine should be endowed and qualified men could give themselves to uninterrupted study and investigation, on ample salary, entirely independent of practice. To this end, it seemed to me an Institute of medical research ought to be established in the United States.

In July, Gates returned to his office in the Standard Oil building with "my Osler" in hand and dictated a memorandum to Rockefeller. He laid out his conclusions about the tragic state of medicine in the United States and its immense potential. He pointed out the usefulness of the Koch Institute in Berlin and the Pasteur Institute in Paris. In support of his recommendation for an American institute, Gates explained to Rockefeller that Pasteur's discoveries about anthrax and diseases of fermentation "had saved for the French nation a sum in excess of the entire cost of the Franco-German War." He also insisted that an institute founded by Rockefeller would encourage other wealthy men and women to found and endow other research centers, with the total effort yielding "abundant rewards."

While the memo to Rockefeller did not result in immediate action, it did provide the coherent rationale six months later for opposing the affiliation of Rush medical college with the University of Chicago, at the time Rockefeller's dearest and largest philanthropy. Rush was a respected school of the regular profession, a follower of the scientific vanguard but not among them. Gates got Rockefeller's support for a letter urging the university's administrators to abandon Rush and offering them instead a new medical center, "magnificently endowed, devoted *primarily to investigation, making practice itself an incident of investigation."* For some reason, probably related to the influence in Chicago of Rush's wealthy and socially and politically prominent practitioner-faculty members, the marriage was consummated anyway. Chicago lost its chance for the proposed institute. Thus was Gates' idea for the institute born and preserved from the clutches of medical sectarianism.

Gates' proposal was carefully considered through 1899 and 1900. Gates and Rockefeller, Jr., who joined the philanthropy staff in 1897, hired Starr J. Murphy, a lawyer friend and Montclair, N.J., neighbor of Gates, to study European institutes and confer with leading medical researchers in this country. L. Emmett Holt, pediatrician to several of Senior's grandchildren and a fellow parishioner at Junior's Fifth Avenue Baptist church in New York, impressed upon Junior the broad and basic biological research that led to the recent discovery of diphtheria antitoxin. What was needed to solve other great problems in medicine, he told the younger Rockefeller, "were men and resources which could be devoted solely to the work of research."[11]

Finally, in December 1900 John Rockefeller McCormick, the elder Rockefeller's three-year-old grandson, fell ill with scarlet fever. On the second day of the New Year he died. Any hesitancy the old man, a follower of homeopathy, felt about endowing scientific medical research was undermined when he was told by respected New York doctors that they knew little about the cause of scarlet fever and had no cure for it.[12]

Gates and the Rockefellers were also concerned about competition for their proposed institute. Andrew Carnegie's rival research institute, endowed with $10 million as the Carnegie Institution of Washington in 1902, was then in the planning stages. Rockefeller, Jr., was sufficiently concerned about the competition to wring an agreement from the steel king that his institution would not enter the field of medical research. At the same time Henry Phipps was founding an institute for the study of tuberculosis in Philadelphia. Competition struck close to home when Rockefeller's daughter Edith and son-in-law Harold F. McCormick unveiled their plans for a tribute to their son, the John Rockefeller McCormick Memorial Institute for Infectious Diseases in Chicago.[13]

By March 1901 Rockefeller committed himself to funding Gates' proposed institute. The Rockefeller Institute for Medical Research began its work with $20,000 a year for grants to medical researchers and soon thereafter a $1 million gift from Rockefeller, a board of directors composed of physicians—including Holt and Welch—with training in pathology and a commitment to bacteriological research, and Dr. Simon Flexner as the executive director.

For more than two years Gates grew increasingly impatient as the "medical gentlemen" restricted themselves to supporting small research projects around the country.[14] Finally, in the fall of 1904, the board opened its first laboratories and began its own program of medical research. In November 1907 Rockefeller gave the institute an additional endowment but held back half the $6 million requested by the directors. Finally, in October 1910, after the institute was reorganized—reducing the board of directors to a lesser role as the Board of Scientific Directors and creating a new board of trustees with Gates as chairman— Rockefeller added to the institute's endowment, providing it with the yearly income from $6.4 million of investments. By 1920 the Rockefellers had given the institute $23 million and by 1928 some $65 million.[15]

The institute was organized independently of any university primarily for reasons of efficiency and to avoid conflict with

Senior's commitment to homeopathy. First, Gates and Rockefeller, Jr., wanted the institute free of any teaching pressures. The objective of the institute was to produce results in medicine in order to reduce the amount of disease in society, and it would be a diversion of resources to ask the researchers to teach.[16]

Second, the handful of scientific medical schools, while nominally above medical sectarianism, were the turf of the regular profession's elite. The elder Rockefeller, a lifelong follower of homeopathy, objected to any move that strengthened the regular profession in its conflict with homeopathists. It was undoubtedly on this basis that Rockefeller in 1898 supported Gates' objection to the alliance between the University of Chicago and Rush Medical College, a creature of the regular profession and an opponent of homeopathy. Columbia and Harvard were briefly considered as recipients of the institute, but they were elite regular medical schools. Although neither Gates nor Junior took the old man's concerns seriously, they had to avoid provoking his objections that they were merely supporting one side, the wrong side in the conflict. With the example of the independent Pasteur Institute before them, the efficiency of a purely research institute as their primary concern, and their desire to assuage Senior's hostility to regular schools, Gates and Rockefeller, Jr., agreed to exclude any university affiliation for their project.[17]

HOMEOPATHY: THE CONFLICT SIMMERS

The conflict over homeopathy continued for some years. It is an illuminating example of the workings of the Rockefeller philanthropies, and it suggests an ideological difference between the robber barons like Senior who built up huge industrial empires and the next generation of corporate capitalists who ran the operations.

Rockefeller continued to express his concerns that within the institute and later in his philanthropies' support for medical education, his money was being used to support the regular profession at the expense of the homeopaths. "I am a homeopathist," he scolded his staff in 1916. "I desire that homeopathists should have fair, courteous, and liberal treatment extended to them from all medical institutions to which we contribute."[18] In

1919, when he was considering a $45 million gift to his General Education Board to support medical education, Rockefeller again warned his son and staff: "Homeopathic teaching should not be excluded . . . it should be provided for, the same as Allopathic."[19]*

His son and his staff firmly and repeatedly explained that "scientific medicine has rendered obsolete the former distinctions between the so-called Homeopathic and the so-called regular or Allopathic schools."[20] The new medicine is free of dogma, free of values. It represents not "preconceived notions" about the world but only "ascertained facts."[21] Medical science is devoid of "medical dogma of any kind."[22]

Furthermore, as the homeopaths and regular schools "are constantly drawing nearer together," a trusted adviser wrote the old man, "the discriminations which formerly were practised against homeopathists are being constantly lessened." Simon Flexner provided assurances that at the Rockefeller Institute "they make no distinction and welcome to their staff qualified men irrespective of the school in which they have been trained."[23]

That John D. Rockefeller personally patronized a homeopathist might seem surprising. However, Rockefeller and homeopathy were both products of the nineteenth century. From the mid-nineteenth century on, homeopathy in the United States appealed primarily to the upper classes. It was safer than the heroics of regular medicine, and it was a sign of affluence and taste since it was very fashionable among the European nobility and upper class, who were aped in many ways by wealthy Americans.[24] Rockefeller, who was twenty-two at the outbreak of the Civil War, grew up believing that homeopathy was medically and socially desirable.

Furthermore, while Rockefeller used chemists and engineers in developing his Standard Oil empire, his chief assets were an unbridled ambition and an intuitive and cunning sense of opportunity and organization. He accumulated the largest fortune among all the robber barons by paying his workers as little as possible and by ruthless methods in the marketplace, extracting huge rebates from the railroads for his shipments and cutting the

---

*"Allopathic" was another term for the regular, or orthodox, sect of the medical profession.

price of refined oil products to drive his competitors out of business. He did not fully share his son's and his later managers' appreciation of the importance of science in developing the base of industrial capitalism.

In his retirement and devotion to giving away his fortune, Rockefeller generally gave free reign to Gates and his son. He knew that his caution in disposing of his fortune was shared by his trusted lieutenants. Within his philanthropies he had the money but did not take the authority to establish policy. It seemed sufficient to him that his name was no longer the object of spittle, but rather gratitude. Except for occasional questions, taciturn consideration of his advisers' requests for millions of dollars, and objections to the treatment of homeopathists, Rockefeller, Sr., left the running of his philanthropies and his financial empire alike to Gates and his son.

Although Gates and Junior worked together in developing programs and prying gifts from the occasionally reluctant father, Junior himself acknowledged that "Gates was the brilliant dreamer and creator," and "I was the salesman, the go-between with father at the opportune moment."[25] Fortunately for history, Gates was a prolific writer of his ideas, leaving his thoughts in letters to Rockefeller, Sr., speeches to the various philanthropic boards, and memos to himself and his staff. Given his central role in the Rockefeller philanthropies and the importance of these philanthropies in the development of scientific medicine, it is illuminating to consider Gates' views of the role and consequences of medical science.

SCIENTIFIC MEDICINE AND CAPITALIST GATES

Gates, the premier Rockefeller medicine man, was attracted to medical science. It was not the appeals from medical science that drew his interest or his money. He was, like most educated people of the late nineteenth century, vaguely aware of the march of progress in medicine. He knew of Pasteur and the germ theory of disease. He had read Osler and understood the potential of medical science. But he never heard of Dr. Simon Flexner or Dr. William H. Welch, and he had no contact with other medical scientists until he initiated the medical institute. Nevertheless, he did "intelligently and clearly see that there was a tremendous need of medical research." Whatever requests for money for medical science crossed Gates' desk, none was taken seriously until 1907, when McGill University asked for aid to replace two medical school buildings that had been destroyed by fire.[26]

Gates was always an autonomous figure in medical philanthropy. He was moved by his own conceptions of the value of medicine and his own strategies for developing its role in American society. He was certainly influenced by medical men whom he respected, above all Simon Flexner and William Welch, but it was because their ideas and contributions conformed to *his* plans for the transformation of medicine. What visions did he have of the role and functions of scientific medicine?

We may grant that Gates had genuinely humanitarian motivations. His ministrations to the sick and dying in his Minneapolis parish undoubtedly evoked sympathy for their suffering. In his later years he credited medical science with standing above all other elements of history. None but medicine has "done so much to promote all the forces of civilization, to increase human happiness or to ameliorate human suffering."[27]

Typical of Gates, his enumeration of the accomplishments of medical science places the relief of human misery after the promotion of the "forces of civilization." This is not a petty criticism, for Gates' preeminent consideration was the development and extension of Anglo-American civilization. What he understood that civilization to represent will become clear in the following pages, but in its essence "civilization" meant the values of work and disciplined living, a social life organized around productive labor and frugal consumption. "Civilization" also meant the right and indeed the responsibility of men of wealth to govern society and of industrial societies to direct economically less developed societies. In brief, "civilization" was equated in Gates' mind with industrial capitalism and imperialism.

What value did scientific medicine have for capitalism? Gates envisioned numerous material and social-political consequences flowing from medical science in a never-ending stream of support for capitalist society.

HEALTHIER WORKERS

The *material* benefit of medicine is a healthier population and thus a healthier work force. What Pasteur's work on anthrax had done for the French cattle industry, medical science could do for the whole society. The findings of medical science were most important when applied to preventing disease. "By keeping well," Gates observed, a person "enjoys all the employments, pleasures, and financial gains of continuous health." Gates insisted from the beginning of his career to its end that "the fundamental aim of medical science ought to be not primarily the cure but primarily the prevention of disease."[28]

Gates believed that events supported his contention. In the first quarter of the twentieth century, "sanitary science and preventive medicine" had reduced sickness by half, he asserted, citing support from U.S. Census Bureau reports of mortality rates, insurance company statistics, and reports of state and local health boards.[29] Although sickness was still a major obstacle to the full utilization of labor, the assault by the forces of science was paying off. Gates cited a report that 20 percent of the employees of large companies were home sick each day, but, he added, triumphantly, "I think that even so high a figure is far below that of the armies of [General] Washington."[30]

Gates was far from a solitary figure preaching the potential of medicine for capitalists. Big business, Gates observed in 1925, sponsored preventive medical care programs on a large scale "because health is found in a variety of ways to be profitable."[31] Healthy workers are profitable because they are an employer's human capital to be utilized for production of salable goods and services. Just as the capital invested in machines needs to be protected by adequate maintenance programs, so too does human capital require maintenance and repair, a perspective long recognized in many contexts.

Southern slave owners and their physicians viewed their black slaves as a capital investment to be saved from disability or death whenever possible, lending credibility to the myth of paternalistic slavery. In a study of the role of medicine in the ante-bellum South, Walter Fisher concluded that the primary reason why slaves were provided with medical care was the tremendous economic investment they represented to slave owners.[32] Every planter understood that "to save his capital was to save his negroes," observed Dr. Richard Arnold, an upper-class physician in Savannah. The self-interest of the slave-owning class in the preservation of its investment made Southern slavery "the only institution in which Interests and Humanity go hand in hand together," Dr. Arnold wryly added.[33]

It was not only racism and slavery that facilitated "paternalistic" self-interest. The U.S. Sanitary Commission, organized in 1861 to provide medical relief to Union soldiers on Southern battlefields, was by its own account no humanitarian enterprise. Run by wealthy Easterners, the commission declared "its ultimate end is neither humanity nor charity. It is to economize for the National service the life and strength of the National soldier." Saving a soldier's life, the commission calculated, reduced the monetary cost of the war and preserved the soldier as a "producer" when he "returned to the industrial pursuits of civil life." Each soldier's life was worth "no less than one thousand dollars" to society.[34]

With the rapid development of an industrial base in the United States during and after the Civil War, employers in many industries viewed their workers as disposable resources. Particularly with increasing mechanization in industrial production, a decreased demand for skilled workers, and an unlimited supply of desperate immigrants, the work force became a sea of men and women to be plucked up by employers as needed and later tossed out. Workers who were maimed, killed, or simply worn out by their jobs were replaced by other bodies from among the unemployed.

As the unemployed work force shrank with the outbreak of war or upswings in the economy, as labor organized to change its working conditions and pay, and as employers found that lost production because of illness and rapid turnover of their workers cost them profits, enlightened businessmen developed new attitudes toward their workers. It was not concern for the workers' needs that led to better conditions and health and welfare programs. Rather these reforms sprang from the industrial unionism and political organization of workers and from the opposing necessity of employers to discipline the work force to the requirements of capitalist production. The firm that improved its working conditions reduced work days lost to strikes. The firm that took pains to keep its workers found increased productivity from its capital investment. The firm that offered company housing, shares of stock, and company medical care increased the dependence of the workers on the company and lessened the threat of unionization. And, in the early years of this century up to World War I, industries that voluntarily acted could reduce the risk of restrictive legislation demanded by the forces of Progressivism. As early as 1892, following the bloody Homestead strike, Andrew Carnegie articulated a more conciliatory policy toward his workers to prevent the loss of experienced workers, though there is little evidence that he or his company followed the policy. "It is impossible," he said, "to get new men to run successfully the complicated machinery of a modern steel plant."[35] Labor stability became an important element in the productivity and profit strategies of modern industries. "It is good business to conserve life and health," observed John Topping of Republic Steel, for thereby "one of the most important items of economy in production is secured."[36]

Industrialists who weathered the marketplace and emerged among the monopolistic leaders of their industry had the capital and foresight to ward off unionization and stabilize their work forces with health and welfare programs. Steel companies, railroads, oil companies, and others created complete medical care systems for their workers, hiring or contracting with physicians and providing dispensaries or hospitals.

The efforts of slave owners and the U.S. Sanitary Commission to preserve lives by curing disease were aimed at conserving human capital, the one "belonging" to an individual and the other profiting a whole class. The medical programs of individual corporations were aimed more at undermining unionization and stabilizing their own work forces, with improved health an added benefit rather than the main purpose. Thus, slave owners and industrial corporations exhibited enlightened self-interest while the upper-class sanitary commissioners demonstrated a more far-sighted plan for investing in the whole society's work force. The latter is an articulated interest of an entire class—the interest of the capitalist class in a stable and healthy work force.

Frederick T. Gates consistently articulated this larger perspective and shaped his philanthropic programs around it. He understood the importance of a healthy work force to the growth of capital and industrial output. The Rockefeller Sanitary Commission, organized by Gates in 1909, sought to eradicate hookworm disease from the southern U.S. population. Charles Wardell Stiles, a government zoologist, convinced Gates and

Junior that the hookworm was "one of the most important diseases of the South" and a cause of "some of the proverbial laziness of the poorer classes of the white population." Whatever genuine pride the Rockefellers and Gates felt in relieving the suffering of thousands of Southerners, their primary incentive was clearly the increased productivity of workers freed of the endemic parasite. Gates observed that the stocks of cotton mills located in the heavily infected tidewater counties of North Carolina were worth less than mills in other counties of the state where fewer people were infected. "This is due," he explained to Rockefeller, Sr., "to the inefficiency of labor in these cotton mills, and the inefficiency in the labor is due to the infection by the hookworm which weakens the operatives." Gates calculated, "It takes, by actual count, about 25 percent more laborers to secure the same results in the counties where the infection is heavier." It also took 25 percent more houses for the workers, more machinery, and thus more capital and higher operating costs. "This is why the stocks of such mills are lower and the profits lighter."[37]

The Rockefellers did not have any significant investment in Southern textile mills. Rather their extensive and widespread investments gave them a concern for the productivity of the entire economy. The Sanitary Commission was a logical extension of their educational programs in the South (discussed in Chapter 1), all directed ultimately to integrating the Southern economy into the national dominion of Northern capitalists.

Through the International Health Commission—the first program of the Rockefeller Foundation established in 1913—the hookworm and other public health programs were extended worldwide. None of these programs was intended to prop up specific Rockefeller investments abroad. They were directed more generally at improving the health of each country's work force to facilitate sufficient economic development to provide the United States with needed raw materials and an adequate market for this country's manufactured goods. Stacy May, an economist and a director of a Rockefeller-controlled international investment corporation, recently reaffirmed the value of such programs. "Where mass diseases are brought under control, productivity tends to increase—through increasing the percentage of adult workers as a proportion of the total population, [and] through augmenting their strength and ambition to work," he observed.[38]

Each of these programs can be traced to Gates' and the Rockefellers' broader concern for the permanent economic and social viability of capitalist society. Gates viewed the public health in a larger capitalist class perspective than probably any other important figure in the various medical reform movements of the period. Although his articulated views on the relation between health and capitalism were more complete than other capitalists of his era, he was not alone in maintaining the importance of such programs.

The American Association for Labor Legislation, a Progressive era alliance of corporate-liberal business leaders, some labor leaders, and upper middle-class reformers, won business support for its proposal for compulsory national health insurance mainly on the basis of the self-interest of employers. "Illness as well as injury occasion a large economic waste to the company as well as to the employees on account of lost time, idle machinery, and ineffective work," reported Howell Cheney of the Cheney Brothers' Silk Mills. "It is to the direct interest of the company as well as to the individual to bring about a reestablishment of health, and consequently efficiency, by supplying the best conditions possible for recovery."[39]

The National Association of Manufacturers committee on industrial betterment supported compulsory sickness insurance against voluntary systems largely because of the importance they attached to a healthy work force. "We know that there are employers who would not comply with the voluntary plan," the NAM committee warned. Even a corporation president who sees the long-run advantages of "enlightened" industrial relations may bow blindly to maximizing this year's profits. This was an important enough issue, they argued, that the State must "subordinate the independence of the individual to the general good."[40]

It was *not* primarily a concern for conserving human life that led America's corporate liberals in the Progressive era to support compulsory health insurance. From Bismarck to the Conservative party in England to the American Association for Labor Legislation and the National Civic Federation, the far-sighted leaders of corporate capitalism believed that government-sponsored sickness insurance, workers' compensation, and other social security measures would reduce the appeal of radical labor and socialist movements.[41] Hoping to depoliticize workers' unhappiness with their lot, corporate leaders joined reformers in calling for such moderate reforms. Despite this expedient application of medical care programs, leaders of many corporations as well as the conservative National Association of Manufacturers believed that medical care, when extended to the whole population, would substantially improve the health of workers and their families, which included future workers.

Sharing the concern of the business class, the vanguard of scientific medicine considered the economic benefits of medicine among its most important effects. The smaller view pervaded the thinking of physicians working in a particular company's health programs. C. W. Hopkins, chief surgeon for the Chicago and Northwestern Railway, told the 1915 annual meeting of the American Academy of Medicine that the railroads found it economically desirable to organize medical care programs because it cost them $500 to train an employee and because experienced and healthy workers were important in reducing accidents that injure passengers and destroy property. "It is now a well-recognized fact among the managements of the railroads," reported Dr. Hopkins, "that it is just as important to care for their sick and injured [workers] as it is to maintain a certain standard of efficiency or perfection of their rolling stock and road bed."[42]

Broader views of medicine's material importance to society guided strategies of men who led the medical reform movement at elite universities and the national level. Charles W. Eliot, the Harvard president who launched major medical reforms beginning in 1869, considered medical research both pure and applied. At the dedication ceremonies for the Rockefeller Institute's laboratories in 1906, Eliot characterized research medicine's primary object as striving for "truth in the abstract" and its secondary objects as preventing "industrial losses due to sickness and untimely death among men and domestic animals," and lessening the negative impact of sickness on human happiness.[43]

William H. Welch, at the same ceremony, asserted with pride that scientific medicine made possible the "great industrial activities of modern times, efforts to colonize and to reclaim for civilization vast tropical regions, [and] the immense undertaking to construct the Panama Canal."[44] For the most part, academic doctors were content to support the uses of medical science laid down by the philanthropic strategists whose funding programs guided the development and utilization of research. The medical profession thus accepted the capitalist definition of health as the capacity to work.

IDEOLOGICAL MEDICINE

AN INDUSTRIALIST WORLD VIEW

For philanthropist and capitalist Gates, the material consequences of medical science were only one of its advantages. Indeed, Gates gave more attention to the other advantages that intrigued him. Probably more than any of his contemporaries, Gates perceived and understood the ideological functions of medicine. Some of his thoughts were implicit understandings of the relation between scientific medicine and industrial capitalist ideology. His most systematic thinking concerned the social value of medical science as ideology and as a cultural force.

Members of any society or social class whose existence is intimately tied to industrialism will find scientific medicine's explanations of health and disease more appealing than mystical belief systems. The precise analysis of the human body into its component parts is analogous to the industrial organization of production. From the perspective of an industrialist, scientific medicine seems to offer the limitless potential for effectiveness that science and technology provide in manufacturing and social organization. Just as industry depends upon science for technically powerful industrial tools, science-based medicine and its mechanistic concepts of the body and disease should yield powerful tools with which to identify, eliminate, and prevent agents of disease and to correct malfunctions of the body.

Gates and other industrial capitalists found a close correspondence between this new medicine's concepts of the body and disease and their own world view. The body, Gates believed, is a microcosm of society, and disease is an invasion of external elements. Medical research must discover the agents of disease and find the means of preventing their destruction of the body or provide a cure. Health, in Gates' view, is the absence of disease.

"Nearly all disease," Gates explained to Rockefeller,[45]

> is caused by living germs, animal and vegetable, which finding lodgement in the human body, under favorable conditions multiply with enormous rapidity until they interfere with the functions of the organs which they attack and either they or their products poison the fountains of life.

Nature's healing methods are strikingly similar to the organization of industrial society.

> When, for illustration, the skin is cut with a knife, nature at once begins to hurry to the point of disaster squadrons of white corpuscles of the blood and other healing forces. Just as the fire engines start from all quarters on the dead run to a fire when the alarm is sounded, healing forces rush from every part of the body to the point of trouble, some to destroy any poisonous germs that may get into the wound, others to unite the wounded parts as before.

The body in which nature works is constructed like a Lilliputian community, complete with modern social organization and industrial plants.

> The body has a network of insulated nerves, like telephone wires, which transmit instantaneous alarms at every point of danger. The body is furnished with a most elaborate police system, with hundreds of police stations to which the criminal elements are carried by the police and jailed. . . . The body has a most complete and elaborate sewer system.

The body's industrial life exists in

> an infinite number of microscopic cells. Each one of these cells is a small chemical laboratory, into which its own appropriate raw material is constantly being introduced, the processes of chemical separation and combination are constantly taking place automatically, and its own appropriate finished product is constantly being thrown off, that finished product being necessary for the life and health of the body. Not only is this so, but the great organs of the body like the liver, stomach, pancreas, kidneys, gall bladder, are great local manufacturing centers, formed of groups of cells in infinite number, manufacturing the same sorts of products, just as industries of the same kind are often grouped in specific districts.

"We are fearfully and wonderfully made," Gates ironically concludes, as though praising some new machine created in God's own image. Because "nature is the great physician," her healing powers have obscured the failing of all pre- and nonscientific forms of medicine. Recovery from disease before the advent of scientific medicine, Gates believed, was due entirely to the power of nature as healer. Homeopathic and orthodox medical sects, Christian Science, psychic healers, osteopaths, Indian herb doctors, and patent medicine men all survived by claiming nature's cures as their own.

Only science was able to comprehend nature. "Science has discovered the laboratories where she has stored her reserves and has robbed her of them for use on human beings." Medical researchers in Gates' day were pressing the campaign against disease on two fronts: "they are trying to break into and expose to the light many more of the secret processes in nature's laboratories," and "they are working to create new chemical combinations that will cure."

Gates thus appreciated the human body as one of nature's puzzles, to be investigated and understood by science. His view, shared by scientific doctors, engineers, professionals of all sorts, and most corporate executives and owners, envisioned health as the absence of disease and medicine as an engineering task. Science was helping industry reshape the organization of production by developing machinery to control and cheapen human labor and more cheaply extract from nature a salable product. Science would also extract from nature the secrets of life itself while medicine would apply them to understand disease and develop methods of preventing or curing these pestilences of life and commerce. Improving the health of the population was thus an engineering job that involved understanding and manipulating nature.

Gates' views were not very different from those generally held by medical scientists of his day. While few directly applied the analogy of industrial society, nearly all conceived the body in mechanistic terms that made such an analogy seem natural. The similarity between the constructs of scientific medicine and the world view of industrial capitalism made it seem natural for the new order to support scientific doctors against all "quacks." The medical profession benefited from the compatibility of its theories with the perspectives of the newly dominant class, but the capitalist social order won extraordinary ideological and cultural advantages.

INDUSTRIAL CULTURE AND CAPITALIST LEGITIMATION

Scientific medicine's singular concern with the microbiological interaction of the human body and specific disease states had political consequences which Gates and a few others envisioned. In brief, Gates embraced scientific medicine as a force that would: (1) help unify and integrate the emerging industrial society with technical values and culture, and (2) legitimize capitalism by diverting attention from structural and other environmental causes of disease.

Gates and other officers in the Rockefeller foundations believed that medicine had an important cultural role to play. Gates believed that the goal of medicine, the "healing ministration," is "the most intimate, the most precious, the superlative interest of every man that lives." After food, water, sleep, and sex, freedom from disease is the great longing of all peoples. The desire for health is a unifying force "whose values go to the palace of the rich and the hovel of the poor." Medicine is "a work which penetrates everywhere." Thus, "the values of medical research are the most universal values on earth, and they are the most intimate and important values to every human being that lives."[46]

With medicine's unique acceptance by all people, the Rockefeller Foundation discovered what the missionaries also knew: Medicine can be used to convert and colonize the heathen. In 1909 the Rockefeller philanthropies added public health programs to their earlier efforts to develop public schools and promote agricultural demonstration projects in the South in part because medical care is so seductive to even the most reluctant people.

In China, Gates switched from supporting religious missionaries to building a Western medical system. This episode is fascinating both because of the greater value that Gates, a man of the cloth, placed on scientific medicine in promoting Western influence and because of the unabashed imperialist motivations he himself attributed to Rockefeller philanthropies abroad. In 1905 Gates urged Rockefeller, a frequent contributor to Baptist missionaries, to donate $100,000 to an organization of Congregational missions.[47] "Now for the first time in the history of the world," Gates explained to Rockefeller,

> all the nations and all the islands of the sea are actually open and offer a free field for the light and philanthropy of the English speaking people. . . . Christian agencies as a whole have very thoroughly invaded all coasts, all strategic points, all ports of entry and are thoroughly entrenched where they are.

For Gates, transforming heathens into God-fearing Christians was "no sort of measure" of the value of missionaries:

> Quite apart from the question of persons converted, the mere commercial results of missionary effort to our own land is worth, I had almost said a thousandfold every year of what is spent on missions. . . . Missionary enterprise, viewed solely from a commercial standpoint, is immensely profitable. From the point of view of means of subsistence for Americans, our import trade, traceable mainly to the channels of intercourse opened up by missionaries, is enormous. Imports from heathen lands furnish us cheaply with many of the luxuries of life and not a few of the comforts, and with many things, indeed, which we now regard as necessities.

Industrial capitalism, however, required not only raw materials and cheap products. It also needed new markets for its abundant manufactured goods. As Gates added to Rockefeller's receptive ear:

> our imports are balanced by our exports to these same countries of American manufactures. Our export trade is growing by leaps and bounds. Such growth would have been utterly impossible but for the commercial conquest of foreign lands under the lead of missionary endeavor. What a boon to home industry and manufacture!

The missionary effort in China was effective for a time in undermining Chinese self-determination. Missionaries were the velvet glove of imperialism, frequently backed up by the mailed fist. Nevertheless, the missionary effort, promoted through schools and medical programs, was still a very transparent attempt to support European and American interests. As J. A. Hobson, an English economist, noted at the time, "Imperialism in the Far East is stripped nearly bare of all motives and methods save those of distinctively commercial origin."[48]

In China, as throughout the world, the Rockefeller philanthropists soon concluded that medicine and public health by
themselves were far more effective than either missionaries or
armies in pursuing the same ends. The Rockefeller Foundation
removed the Peking Union Medical College from missionary
society control, established it under foundation direction, and
developed it into a completely secular, world renowned medical
center, spending a total of $45 million for the China medical
program.

In the Philippines, the foundation's International Health
Commission outfitted a hospital ship to bring medical care and
the "benefits of civilization" to the rebellious Moro tribes. The
foundation officers were ecstatic that such medical work made it
"possible for the doctor and nurse to go in safety to many places
which it has been extremely dangerous for the soldier to approach." Their medical work paved "the way for establishing
industrial and regular schools" and served as "an entering wedge
for permanent civilizing influences."[49] Thus, in subduing primi-
tive peoples and bringing them into desired colonial relations,
medical care has, in the words of foundation president George
Vincent, "some advantages over machine guns."[50]

Given the openly imperialist ambitions of the United States
early in this century, the Rockefeller philanthropy officers could
publicly acknowledge their use of medicine to integrate dissenting
people into industrial and capitalist society. Their domestic
medical programs had exactly the same ends, though Gates and
others were far more circumspect in discussing them.

Medicine was increasingly replacing religion as the intimate
arm of the social order. In education the teaching of values was
obvious, and attempts to reform the schools provoked angry
responses from a class-conscious society.[51] In 1914 the National
Education Association's attacks on the Carnegie and Rockefeller
foundations were joined by many newspapers that condemned
the foundations for trying to turn "our schools into mills for the
manufacture of men and women made according to Rockefeller
and Carnegie specifications."[52] Medicine was more insidious.

For Gates to see medicine as a desirable replacement for
religion was indeed an interesting turn of events. Gates, it will be
recalled, was successively a Baptist minister, executive secretary
of the American Baptist Education Society, and Rockefeller's

chief lieutenant in charge of the industrialist's philanthropy and a large part of his financial empire. Like other members of the managerial stratum, Gates identified his own interests and destiny with those of his employer.

Shortly after his move from the ministry to directing the largest philanthropic and financial empire in the world, Gates' views on religion began to change. He began to read the Bible more critically and was soon convinced that "Christ had neither founded nor intended to found the Baptist church, nor any church; that neither he nor his disciples during his lifetime had baptized; that the communion was not conceived by Christ as a church ordinance, and that the whole Baptist fabric was built upon texts which had no authority, and on ecclesiastical conceptions wholly foreign to the mind of Christ."[53] Gates found himself converted from Baptism to capitalism and scientism!

Medicine was a fundamental part of his new "religion." While theology was being "reconstructed in the light of science," scientific medicine was promulgating "new moral laws and new social laws, new definitions of what is right and wrong in our relations with each other." For Gates, the Rockefeller Institute for Medical Research was a "theological seminary, presided over by the Rev. Simon Flexner, D.D."[54]

Gates did not fully explain the meaning of his metaphor, but it seems clear that he viewed medicine as industrial society's counterpart to religion, carrying moral precepts, "new duties," and the values of science to all people through its universal appeal and irresistible intimacy. This function was understood by leading members of the medical profession as well. Dr. John B. Roberts, in his presidential address to the American Academy of Medicine in 1904, laid out "The Doctor's Duty to the State." The physician "should teach the laity that mental hygiene, or discipline, is as essential to proper living and happiness as physical hygiene," Roberts said. "Hygiene of the body gives a spirit of religious toleration and calm" while "hygiene of the mind gives a healthy digestion and a good income-making body and fits man for this world as well as the next."[55] Scientific medicine was thus an ideal instrument to help unify and integrate the new industrial society and indeed a world order in the values and culture of science, technology, and capitalism.

Western scientific medicine was an uncommonly good vehicle

for United States efforts to dominate Latin America, Asia, and Africa. But it was equally useful in bringing rural and technologically and industrially naive North Americans to accept the domination of their lives by science and technology. Science had provided a basis for rationalizing industry, for organizing production consistent with the imperatives of profit and the growth of capital, and simultaneously for undermining the arguments of workers that the new technology eliminated their control over the productive process. The application of science to industry in fact depoliticized the whole productive process and created the appearance that progress is technology's own imperative. Beneath that rule by technology lay the more fundamental imperative—capitalism's need for economic growth. The march of scientific and technological progress appears as an independent variable on which essential economic growth depends. Science and technology are developed mainly in ways useful to capitalist society, and as Jürgen Habermas has shown, "the development of the social system *seems* to be determined by the logic of scientific-technical progress."[56]

The same mystification that the technological "imperative" pulls over the productive process is extended to all social spheres. Mechanical engineers, led by Frederick Taylor, developed more "efficient" ways of utilizing human labor in the factory, mainly by separating mental from manual labor, reorganizing the labor process under management's control, and substituting unskilled for skilled labor wherever possible. Although it did not particularly increase profits, Taylor's "scientific management" proved a very effective form of social control.[57] It provided a moral rationale for demanding obedience to capitalist values of hard work and disciplined living. "Too great liberty," Taylor wrote to Harvard president Charles Eliot, "results in a large number of people going wrong who would be right if they had been forced into good habits."[58] Housewives and mothers were similarly exhorted to be more efficient, for the home was "part of the great factory for production of citizens."[59] Industrial and social leaders of the Progressive era, whether themselves Progressives or not, hoped to rationalize all social relations. The cult of efficiency firmly established in American culture and intellectual life the notion that technology must be served. Added to the already widespread view that science and technology are value-free, the technological imperative became a powerful moral force.

Corporation heads, presidents of elite universities, and philanthropists all joined in support of the new religion of science. "Respect for the man who knows and loyalty to demonstrated truth," preached Nicholas Murray Butler, president of Columbia University, "are characteristics of a civilization that is founded on rock."[60]

Research institutes were the temples of the new religion. The Rockefeller Institute for Medical Research will be important in three ways, Butler told the dignitaries assembled for the opening of the institute's laboratories. It will add to mankind's knowledge of medicine, it will help train needed scientists, and it "will help spread abroad in the public mind a respect for science and for scientific method." Each of these contributions is a public service, he added, "but the last named is perhaps the greatest."[61]

Scientific medicine, as part of the fervent campaign for science, helped spread *industrial culture*, albeit a *capitalist* industrial culture, throughout the land and indeed the world. But scientific medicine also developed into an ideological perspective that *legitimizes* the great inequalities of capitalist societies and the misery that results from the private appropriation of human and environmental resources.

At one time, many physicians were in the vanguard of progressive social reform movements. By the mid-1800s social medicine was a highly developed field. Villermé, Buchez and Guérin in France, Neumann, Virchow, and Leubuscher in Germany, and dozens of lesser-known doctors studied the economic, social and occupational causes of disease and worked for reforms to eliminate them. Rudolf Virchow, one of the fathers of modern cell physiology, argued that medicine "must intervene in political and social life. It must point out the hindrances that impede the normal functioning of vital processes, and effect their removal."[62] Many physicians and sanitarians identified and statistically documented inhuman and dangerous working conditions, unemployment, miserable living conditions, malnutrition, and general poverty as the major causes of the high disease rates and early deaths among Europe's working classes.

The failure of the revolutionary movement of 1848, in which many of these physicians participated, did not halt their efforts to change the conditions they opposed.

From the time of Pasteur and Koch, however, a more conservative outlook dominated medical research. The clinical, or medical, model focused attention on the individual, while bacteriological research identified discrete, external, and specific agents of disease. This perspective encouraged the idea of specific therapies to cure specific pathological conditions, and it diverted attention from the social and economic causes of disease. When Koch presented his discovery of the tubercle bacillus to the Berlin Physiological Society in 1882, many medical scientists did not share Koch's view that this bacillus *causes* tuberculosis. Virchow and others argued that since pathogenic micro-organisms lived in healthy bodies, they are not *the cause* of disease. In their view, invading micro-organisms could cause disease only after the host organism had been weakened by some physiological or environmental misery.[63] Pasteur and Koch, nevertheless, won deserved plaudits for their technical accomplishments; they and their followers also won extensive financial support from their governments and wealthy individuals alike. In Europe and the United States elite physicians perceived the opportunities opening before them, and leading capitalists showed their appreciation for medical science's ideological role.

Ideologues for capitalist society promulgated the insufficiency of our mastery of nature, the inadequacy of our technological development as the fundamental cause of misery. "The trouble is," Gates wrote Rockefeller, "that the blanket of happiness seems to be too short. If you pull it up at the head you expose the feet; if you tuck it in on the one side you uncover the other side." While there is probably no way to increase the "sum total of human happiness," it is certain that the Rockefeller Institute "is actually and enormously decreasing the sum total of human misery."[64]

It is clear whence comes the unhappiness. It comes *not* from unequal distribution of wealth, sickening working and living conditions, miserable and alienating work, tension caused by frequent and prolonged unemployment, economic insecurity, and competition among those whose sights are set on higher stations in life. "*Disease* is the supreme ill of human life," Gates proclaimed, "and it is *the main source of almost all other human ills,* poverty, crime, ignorance, vice, inefficiency, hereditary taint, and many other evils."[65] It is not poverty or one's place in the capitalist class structure that breeds misery; it is disease that is the cause of the misery commonly attributed to poverty. Misery is a technical not a social problem.

While "the great mass of charities of the world" go around helping an individual poor family or indirectly "relieving or mitigating such evils and miseries of society as are due mainly to disease," the Rockefeller Institute reaches "the root of the evil" and cleanses "the very fountains of human misery."[66] This human unhappiness can be eradicated through science and technology. The same forces that helped create America's vast and growing industrial base could be turned to eliminating her misery as well. Gates thus joined with others in "medicalizing" all social problems, defining them out of political struggle and even religious morals, and giving them over to technical expertise and professional management.

Rockefeller money did not support medical research that investigated the relationship of social factors to health and disease. In its first decade, the Rockefeller Institute focused its resources on chemistry, biology, pathology, bacteriology, physiology, pharmacology, and experimental surgery.[67] It ignored the impact of the social, economic, and physical environment on disease and health. In later years, institute researchers touched on the role of nutrition as a contributing factor in malaria and some other parasitic and infectious diseases, but even then they did not extend their conclusions to the actual social conditions in which people lived.[68] Of the more than 650 men and women who contributed their skills to the Rockefeller Institute, few—with the notable exception of René Dubos—seemed even to understand the role of society and environment as forces affecting the very diseases they studied.

This orientation to biological reductionism pervaded the Rockefeller medical philanthropies. When Gates, Junior, and other men in the Rockefeller Foundation decided to establish the first public health school in the United States, they selected Dr. Welch and Johns Hopkins University as their vehicles, knowing the new school would have a heavy emphasis on the basic sciences and not stray too far into social issues.[69] Charles Wardell Stiles, the government zoologist who brought the hookworm to the attention of the Rockefeller philanthropy and was named scientific director of the campaign to eradicate the parasitic disease, exhibited a capacity for keeping his nose to the parasites and not being distracted by social concerns. In an article on "The Chain Gang as a Possible Disseminator of Intestinal Parasites and Infections," Stiles offered not one word of criticism of chain gangs per se. He limited himself to criticizing the lack of privies and bemoaned the missed "opportunities for rigid discipline" that could "make these penal institutions admirable schools in which the State might easily give its charges some good lessons in cleanliness, hygiene, and sanitation."[70]

GATES' DIGRESSION

Gates genuinely believed in technical solutions for problems of social happiness. But there was another side to Gates. There was a side that recognized the exploitation of labor by capital, that felt compassion for the oppressed men and women of the industrial working class. As a member of the board of directors or chairman of the board of more than a dozen corporations, but not a part of day-to-day management, Gates was never personally involved in labor disputes. From his lofty heights at the top of the Rockefeller financial and philanthropic empires, Gates had a broad view of the needs of his class and a measured strategy for meeting them.

In 1916, two years after the clamorous criticism over the Ludlow massacre and a time when "labor is demanding more wages everywhere," Gates asked himself the strategic question, "shall one oppose this demand or favor it?" In a memorandum for himself, Gates developed his position on "Capital and Labor."[71] First, unionism is selfish, violent, ignorant, perverse, and mistaken, he believed. Through unions, labor demands "the largest possible wage" and does "the least possible work" whereas the public-spirited citizen, whether wealthy capitalist or poor laborer, does the "largest possible service" and consumes the "least possible amount of the public wealth" by accepting private economy and saving.

Second, the object of labor should be to increase its *real* wages, not merely get a jump on the next guy. "If a few crafts become thoroughly unionized and secure their demands, it must be," Gates observed, "at the expense of all other crafts that are not so unionized." Unions seemed to care little that raising the wages of any one group will result in an increase in the cost of living for all other groups since employers will pass on to workers-as-consumers the increase in wages they grant. The wage earner will have won his battle, Gates concluded, "not merely when he has got his wages, but when he has so got them that they will buy more." Higher wages without a higher cost of living is the object, "and the only way under heaven in which that can be done is by taking the wages out of the returns of the capitalist."

Gates believed labor's demand for a greater share of the wealth was just. The laboring classes are "degraded" by the kind of work they have to do, the amount of work required of them, and "the deprivations that they have to suffer." The differences between rich and poor, capitalist and laborer, "are due not to heredity but to environment." The rich and aristocratic have no purer blood than the "misshapen, ill-dressed, half-brutalized men and women" who have worked the mines from childhood.

> Shall we hate and despise and look down upon these people whom our social system has made what they are, or shall we pity them and shall we blame ourselves for having made them what they are, for keeping them where they are, and for clothing ourselves with the fruits of their unpaid labor?

Frederick Engels was not more eloquent!

Gates concluded that it was necessary and desirable for capital to voluntarily reduce its return on investments from the prevailing 5 percent to 2 percent and give the balance to the workers.

> Cut down their hours of labor. Improve their living conditions. Give them opportunities for music, for pictures, for whatever can cultivate them in mind, whatever can beautify and adorn them in body. Let us ourselves share to some extent the manual labor of the world, and instead of a few rising to the top on the backs of the many, let us undertake to build up society in all its parts as a whole to a higher level.

Gates was moved not by compassion but by fear. He and other members of America's ruling class were shaken by the violent labor struggles, widespread working-class consciousness and support for the Socialist party, and unrest among middle-class Progressives. Most of this class antagonism was aimed at the great concentrations of wealth in the industrial monopolies and the flaunting of wealth by the Vanderbilts and the Astors. Always an advocate of inconspicuous consumption, Gates now privately and momentarily looked to corporate-liberal social reforms to head off the anticipated cataclysm.

With the entrance of the United States into the European war, full employment and patriotism overwhelmed the Progressive reform movement and justified repression of the Socialists and militant working-class organizations. The immediacy of the internal threat passed, and Gates abandoned even his private thoughts of redistributing the wealth. Promoting physical and social science research continued unaltered as the primary foundation program for ameliorating misery although the junior Rockefeller developed new programs in the arts to uplift the people's culture.

A PERMANENT INVESTMENT

In addition to the expected material and political benefits of medical science, Gates believed that endowing the Rockefeller Institute was an ideal investment because of the permanence of its findings. Each generation takes from the past and hands on to the future "only the things that are proven to be permanently useful." The "useless baggage" is dropped and left behind. The one thing that "humanity has got to live with" is "old Nature and her laws in this world," Gates told his friends at the Rockefeller Institute. "These laws do not change and humanity will never outlive them. Whatever we discover about Nature and her forces, and incorporate into our science, that will be carried forward, though all else be forgotten."[72]

Despite his naive view of science, Gates viewed endowments for scientific research as permanent social capital, an investment that would continue to return dividends into the distant future. Given his broad and long-range perspective of the needs of capitalist society, Gates was very attracted to this feature of scientific research.

Aside from its permanence, an investment by Rockefeller in an institute for medical research would call forth more money into medical research. This one act of philanthropy would "call public attention to the importance of research" and encourage "many thoughtful men of wealth" to endow research in scientific medical schools throughout the country.[73]

In the end, private fortunes and public taxes alike flowed in ever-increasing amounts into medical research. In 1911 Gates was pleased that other rich men and women had indeed followed the example of Rockefeller.[74] By the mid-1920s Gates felt assured that his strategy of encouraging public and private grants had paid off. "Never before were the common people so ready to grasp the extended hand of a liberal philanthropy," he told fellow trustees of the Rockefeller Foundation, "and to cooperate by legal enactment, liberal taxation, and private munificence."[75]

All this financial support for medical science and the social recognition heaped upon the scientific medical profession by members of the upper class had given physicians a higher and more secure status. Medical research institutes, Gates observed, "have conferred dignity and glory upon medicine," with the consequence that the medical profession was awakening "to a proud and healthy consciousness of the dignity of its vocation." Quite uncynically, Gates believed that "the elevation of the medical profession" would further the interests of the profession itself and help stabilize a sometimes shaky class structure.[76] Capitalist society was gaining another firm supporter as the medical profession, cleansed of any social conscience, increasingly recognized its duty to preserve the existing social order.

The philanthropic capitalists who supported medical science believed it would do more than demonstrate their good works. First, reductionist scientific medicine bore a striking, and not incidental, similarity to the capitalist world view. Second, scientific medicine would help integrate all members of society, whatever their occupations or social standing, into an industrial-technical culture, unifying the fragmented and often fragile industrial-capitalist social order. Third, scientific medicine would help replace the widespread class theories of misery with the perspective that inequalities and unhappiness are technical problems susceptible to engineering solutions, thus depoliticizing medicine and legitimizing capitalism. Finally, scientific medicine would help elevate the medical profession, encouraging a stronger identification of its members with the highest class in society and the capitalist order itself.

Gates believed that all these characteristics and consequences of scientific medicine were good for society, just as he considered socially beneficent the accumulation of wealth by Rockefeller and his private decisions as to how it should be spent. Gates' views on the benefits of scientific medicine and medical research were clearly shared in practice by other capitalists, government officials, and members of the profession. Seldom laid out for us with even Gates' minimal explicitness and coherence, their perspectives were nevertheless clear in their programs and articulated concerns. Gates' views on scientific medicine were influential beyond the support given the Rockefeller Institute and encouragement given to other programs of medical research. Gates had the interest, the ideas, and the money at his disposal to formulate and launch numerous programs to develop and extend public health work and a major program to reform medical education.

John D. Rockefeller, whose Standard Oil fortune financed the vast philanthropies in his name, and John D. Rockefeller, Jr., who took over his father's financial empire and philanthropies (1921). *Rockefeller Archive Center.*

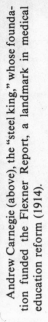

Andrew Carnegie (above), the "steel king," whose foundation funded the Flexner Report, a landmark in medical
education reform (1914).

Carnegie Foundation for the Advancement of Teaching

Henry S. Pritchett (right), first president of the Carnegie
Foundation (about 1925).

Carnegie Foundation for the Advancement of Teaching

Frederick T. Gates, Baptist minister who became architect of the Rockefeller philanthropies and chief of Rockefeller's financial empire (1922).   *Rockefeller Archive Center*

Abraham Flexner, author of famous Carnegie Foundation report on medical education and first director of the Rockefeller philanthropy programs in medical education.
Rockefeller Archive Center

Frederick T. Gates (seated) and Dr. Simon Flexner, creator and first director, respectively, of the Rockefeller Institute for Medical Research. *Rockefeller Archive Center*

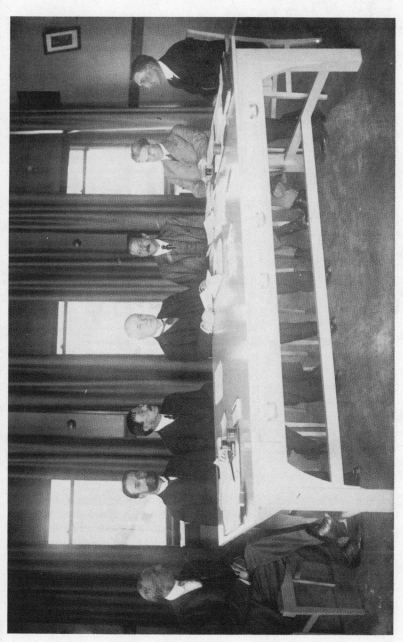

The original Board of Directors of the Rockefeller Institute for Medical Research. *Left to right*: Simon Flexner (director), Theobold Smith, Hermann M. Biggs, William H. Welch (first dean of the Johns Hopkins Medical School), T. Mitchell Prudden, L. Emmett Holt, Christian A. Herter.

Rockefeller Archive Center

Trustees of the General Education Board, the first Rockefeller foundation, at a retreat in Rockland, Maine, in July 1915. *Front row, from left*: Edwin A. Alderman, Frederick T. Gates, Charles W. Eliot (former president of Harvard University), Harry Pratt Judson (president of University of Chicago), Wallace Buttrick (executive officer of the Board). *Second row, from left*: Wickliffe Rose (head of the Rockefeller public health programs), Hollis B. Frissell, John D. Rockefeller, Jr., E. C. Sage, Albert Shaw, Abraham Flexner. *Third row, from left*: George E. Vincent (president of the Rockefeller Foundation), Anson Phelps Stokes, Starr J. Murphy, Jerome D. Greene.   *Rockefeller Archive Center*

Reforming Medical Education: Who Will Rule Medicine?

BY THE END of the nineteenth century, American physicians were still complaining bitterly of their "poverty" and low status in American society. Those who had studied in Europe were especially struck by the low esteem in which American doctors were held compared with their German colleagues. The disparity among physicians' incomes left some well off and some poor. As the New York State Medical Society's journal put it, "There is a handsome income for a few, a competence for the many, and a pittance for the majority."[1]

Most professional spokesmen blamed the relative poverty of doctors on "overcrowding" in the profession. The AMA *Journal* argued in 1901 that through death and retirement of old doctors and the increase in population, there was "room for nearly 3,300 new doctors each year," but the nation's 160 medical colleges were producing nearly double that number.[2]

To deal with these problems, the medical profession adopted an effective strategy of reform based on scientific medicine and the developing medical sciences. Their plan was to gain control over medical education for the organized profession representing practitioners in alliance with scientific medical faculty. Their measures involved large expenditures for medical education and required a major change in the financing of medical schools. Dependent on outside capital, the profession opened the door to outside influence. The corporate philanthropies that intervened turned the campaign to reform medical education into a struggle for control between private practitioners, on the one hand, and academic doctors and the corporate capitalist class, on the other. The conflict over who would rule medical education, to which we now turn, was fundamentally a question of whose interests the medical care system would serve.

PRACTITIONERS GAIN A FOOTHOLD

By 1900 the strategy evolved by elite physicians to reduce the number of doctors, increase incomes, and raise the social class base of the profession began to pay off. Medical research, despite its limited financial support, was building public confidence in modern practitioners. Reforms were being pressed in some leading universities, setting a new standard that others would soon be forced to follow. Most states had established medical licensing boards, however varied the standards they imposed. The Illinois Board of Health in particular had begun a crude evaluation of all medical schools in the United States and Canada. Its report published in 1889 shook more than a few of the 179 schools of the regular sect, twenty-six homeopathic, twenty-six eclectic, thirteen miscellaneous, and thirteen schools condemned as "fraudulent."[3]

All these advances did not yet resolve two major obstacles to professional uplift. First, medical schools remained unregulated. In the final quarter of the nineteenth century more than 114 new schools had been founded.[4] The finances of medical schools forced their faculties to oppose the reformers' strategy of promoting scientific medicine to reduce output. Medical schools were for the most part small profit-making enterprises, owned mainly by their faculties. The only commodities they could sell were medical degrees. Dependent for their survival as well as their profits on student fees, the schools continued to pour forth their products. Being proprietary in character but profitable only to the faculty directly involved, they were unable to attract outside capital or operating funds to support expensive teaching and research programs necessary to scientific medical education. Thus, "scientific medicine" was taught at only a few university medical schools, and to a limited extent even in those—except for Johns Hopkins, which was far from the norm.

The second obstacle to implementing the reform strategy was the organizational disarray of the profession itself. The AMA had failed in its mission. It was by-passed in the last part of the century by specialty societies which formed an alliance in 1888 in the American Congress of Physicians and Surgeons. The American Academy of Medicine and other groups were formed to fill the reform role left vacant by the AMA. Membership in local and state medical societies did not confer membership in the national association, isolating it from the majority of practitioners. By 1900, only 8,400 physicians were members of the AMA.[5] The national leadership, without structural ties to state and local societies, operated within a vacuum. Structurally weak, numerically small, dominated by traditional doctors only half-heartedly committed to scientific medicine, the "voice of the medical profession" seemed to have laryngitis.

Before the medical profession could secure reforms in medical education, it had to strengthen its own organization. After some stalled attempts at reorganization at the end of the nineteenth century, the reformers won support from state medical societies and completely reorganized the AMA at the 1901 convention in St. Paul. The new organization, which continues to this day, made the local medical society the basic unit of the association. Individual physicians would join a local society. The local society would send representatives to a state society, which in turn would elect delegates to the newly formed house of delegates, the legislative body of the national association. The president of the AMA and a board of trustees were given substantial powers. With the campaign skillfully managed by Dr. George H. Simmons, the reform leader recently appointed secretary of the AMA and editor of its *Journal,* and with the convention sessions presided over by Dr. Charles A. L. Reed, the reorganization plan was instituted without discussion.[6]

The reorganization created a hierarchical, representative structure. The direct line of authority depended on the strength of the local societies, always the strongholds of professional interests. The new structure gave the state and national organizations stable leadership, which could more effectively coordinate and mobilize resources for the profession's interests. The plan was intended, and succeeded, to federate state societies into the national association and, in the words of the committee on reorganization, "to foster scientific medicine and to make the medical profession a power in the social and political life of the republic."[7]

Doctors with a vision of uniting the profession behind a campaign to elevate it moved from the wings onto center stage. George Simmons invigorated the *Journal* with the mission of the reform movement. AMA leaders asked physicians around the country to spur legislative reforms, control state licensing boards, and goad medical schools into altering their admission criteria and curricula. The increased effectiveness of the AMA brought support and membership from the many specialists who seemed to have forgotten that they were physicians first and surgeons or gynecologists second. Private practitioners of all types rose to support the coordinated local-state-national vehicle for their common interests. By 1910 some 70,000 doctors were AMA members, more than eight times the membership at the turn of the century.

Although many rank-and-file physicians were unhappy with the centralized control emanating from the AMA's Chicago offices and with the reform strategy itself, most physicians undoubtedly supported the movement.[8] Most physicians resented the economic and social conditions of the profession, particularly when they realized that things could be better. They understood that competition among physicians for a greater share of the available medical dollars would help only a few and that the interests of every physician were tied to the interests of the profession as a whole.

The reform leadership, representing a coalition of private practitioners and medical school faculty, articulated the desires of most doctors for financial and social uplift, and offered a viable strategy for achieving them. This coalition controlled the AMA from the end of the nineteenth century until World War I, sharing the association's presidency and jointly implementing its reform strategy.[9]

COUNCIL ON MEDICAL EDUCATION

Once in control of the reorganized AMA, the reformers launched their most effective tool for transforming the profession. In 1904 the AMA replaced its temporary committee on medical education with a permanent Council on Medical Education, headed by the energetic and resourceful Arthur Dean Bevan, a successful surgeon and part-time professor at Rush Medical College in Chicago. The new council was armed with a staff to help it exert "a national influence and control of medical education."[10]

To facilitate that control, it invited state licensing boards to a national conference in 1905 to review the status of medical education and set standards. There the council adopted "an ideal standard to work for in the future"—one that would raise U.S. medical education to the same basis as England, France, and Germany—and "a minimum standard for the time being." The temporary standard was: (1) a preliminary education of four years of high school, (2) a four-year medical course, and (3) passing an examination before a state licensing board.[11]

Bevan urged local and state medical societies to become more active in the reform movement and to see that "the right sort of men" were appointed to the licensing boards. Within two years the state medical societies, under the guidance of the Council on Medical Education, dominated the state boards. Through the influence of the state societies and direct contact by the council, the licensing boards increasingly became agents of the council's plan of action.[12]

The more the state boards cooperated with the council to accept diplomas only from medical schools "in good standing" and to gear their examinations to the curricula of scientific medical schools, the more uncertain was the future of all medical schools except those elite schools already geared to the needs of scientific medicine. Those schools that could tap sufficient resources to provide laboratories, "clinical material," and scientifically trained faculty had a reasonably good prognosis. The graduates of such schools were allowed by the state boards to take their licensing exams, and they had a fairly good chance of passing. There was little incentive for students to attend and pay the fees of unapproved schools and schools whose graduates tended to flunk the licensing examinations. But state boards were not uniformly in the hands of the state medical societies, so the council developed a new tactic to upgrade medical education, close more schools, and develop a controlling role for itself in the field.

In 1906 the council inspected every one of the country's 160 medical schools. Each school was personally visited by council secretary Dr. N. P. Colwell or another council member and was rated on the percentage of its graduates who passed the state licensing exams, enforcement of preliminary education require- ments, curriculum, laboratory and clinical facilities and instruc- tion, laboratory science faculty, and whether the school was run for a profit. Reports on each school were sent to the state licensing boards, and the percentage of each school's graduates who failed state board examinations was published in the AMA *Journal.* [13]

In 1907 the council divided medical schools into classes A, B, and C, depending on their ratings. Of the 160 schools inspected, eighty-two were rated as class A medical colleges, forty-six were class B, and thirty-two class C. The impact of the council's report was significant. Fifty schools agreed to require one year each of college physics, chemistry, biology, and a modern language before admission to the medical program. Sensing doom, a number of schools consolidated with other medical schools in their cities, combining facilities and staffs. Other schools realized that they did not have the resources to survive the heightened competition. By 1910 the number of schools had fallen from a high of 166 to 131. [14]

While the practitioner reform leaders were pressing for stiffer standards within medical education, the medical schools them- selves were doing their best to survive. The Association of American Medical Colleges (AAMC), representing about a third of all American medical colleges, sought to differentiate its member schools—"the better classes of medical colleges"—from run-of-the-mill schools. They were concerned that rising stan- dards in admission and instruction would bankrupt even the best schools. As the representative of the elite portion of scientific medicine's rear guard—the schools themselves—the AAMC favored cooperation between itself, the Council on Medical Education, and the association of state licensing boards. The AAMC sought uniform minimum standards for all states so that each state's requirements of medical schools would come "up to, but not beyond," the standard recommended by a joint commit- tee of all three bodies. [15]

Although the Council on Medical Education had neither legal powers nor authority within the profession, council chairman Bevan, AMA secretary and *Journal* editor Simmons, and other professional reformers well understood the role of leadership and the powerful advantage of articulating a strategy consistent with historical forces. Science's time had arrived in medicine: A middle and upper class whose dominance depended on industrialization was receptive to what scientific medicine advocates within the profession offered. State licensing boards, under the influence or in the hands of the medical societies, assured the dominance of scientific schools and the competitive disadvantages of economically weaker schools. The cost of a scientific medical education was shattering the financial arrangements of proprietary medical schools. The council could not order schools closed, but it rallied political allies in the state boards and the forces of the marketplace to wreck the *ancien régime*.

MONEY FOR MEDICAL EDUCATION: WHO WILL PAY?

The reforms initiated and pressed by the AMA leadership were clearly having their desired impact. But the profession's power to accomplish its ultimate goals was limited. Scientific medicine was an expensive affair. Nearly all medical schools at the end of the nineteenth century relied for most of their support on students' tuition fees. Most independent medical colleges and many of those nominally associated with universities had no other source of income. Yet the teaching of scientific medicine required expensive laboratory buildings, a teaching hospital and teaching clinic, and equipment. Some of these facilities could be obtained from local men and women of wealth if faculty members had fashionable private practices. Some facilities could be had if the medical school was affiliated with a well-endowed university. However, more than facilities were needed.

The largest operating expense for a scientific medical school was the faculty to teach the laboratory science courses. A practitioner might be good enough to teach clinical courses, but he usually was not expert enough in physiology, bacteriology, or pathology. The basic medical sciences had to be taught by medical scientists who were specially trained in that area and whose on-going research kept them abreast of developments in their field. These faculty had to devote their full time to teaching and research, and they were the largest operating expense of a turn-of-the-century scientific medical school.

The cost of a scientific medical education was beyond the

means of students. "It costs more to educate a medical student," Bevan noted, "than he can pay in the way of fees."[16] The capital investment and operating costs for scientific medical education were also beyond the means of the profession itself. Wealthy physicians might provide a small portion of the capital for a medical college, but the reformers recognized early that most of the capital for scientific medical schools would have to come from outside the profession.[17] States might be persuaded to support state institutions, but most medical schools and universities—and certainly the most elite—were privately controlled. "The public must be taught the necessities and the possibilities of modern medicine," Bevan argued, and philanthropists must be shown that medicine deserves their endowments.[18] Because of the amounts involved, much of the money would have to come from the fortunes of the very wealthiest men and women in America.

The medical reformers were well aware of the dangers of help from the outside. "Rich men may injure the cause of medical education," the AMA *Journal* warned in 1901, unless their giving is directed by the profession itself.[19] With the blessings of the rest of the profession's leadership, Bevan took on the task of getting and guiding endowments for medical colleges. "We must secure for them state aid and private endowment," he told the council's 1907 national conference. "We must start an active, organized propaganda for money for medical education."[20]

HELP FROM THE CARNEGIE FOUNDATION

Impressed with the impact of the council's own survey, Bevan turned to the Carnegie Foundation for the Advancement of Teaching. He sought the foundation's help, not just to replicate the council's own work, but to add to their campaign the foundation's developing prestige and image of "objectivity." Bevan understood the foundation's potential for molding public opinion and providing a credible blueprint for philanthropists to follow while channeling their money into medical education. It was also clear that an agency outside the profession could openly attack medical schools that resisted reorganizing themselves or going out of business without once again splitting medical school faculty off from the reform leadership. At the council's first national conference in 1905, Bevan criticized proprietary medical schools as an obstacle to reform, but he felt compelled by the need for diplomacy to urge leniency because of the "property and professional interest" invested in them.[21]

In 1907 Bevan invited Henry S. Pritchett, president of the Carnegie Foundation for the Advancement of Teaching, to examine the survey materials collected by the council. Meeting at the Chicago Club, Bevan and Pritchett saw eye-to-eye on the value of a Carnegie-sponsored study of medical education. For Bevan the Carnegie study would be the big guns in the campaign for medical education reform. Pritchett was sympathetic to that concern, but mainly in the context of the foundation's program to reform and rationalize the nation's colleges and universities, including its professional schools.[22]

The foundation had been established in 1905 to upgrade the status of college teachers while creating a uniform system of higher education. Out of discussions between Andrew Carnegie and Pritchett emerged a plan to advance teaching by the carrot-and-stick method. The new foundation provided an initial endowment of $10 million to support a retirement program for college teachers. The pensions would be given without any cost to the institution or its individual teachers, but each college must meet the conditions laid down by the foundation. Denominational colleges were not eligible for the pension plan. Religion was, of course, an important moral force, but it would not promote the universality of science; colleges controlled by competing denominations would be more concerned with propagating the faith than with training scientists and engineers. Denominational colleges, hoping to make themselves more attractive to faculty, besieged the foundation with inquiries about how to amend their charters to make themselves eligible for free pensions. In addition, the foundation imposed academic and financial requirements designed to force the poorer colleges to match the academic standards of the better colleges and to make higher education follow a uniform pattern throughout the country.[23]

Thus, Bevan's request for a study of medical schools fit well with the foundation's general program and provided an opportunity for the foundation to move into reforming professional education. Pritchett discussed the proposed study with Charles Eliot, president of Harvard and a trustee of the Carnegie

Foundation, Rockefeller's General Education Board, and the Rockefeller Institute for Medical Research. He also talked with Dr. Simon Flexner, director of the Rockefeller Institute. Flexner suggested a director for the study, his brother Abraham. The suggestion meshed well with Pritchett's conception of the study as contributing to the reform of higher education.[24]

Abraham Flexner was a professional educator. He got his bachelor's degree from Johns Hopkins in two years of diligent and hard work. He later founded and ran his own college preparatory school in Louisville and afterwards spent a year in advanced study in education at Harvard. While in Heidelberg in the summer of 1908, Flexner wrote *The American College,* which, in his own words, "fell quite flat." Late in the summer of 1908 Flexner returned from Europe unemployed and "prepared to do almost anything." Hoping to get a job, Flexner initiated a meeting with Pritchett. They talked about higher education and its problems and found they agreed on the necessity for reform. "When I next saw him," Flexner later recalled, "he asked me whether I would like to make a study of medical schools." Flexner was enthusiastic, "but it occurred to me that Dr. Pritchett was confusing me with my brother Simon at the Rockefeller Institute, and I called his attention to the fact that I was not a medical man and had never had my foot inside a medical school."

"That is precisely what I want," replied Pritchett. "I think these professional schools should be studied not from the point of view of the practitioner but from the standpoint of the educator. I know your brother, so that I am not laboring under any confusion. This is a layman's job, not a job for a medical man."[25]

A report on medical education by a physician would lack credibility, and it would feed the divisions between practitioners and part-time medical school faculty. Moreover, Pritchett, while certainly not adverse to aiding medical professionals, wanted medical education integrated into a general system of education. A report by an educator sold on the importance of a scientific medical profession would provide both the right perspective and credibility.[26]

At their November 1908 meeting, Pritchett asked the Carnegie Foundation trustees to authorize the study and appropriate the necessary funds. With their approval, Flexner immediately began his study.[27] Bevan directed the reform campaign, Pritchett financed it with Carnegie's money, and Abraham Flexner implemented it.

THE "FLEXNER REPORT"

A scholarly technician, Flexner began by reading up on the history of medical education in Europe and America. He went to Chicago to discuss the study with George Simmons, secretary of the AMA and editor of its *Journal.* He also met with Bevan and Colwell, secretary of the Council on Medical Education. He read Colwell's reports on medical schools and found them "creditable and painstaking documents" but "extremely diplomatic."

Flexner then visited his alma mater, Johns Hopkins, where he met with the medical school's leading faculty members, Drs. Welch, Halsted, Mall, Abel, and Howell. Flexner found Hopkins "a small but ideal medical school embodying in a novel way, adapted to American conditions, the best features of medical education in England, France, and Germany." Hopkins became the living model for Flexner. "Without this pattern in the back of my mind, I could have accomplished little."[28]

Flexner saw his mission as translating the Hopkins medical school into a standard against which to judge all other medical education in the United States. All others paled before this "one bright spot." Flexner's praise of Hopkins grew ecstatic:

> It possessed ideals and men who embodied them, and from it have emanated the influences that in a half-century have lifted American medical education from the lowest status to the highest in the civilized world. All honor to Gilman, Welch, Mall, Halsted, and their colleagues and students who hitched their wagon to a star and never flinched![29]

Flexner visited every one of the 155 medical schools in the United States and Canada. Colwell, of the AMA, went with him to most of them. In nearly all cases, the school administrators and faculty laid bare the facts of their existence—facilities, laboratory equipment, numbers of faculty and their qualifications, numbers of students and their preparation, the curriculum, patients available as teaching material, income from student fees, and endowments.[30]

Even administrators and faculty who knew their schools were

deficient in many assets the Council on Medical Education believed important permitted Flexner and Colwell access to facilities, staff, and account books. Many of the schools were run by doctors who were committed to elevating the profession and saw the importance of creating scientific medical schools. Even more persuasive in opening medical schools to inspection was that deans, faculty, and trustees of most medical schools believed that Flexner's visit "would be followed by gifts from Mr. Carnegie to set things right." Whatever fear the medical school deans and faculty had of the consequences of public criticism, they understood that failure to comply with the Carnegie study would result in their rapid demise. The market for medical students was very competitive, and bad publicity would do serious injury. But riskier still were the dynamics of the competitive market. If many competing medical schools that cooperated with the Carnegie study got a large advantage—for example, a new laboratory or an endowment—the financial collapse and demise of the disadvantaged was assured.[31]

Some colleges resisted inspection, but resistance was grounds for suspicion. To the recalcitrant medical schools, Pritchett let it be known that "all colleges and universities, whether supported by taxation or by private endowment, are in truth public service corporations," and, therefore, the foundation, the medical profession, and the public had a right to know about their finances and educational practices. Rather than fear intervention by outsiders, the leading reformers in the profession savored this attitude of the foundation. Not only did this attitude support their campaign, but it recognized medicine as a vital societal function.[32]

FLEXNER'S FINDINGS

Flexner visited the medical schools and wrote his report in the space of eighteen months. His whistle-stop tour and his acerbic comments on what he saw gave him a reputation, even among medical reformers, for being "erratic" and "hasty in judgment." The medical faculty at Harvard were insulted and in return cast aspersions on his ability while the faculties at lesser schools merely bristled.[33]

Not coincidentally, Flexner's criticisms of American medical schools and his recommendations for reform were perfectly consistent with those of the leading medical profession reformers. Flexner attacked medical schools for producing too many doctors, for requiring too little education before admission to medical school, for having inadequate facilities and faculty and providing inadequate training, and for creating a social composition for the medical profession that was inappropriate to its important social role.

Flexner and Pritchett both attached great importance to medicine's changing role in society. The physician's function in society, traditionally "individual and curative," was rapidly becoming "social and preventive."[34] If "society relies" on doctors for important social functions, then "the interests of the social order" must be considered first in any public policy for reforming the profession.[35] What was wrong with the medical profession from society's point of view?

Overcrowding was the most serious problem with the profession, according to Pritchett and Flexner. If Germany could thrive with one doctor for every 2,000 inhabitants, then the United States, with an average of one doctor for every 568 persons, suffered from a severe oversupply of physicians. Overcrowding forces professionals into competition with one another, fighting for a relatively inelastic market of patients and encouraging one another to perform unnecessary services to increase their incomes. Overcrowding "decreases the number of well-trained men who can count on the profession for a livelihood," reducing the attractiveness of a medical career to competent men. "The country needs fewer and better doctors," Flexner argued, and *"the way to get them better is to produce fewer."*[36]

The main reason for the overcrowding of the profession, as well as for its generally low standards, was the prevalence of "commercial" medical schools. Only fifty of the 155 medical colleges were integral parts of universities. The rest, whether independent or nominally affiliated with a university, were in reality run by the medical faculty alone without any outside control. These proprietary schools depended on students' fees, which were divided up among the local practitioners who were lecturers in the school. Many of the faculty fattened their incomes through "the consultations which the loyalty of their former students threw into their hands." Faculty chairs in the commercial schools were bought and sold, sometimes for as much as $3,000.[37]

Commercial medical schools dragged down medical education in its entirety, argued Flexner. Their incomes based entirely on student fees, the schools tended to admit as many students as possible and to reduce their expenses as much as possible. Since lectures were the cheapest form of education—in which the income from student fees went directly to the faculty instead of being invested in buildings, laboratories, or equipment—medical education came to consist almost entirely of lectures until the 1880s. The necessity of laboratory and clinical training for the scientific medical doctor greatly strained the resources of proprietary medical schools. The choice was clear. "The medical profession is an organ differentiated by society for its own highest purposes, not a business to be exploited by individuals according to their own fancy."[38] To assure its public service character, medical schools must be made integral parts of universities.

The social importance of the medical profession meant not only that medical education should not be left to proprietary organization, but that it should be reserved for those who could afford "a liberal and disinterested educational experience." Proprietary medical schools, with their admission requirements of four years of high school or its "equivalent," attracted "a mass of unprepared youth . . . drawn out of industrial occupations into the study of medicine." Neither "the crude boy" nor "the jaded clerk" were suitable material for a career in medicine.[39] Flexner proposed a minimum two years of college for admission to medical school at a time when only 15 percent of the high school age population was enrolled in high school and only 5 percent of the college age population was enrolled in a college or university.[40]

Consistent with the racism of his period, Flexner argued that "the practice of the Negro doctor would be limited to his own race." However, "self-protection not less than humanity" should encourage white society to support improved training for black physicians: "ten millions of them live in close contact with sixty million whites." In addition, the importance of black physicians in facilitating "the mental and moral improvement" of their race required creating an elite core of scientific black doctors. Applying the formula of "the fewer, the better," Flexner recommended that of seven black medical schools then in existence, only Meharry and Howard be continued.[41]

Flexner also recommended closing the three women's medical colleges. Schools for women alone were unnecessary and ineffi cient since "medical education is now . . . open to women upon practically the same terms as men." If the number of women medical students was declining, it demonstrated a lack of either "any strong demand for women physicians or any strong ungrati- fied desire on the part of women to enter the profession," or both. Flexner seemed to believe, with most of his peers, that women are seldom equipped for the mental rigors of medicine and, if middle or upper class, women make better patients than doctors.[42]

The very clear consequence was to be an across-the-board reduction in the production of doctors, with especially large reductions in the numbers of poor and working-class young men, blacks, and women entering the medical profession. The social class and status of medicine would be raised, together with the incomes of physicians, to a level appropriate to its role in society. These changes were made necessary, according to Flexner, by the requirements of scientific medicine as well as by medicine's new social role.

Flexner found that only twenty-three of the country's 155 medical schools required two or more years of college prelimi- nary to medical school. And 132 schools admitted students with a high school education or its "equivalent." The latter would be a tolerable "temporary adjustment" where there were not enough college students to fill the medical school openings, but two years of college provides "the varied and enlarging cultural experi- ence" necessary to a modern physician.[43]

Instruction in biology, chemistry, and physics should be required before the student could enter medical school. The medical college curriculum was to proceed from there. In the first two years the student would study anatomy, physiology, bacteri- ology, pathology, and pharmacology. With this thorough ground- ing in the laboratory sciences, the student would spend his or her third and fourth years in supervised clinical study. Only the better medical schools, affiliated with universities and requiring two years preliminary college education, provided the model curricu- lum.[44]

Flexner's report thus sought to place medical education on a uniform basis consistent with the needs of scientific medicine and to elevate the status of the medical profession to a position consistent with its important social role. This mission required eliminating both proprietary schools and the lower classes, restricting the opportunities of women and blacks to enter the practice of medicine, as well as increasing the preliminary requirements and standardizing the curriculum into a graded, four-year program. Reducing the supply of physicians was no mere by-product of Flexner's program. "The improvement of medical education cannot," he argued, "be resisted on the ground that it will destroy schools and restrict output: that is precisely what is needed."[45]

Flexner's analysis and recommendations were strikingly like those of the leading reformers of his time within the profession. For at least a decade before Flexner's report was published in 1910, medical journals argued that the profession was overcrowded and that improving medical education was the best means of restricting output. "We raise the standard of medical education year by year, yet the mushroom colleges do not go," Frank Lydston complained to his colleagues in 1900. "We have done the best we could to breed competition by manufacturing doctors."[46]

In 1901 the AMA *Journal* warned that the growth of the medical profession should be stemmed "if the individual members are to find the practice of medicine a lucrative occupation."[47] And in 1905, Council on Medical Education member V. C. Vaughan told the council's first national conference that "the supply quite equals the demand, and for this reason the time is propitious for raising the barrier to admission one notch higher."[48] The argument that medical students should be drawn only from the better classes likewise did not originate with Flexner.[49]

At their 1905 national conference and in the following year, the council had urged a temporary preliminary education requirement of high school graduation and one year each of university physics, chemistry, and biology. The council had also recommended a curriculum of four years, with anatomy, physiology, pathology, pharmacology, and bacteriology in the first two years and supervised clinical study in the last two.[50]

Strict university affiliation had been a cornerstone of the medical education reform movement for at least forty years by the time Flexner published his report. The university affiliations of most nineteenth-century medical colleges provided the medical school with prestige and legitimacy and gave the university credit for having a medical school, but there were few administrative or academic ties. Charles Eliot, when he assumed the presidency of Harvard in 1869, asserted the authority of the university over the medical faculty and turned the medical school over "like a flapjack," in the words of Oliver Wendell Holmes, then a faculty member in the school. Eliot's new regime raised entrance requirements, instituted scientific medical courses, and forced the faculty to submit to the normal university administrative and academic authorities. Eliot hoped to attract an endowment by demonstrating that the medical school was no longer a private venture "for the benefit of a few physicians and surgeons." His plan was successful. Subordination of the medical school to the university became a key plank in the platform of medical education reformers.[51]

The coincidence of Flexner's and the profession's analysis and recommendations could be due to the compelling claims of scientific medicine. That is, any two investigators of the medical profession at that time might have been led to more or less the same conclusions because, within the strategy of developing medical science, the deficiencies of the profession and medical training were obvious. But the relationship of Flexner to the profession was close. His brother was director of the country's leading medical research institute, and he consulted at great length with the AMA leadership throughout his study.

In fact, it was explicitly understood from the beginning that the Carnegie study would be part of the council's campaign, lending credibility to the council's plans for reforms. Six months before Flexner's report was published, Pritchett, president of the Carnegie Foundation, wrote Bevan:

> In all this work of the examination of the medical schools we have been hand in glove with you and your committee. In fact, we have only taken up the matter and gone on with the examination very much as you were doing, except that as an independent agency disconnected from actual practice, we may do certain things which you perhaps may not. When our report comes out, it is going to be ammunition in your hands.[52]

Bevan, anxious to start getting mileage out of the Carnegie study, wanted Flexner and Pritchett to speak at an AMA meeting several months before the report was to be published. Pritchett was concerned that if the conspiracy between the foundation and the AMA was made visible—and especially before publication— the report would lose some credibility, and the foundation's "disinterested" image would be tarnished. "It is desirable," he privately added to Bevan, "to maintain in the meantime a position which does not intimate an immediate connection between our two efforts."

This sort of deception increased the credibility of the Flexner report, but it was not essential to the transformation underway. It merely helped along the social and economic forces already in motion.

IMPACT OF THE REPORT

When the Flexner report was published as "Bulletin Number Four," the Carnegie Foundation found itself the object of "more stone-throwing than was to be expected" for its association with the "Medical Trust"—the AMA and its Council on Medical Education. Pritchett was embarrassed by the "somewhat dogmatic appearance" of the report which lent credibility to charges of collusion with the AMA, but Bevan and the AMA felt "very much flattered by such an association." Regardless of how Pritchett felt about the public impugning of the foundation's reputation, neither he nor the foundation backed down from its support for the AMA.[53]

Pritchett did not consider that aligning his foundation with the medical professionals might compromise the foundation's larger objectives. Only in 1913 did he begin to see a conflict developing between the profession's objectives of closing medical schools right and left and the foundation's goals of rationalizing higher education and providing for a professional group to fulfill an important function in society. The council's demand for one year of college preparation for admission to every medical school in the country did not take account of regional differences and especially the relative backwardness of the South. Pritchett feared that the very classification scheme that so impressed him in 1907 was being used to set medical education off from the rest of the school system, rather than gradually pressuring the lower schools to meet the preliminary training needs of the medical schools. He accused the council of disregarding "the educational results which the school system itself can turn out," and he warned that "your power will quickly disappear if you advocate courses which are educationally indefensible."[54]

Pritchett gradually came to realize that the medical profession's interests would lead it to actions that conflicted with the interests that the foundation wanted to further. By 1918 it was clear to Pritchett that the AMA would wreck all medical education for blacks if left to its own devices. Believing in the social importance of black doctors among black people, the Carnegie Foundation was supporting the Meharry medical school while the council was rating it a class B school. Pritchett protested the "grave injustice done to the negro [sic] schools" by the council's de facto policy of not extending to them the same leniency given to white schools in the South. The policies of the zealous AMA reformers were closing medical schools and disrupting the attempts to build a uniform school system, all without regard for the public interest as defined by the leading foundations. Pritchett threatened to call a meeting of his and the Rockefeller foundations, representatives of some licensing boards, and the dozen "stronger medical schools" to force the council to "revise its present classification of medical schools."[55] Within a decade of his cordial meeting with Bevan at the Chicago Club, Pritchett had come to view the council's power in much the way Dr. Frankenstein viewed his own creation.

Pritchett's dismay at the council's use of its power was undoubtedly made more painful because of the influence exerted by the Carnegie report. It is sometimes forgotten that the report did not create the movement for medical school reform. The movement for scientific medical education had borne its first fruit four decades earlier. Charles Eliot had led the reform of the Harvard medical school beginning in 1870. Also in the seventies the first teaching hospital was founded by an American university in Michigan, state medical licensing boards were reestablished, and the Illinois board had begun a series of influential reports on medical schools. The Council on Medical Education's own survey of medical schools in 1907 was, of course, the model for Flexner's study and had a substantial impact itself. The profession's increasing control of state boards made rapid "progress" possible.[56]

Flexner noted that even before his study was published, great strides had been made in reforming medical education. Medical school programs had been extended to four years, clinical teaching had been added to didactic methods, laboratories were widely available and had been expanded, admission standards had been adopted and were lived up to with varying degrees of commitment, and state boards—the police power behind the reform movement—had been created in most states. The consequences of these changes were admirable. The number of medical schools was declining, he noted, and independent and commercial schools were rapidly giving up the ghost.[57]

Flexner's report thus aided a process already underway. The rate of consolidation and elimination of medical schools was as rapid before the report as after. Between 1904 and 1915 some ninety-two schools closed their doors or merged, forty-four of them in the first six years to 1909 and forty-eight in the second six years to 1915.[58]

Cut off from sources of funding, in part by Flexner's recommendation, the five disapproved medical schools for blacks soon closed. With racism as rampant in white medical schools and medical societies as throughout the rest of the society, medical care for blacks declined even further. In 1910 there was one black doctor for every 2,883 black people in the United States (compared with one physician to every 684 people for the nation as a whole), but by 1942 the ratio had grown further to one black physician for every 3,377 black people.[59] Flexner's attitude toward women in medicine, more extreme than the views of many of his contemporaries, certainly contributed to keeping women at an average of less than 5 percent of all medical graduates from 1900 until World War II. Today women constitute about a fifth of all medical students and blacks about 6 percent, both far less than their proportions in the population but substantially higher than a decade earlier because of the recent struggle for an affirmative action policy in medical school admissions.

Flexner's report also contributed to eliminating sectarian medical colleges. Scientific schools no longer called themselves "regular." By 1932 Arthur Dean Bevan was able to say appreciatively, "We were, of course, very grateful to Pritchett and to Flexner" for enabling "us to put out of business" the homeopathic and eclectic medical schools in existence in 1910.[60] Flexner's contribution was not as substantial as Bevan remembered: The 31 homeopathic and eclectic schools surviving in 1910 were down a third from their number in 1900.[61]

The report's direct impact on the profession was moderate, but its consequences were indirectly monumental. As Flexner himself pointed out, the report spoke to the public on behalf of the medical reform movement. It helped "educate" the public to accept scientific medicine, and, most important, it "educated" wealthy men and women to channel their philanthropy to support research-oriented scientific medical education. The Flexner report and the Carnegie Foundation's support brought economic and political power into the war as partisans of the "regular" doctors cum-scientific medical men.

Within a year following the report's publication, the General Education Board entered the fray in earnest. By 1920 the GEB had appropriated nearly $15 million for medical education and by 1929 a total of more than $78 million. By 1938 contributions from all foundations to medical schools exceeded $150 million.[62] The frequently used matching grant policy, requiring the recipient institution to raise an equal sum itself, greatly increased the impact of their funds. Because the foundation grants were conditional on specific reforms in the medical schools, the foundations exerted a major influence. They forced schools to adopt a research orientation, required teaching hospitals to subordinate their autonomy and patient care to the needs and authority of a university medical school, and established salaried clinical professorships.

The foundations' power was in providing the outside capital for the reform of medical education and the profession itself. As the suppliers of that capital, they were able to dictate terms to the profession. In the earliest years, however, it was the profession that defined the goals and the strategy. The Carnegie Foundation had provided its resources to the leading medical professionals. The Flexner report united the interests of elite practitioners, scientific medical faculty, and the wealthy capitalist class. The report validated the elite professionals and enabled them to speak to philanthropists with a single voice, amplified by the Carnegie

Foundation. Without the Carnegie report, the fears of "misdirected generosity," voiced by the AMA *Journal* in 1901,[63] might have been even more justified than they turned out to be.

THE GENERAL EDUCATION BOARD: MEDICAL EDUCATION GETS A DIFFERENT DRUMMER

While Pritchett was parrying blows from critics and soaking up support from the medical profession reformers, Flexner was sent abroad by the foundation to study European medical schools. Back home in New York in the spring of 1911, while he was writing the report of his personal investigation, he was invited to lunch by Frederick T. Gates.

As Flexner recalled the momentous meeting years later, Gates complimented him on Bulletin Number Four and asked him, "What would you do if you had a million dollars with which to make a start in reorganizing medical education in the United States?"

"Without a moment's hesitation" Flexner recommended giving it all to Welch and the Johns Hopkins medical school. Flexner could not have recommended anyone in medicine more dear to Gates' heart. Gates asked Flexner to obtain a leave for a few weeks from the Carnegie Foundation to go to Baltimore as an agent of the General Education Board and report back on his findings at Johns Hopkins. Flexner was delighted and went off to Baltimore assured that the million dollars was available.[64]

In Baltimore Flexner went directly to Welch and explained that the GEB might add a million dollars to the Johns Hopkins medical school endowment and that he was there to study the situation and report back to Gates. Welch arranged a dinner that night at the Maryland Club and invited two of Hopkins' most illustrious medical faculty, Franklin P. Mall, an anatomist who in effect represented the medical science faculty, and William S. Halsted, a surgeon and de facto representative of the clinical faculty.

Mall spoke without hesitation: "If the school could get a sum of approximately $1 million, in my judgment there is only one thing that we ought to do with it—use every penny of its income for the purpose of placing upon a salary basis the heads and assistants in the leading *clinical* departments." That, Mall added, "is the great reform which needs now to be carried through."[65]

Mall's suggestion was the focus of Flexner's report to Gates. Flexner recommended a grant of $1.5 million to reorganize the medical, surgical, obstetrical, and pediatric departments, placing the clinical faculty on a full-time basis. The "full-time plan" would require the clinical faculty, at that time earning roughly $20,000 to $35,000 a year from consultations, to become salaried employees of the medical school and to *turn over all their consultation fees to the school*. Incomes would thus drop to $10,000 for a department head, still a very high salary for the period, and $2,500 for his assistants.

Flexner's report, in the same tradition of thoroughness as his Bulletin Number Four and Gates' own reports to Rockefeller nearly two decades earlier, greatly impressed Gates. The recommendation was informally adopted as policy, and, at Gates' request, Flexner returned to Baltimore and personally explained it to Welch and gave him an informal and confidential assurance that a Hopkins application for $1.5 million to institute the reforms would be approved by the GEB. It would be up to Welch to convince his faculty and the university trustees to make the reform, for it was to be the only basis of the GEB's grant. "No pressure was used," Flexner recalled, "no inducement was held out." Just $1.5 million.[66]

When Flexner brought the proposal to the GEB, the full-time plan already had a powerful advocate within the board. Three years earlier Gates had been instrumental in establishing the strict full-time provision for physician-researchers at the Rockefeller Institute's new hospital.[67] With a view to the needs of maintaining and further developing capitalist society, Gates believed the full-time plan would encourage the application of science to medicine and reduce the independence of the medical profession.

Gates, a director of industry, finance, and philanthropy, believed, as did other men in his position, in the *usefulness* of science and technology. Science could discover the causes of diseases, and technology could develop the means to prevent or cure disease. But medical science could neither relieve the misery of the world nor make the work force healthier if people could not afford its services. Likewise, the cultural and legitimizing functions of medicine could not be performed if medical services were priced out of the reach of the working population. The financial independence of the medical profession was an obstacle to bringing the benefits of science to the people. "This practice of fixing his own price granted to American physicians by custom," Gates wrote to the other GEB trustees, "is the greatest present American obstruction to the usefulness of the science of medicine. For it confines the benefits of the science too largely to the rich, when it is the rightful inheritance of all the people alike, and the public health requires they have it."[68]

Commercialism was fine in the economic sectors that should be reserved for profit making, but in medicine it violated the needs of capitalist society. The full-time plan was adopted by the GEB as its central policy in medical education to help bring the medical profession to heel and subordinate its practices to the needs of industrial capitalism for fully accessible medical care, or, as board member Jerome D. Greene put it, to abate "commercialism in the medical profession."[69] If the elite, standard-setting medical schools supported by the GEB adopted the fixed-price schedule for medical services, Gates argued, "public sentiment, in no time, will enforce those schedules, if reasonable, not only throughout their cities but other cities and finally the country at large."[70]

The full-time plan played a central role in foundation funding of medical education for the following important decade of development. The new arrangement altered the relationship of the medical profession to university medical schools. And it caused deep divisions between the reform-minded elite practitioners in the medical societies and the Rockefeller philanthropies.

FULL TIME: "GOLD OR GLORY"

As Flexner himself has pointed out, the full-time plan for clinical faculty was suggested to him by Mall, though it had first been advocated publicly in 1902 by Lewellys F. Barker, a former colleague of Mall's at Baltimore and then a professor of anatomy at Chicago.[71] The earlier origins of the idea can be traced to more obscure beginnings in German medical laboratories, but its introduction to the United States is of interest here.

The full-time plan was first instituted in the United States in 1893 when the Johns Hopkins medical school opened its doors. Because of the new school's emphasis on research and the widespread experience that local practitioners do little research in the laboratory sciences, the university provided full-time faculty positions in anatomy, physiology, pathology, and pharmacology. The models for the Hopkins reform were the German medical laboratories and universities where Welch and the other Hopkins medical faculty got their scientific training. For some of the new faculty who had previously split their time between private practice and teaching laboratory sciences, the Hopkins plan meant giving up an income of $10,000 a year or more, in return for a salary of $3,000 or $4,000. But the bright young men who were actively recruited were, like Welch and Mall, struggling to survive without private practice.[72] For these men, medicine was science and laboratories, not patients and housecalls.

Welch himself had never wanted to be a physician. After graduation from Yale, he wanted to be a tutor in Greek, but the prospect of unemployment thwarted his ambition and drove him to follow his father into medicine. His interest in medicine soon bloomed though not with visions of a bedside practice. Welch was "fired in the dissecting and autopsy rooms with the desire to become a professor of pathological anatomy," wrote Simon Flexner, "to study and examine for the rest of his life without having to make his living as a practitioner." The development of scientific medicine in the United States opened to Welch the possibility of a new kind of medical career, and he ambitiously set about building a future for himself in the medical sciences. Returning from his postgraduate medical studies in Europe, Welch, with a little financial help from his friends, founded the first pathology laboratory in the United States at Bellevue Hospital medical school in New York. From there he was invited to Johns Hopkins by president Gilman as one of the first full-time faculty in the laboratory medical sciences and was soon made dean of the distinguished medical school. Welch devoted his life to building the first medical center "empire," seeking favor with philanthropists, initiating reforms in medical education and research, and planning and organizing new programs and institutions.[73]

Franklin Paine Mall, after receiving his medical degree from the University of Michigan in 1883, went to Germany for additional clinical training and came back a dedicated medical scientist. In Ludwig's and other laboratories Mall learned to love science and to appreciate the freedom to study what interested him. In his anatomy laboratory at Johns Hopkins, Mall was an efficient and organized administrator. He knew the investments of all the major universities and foundations and was good at bringing research grants to his laboratory. Mall put great value on original research as part of the training of physicians. If dissertations were required for the M.D. degree, he urged hopefully, "it would stimulate scientific work in the medical schools, would tend to reduce the number of graduates, and would improve the quality of the physician."[74]

It was Ludwig in Germany who put the bug about full-time clinical teaching into Mall's ear. Mall brought it back to Baltimore and Chicago and spread the idea among Barker and other colleagues. Mall saw the struggle over the full-time plan as a contest between the clinical faculty and practicing physicians, on the one hand, and the laboratory science faculty, on the other. Reform practitioners had demanded full-time laboratory faculty for the first two years of basic science in medical school, and now "it falls to us to demand of the last two years of medicine what they demanded of the first two." With a sense of victory occasioned by the GEB's proposal to Hopkins, Mall added that "the day of reckoning is at hand." The lesser salaries of full-time faculty should not deter brilliant men and women from entering the field. As Mall liked to put the issue, a physician must choose "which 'G' to worship—Gold or Glory."

Other laboratory science faculty had similar motivations. Many were undoubtedly drawn to the medical sciences partly by the field's growing prestige, partly by their interest in the single-minded pursuit possible in a laboratory, and partly for escape from hustling patients and dealing with the mundane business of medical practice.

To the laboratory scientists, limiting clinicians to their salaries would accomplish several things at once. First, they believed that medicine should be fundamentally a science devoted to finding the bio-physical causes of disease and less an art of bedside diagnosis and hopeful therapies. Second, since the medical sciences prospered most with faculty devoting themselves entirely to research and teaching, it followed in their thinking that clinical instruction would also benefit from the clinical faculty's singular devotion to research and teaching. Third, since the medical school competed with the clinicians' private practice for their time and energy, eliminating private practice would unify and rationalize the organization of the medical school. Clinicians would no longer be responsible to an outside practice. Finally, eliminating clinicians' private practices would unify the *material* interests of all the faculty in the medical school. Clinical faculty, leaving behind large and fashionable private practices, would derive their incomes and reputations from the same source as the laboratory faculty. From at least the days of Benjamin Rush, practitioners had used their faculty positions in medical schools to build large, prestigious, and very lucrative private practices. The proposed full-time plan would reduce such practices, making the main clinical faculty captives of the medical school, with loyalties no longer divided between personally lucrative consultations and the needs of the school for research and teaching.

Some practitioners as well as academic doctors were mindful of the need for faculty who would commit themselves mainly to teaching. As early as 1900, the AMA *Journal* argued that clinical departments should be headed by physicians "who are properly paid and of whom more may be demanded than of those who regard their clinical services merely as a means of rapidly acquiring a large private clientele."[75]

But as news of the Hopkins plan spread, the outrage among private practitioners grew. The AMA appointed a special committee on the reorganization of clinical teaching. Its chairman, Victor Vaughan of Michigan, tried to steer a middle course, rejecting extreme involvement in private practice by clinical faculty while expressing the committee's considerable skepticism of the full-time plan. Vaughan concluded that even if the plan were ideal, it would not be feasible for any but a few medical schools that were well endowed.[76]

Many clinical faculty charged that full-time medical school faculty, based in laboratories and wards, made "poor practitioners" because they were more concerned with research than with patients as suffering human beings. They claimed that without a private practice a physician would lose touch with the real practice of medicine and be a poor example for medical students. William Osler, the renowned professor of medicine at Hopkins who had introduced a number of reforms in clinical teaching, had always been an advocate of "medicine as art" as well as science. He frequently argued with Mall, who conceived of medicine as simply a research science. When Osler left Hopkins for Oxford in 1904, he bitterly conceded to Mall, "Now I go, and you have your way."[77] The initiation of the full-time plan at Hopkins must not have surprised him, and he wrote from England his severe criticisms of the proposed change. Similarly, the highly regarded Society of Clinical Surgery, including such celebrated surgeons as Charles Mayo and George W. Crile, registered their opposition to the plan. Other general and specialty societies joined the chorus.[78]

Practitioner attacks on the full-time plan exposed their ideological, material, and political differences with academic physicians, particularly the laboratory scientists. Although the practitioners' and academics' common interest in promoting scientific medicine had united them at the end of the nineteenth century, differences quickly developed as to just what that meant. Academics differed with practitioners over the relative weight of science and art in medicine, the financial interests of practitioner-clinicians, and who should control medicine.

Medical scientists and their foundation allies believed that medicine was at its best as an exact science, isolating variables in the laboratory and finding a cure under very precise laboratory conditions. Practitioners, in the business of selling cures to patients, seldom saw the relevance of laboratory controls to treating individuals in the real world. With all their deficiencies, the proprietary schools had, in the words of Rosemary Stevens, "at least been firmly attuned to the average practitioner."[79] The medical ideology implicit in the full-time plan was now driving practitioners and academics apart.

Whether the practitioners were driven more by their commitment to practice or by consideration for their bank accounts is, of course, a moot question. The issues were so intertwined that it was never clear whether the argument that medicine is an art was simply a ruse to hide pecuniary motives. Clinicians fiercely defended their material interests against the infringements of the full-time plan. Arthur Dean Bevan denounced the plan as "unethical and illegal" because it deprived clinical faculty of their fees.[80]

Finally, the full-time plan exposed a political conflict that grew out of the different material conditions of practitioners and academics. The AMA sought to control medical education as a vehicle for controlling entry into the profession and thereby medical care itself. The scientific medical school faculty, on the other hand, thought that *they* should control medical care. Medical scientists, remarked a prominent British physiologist in 1914, ought to "remodel the whole system so as to fight disease at its source. . . . Surely it is a time when those who have laid the scientific foundations for the new advances should take counsel together, assume some generalship, and show how the combat is to be waged."[81] The Rockefeller philanthropists clearly sided with the medical scientists and cast their weighty fortune with the armies of academe.

Behind the passion of the AMA's attacks were the realizations that the position of medical faculty would no longer be a lucrative supplement for private practitioners *and* that the full-time clinical faculties' main loyalties would be to medical schools and not the organized profession. Elite practitioners would now have to choose either a grand income or a respected teaching and research position. But even more important to the strategy for controlling medical education, the full-time plan, by reducing the clinician's income and monopolizing his loyalties and material interests in the medical school, would cut the clinical faculty off from private practitioners. Instead of linking together the interests of the elite practitioners with those of the medical schools, full-time clinical faculty would help separate the medical schools from the organized private practice profession. The full-time plan would reduce the power of the organized profession, in particular, the AMA and its Council on Medical Education, within the medical schools.

Of course, things were different in the 1910s from the way they had been at the turn of the century. The profession's reform strategy had accomplished much of what it set out to do: It had established scientific medicine as the ascending model of medical practice and education; it had reduced the number of schools considerably and thereby the output of new physicians; and it had secured supportive legislation and licensing laws. But the plan had just begun to work, physicians' incomes and prestige were rising, and the end was not in sight. Medical schools were still considered key to the strategy and to continued control by the organized profession of its own material conditions. And the

AMA leadership was not about to let that control slip from its grasp. The profession launched a campaign to discredit and oppose the full-time plan.

SELLING THE FULL-TIME PROPOSAL

Welch, an astute medical politician, anticipated the furor the plan would provoke. Four years before Mall suggested the idea to Flexner, Welch had called for reforms that would allow clinical department heads to "devote their *main* energies and time" to teaching and research, "without the necessity of seeking their livelihoods in a busy outside practice and without allowing such practice to become their *chief* professional occupation."[82]

When the GEB proposed to fund full-time organization of Hopkins' clinical departments, Welch faced the dilemma of mediating the interests of the laboratory science faculty with those of the clinicians. Welch asked the GEB to allow some exceptions to the full-time rule, enabling the university president or "some other responsible authority" to permit some full-time, salaried professors to keep their consulting fees.[83] The board adamantly refused to allow any exceptions.

The laboratory faculty unanimously endorsed the plan, but, Flexner later recalled, "there was a rift among the clinicians."[84] Within two years Welch won sufficient support from the clinical faculty. Lewellys Barker, the Hopkins professor of medicine who had publicly advocated the full-time plan in 1902, stood in the way of its implementation at Johns Hopkins. He chose "gold" over "glory" and resigned his professorship, agreeing to become a "clinical professor," drawing a small salary from the medical school but being able to devote most of his time to a lucrative private practice. In his place, Theodore Janeway gave up his chair at the College of Physicians and Surgeons and an elite practice in New York to become the first full-time professor of medicine in the United States. William Halsted was named professor of surgery and Charles Howland, professor of pediatrics. In October 1913 Welch formally applied for the grant, accepting the condition that the full-time clinical faculty at all ranks—assistant professor to professor—would "derive no pecuniary benefit" from any professional services they rendered. The board immediately voted its approval and a grant of $1.5 million.[85]

Three months later the GEB decided to devote all its funds in medical education to "the installation of full-time clinical teaching." Flexner had been hired by the board to administer their program in medical education, and he applied himself with his usual energy.[86]

Within a year Welch reported that "the full-time system is a great success" at Hopkins.[87] Halsted and Howland found the system to their liking, but Janeway resigned his position in 1917 to return to private practice in New York. He was dissatisfied with the full-time arrangements, he wrote in a widely publicized journal article, both because "outside engagements" had been a major source of clinical knowledge to him and because he and his family were used to a higher standard of living than he could afford on his salary. It was "unnatural and repugnant to the patient's sense of justice," he said with great sympathy for his patients, "that a consulting physician should not receive the usual fee for such service."[88]

In 1919 even Osler backed off from his opposition. He asked Welch to use his influence to persuade the GEB to "help McGill start up-to-date clinics in medicine and surgery." Osler made it clear that he did not favor the full-time scheme, but he believed it was now necessary at the Canadian school because "new conditions have arisen" which would leave McGill behind the other first-class schools that had instituted full-time teaching in medicine and surgery.[89]

Over the next few years the board voted more than $8 million from its general funds for similar reorganizations on a full-time basis of the medical schools at Washington University at St. Louis, Yale, and the University of Chicago. With the matching grant policy, these funds represented several millions more in support for the reforms. Between 1919 and 1921 Rockefeller, Sr., contributed $45 million to the General Education Board specifically for medical education.

The first appropriation from this special fund was a grant of $4 million to Vanderbilt University to make the Nashville medical school a model for the South. The GEB considered Nashville its "strategic point" in the South and Vanderbilt the institution that would lead the drive to improve Southern "public health and industrial and agricultural efficiency."[90] By 1960 Vanderbilt, the board's major white university in the South, received a total of $17.5 million from the GEB for medical education. Meharry

Medical College, the board's model black medical school and one of only two that Flexner had argued should survive, received less than half the sum given to the white institution.[91] Despite its relative stinginess toward black medical education, the board firmly believed that scientifically trained black doctors were necessary to improve the health of blacks, protect the health of neighboring whites, and provide an elite and "responsible" leadership for the black population. Through its annual grants to Meharry, it exerted substantial control and even instituted full-time teaching in medicine and surgery in the 1930s, with approved white faculty members in charge and a hand-picked white president.[92]

The board used its $45 million to foster, if not force, acceptance of the full-time plan at the major medical schools in the country. But not all the schools were won over as easily as Hopkins.

BOSTON BRAHMINS RESIST

Harvard staunchly refused to accept the full-time plan. In 1913, while negotiating the details of the Hopkins grant with Welch, the GEB invited the Harvard medical school to apply for a grant to place their clinical departments on a full-time basis. The debt-ridden medical school sought a windfall through subterfuge. The faculty asked for $1.5 million to reorganize all its clinical departments "on a satisfactory university basis." The clinical professors would "devote the *major* part of their time to school and hospital work," but they could still collect fees from their private patients whom they would see in offices provided by the teaching hospital. This proposal was hardly consistent with the GEB's by then well-known interpretation of full time.[93]

The opposition to the GEB's strict full-time policy was led by two powerful members of the Harvard clinical faculty, Harvey Cushing, a renowned neurosurgeon and chief-of-surgery at Peter Bent Brigham Hospital (a Harvard teaching hospital), and Henry A. Christian, former dean of the medical school. Cushing and Christian, like other members of Harvard's clinical faculty, had lucrative private practices, which they refused to give up. They felt it was enough for the clinical faculty to devote themselves to working in the teaching hospital and "to confine their professional activities within its walls." In return, they wanted to accept fees from "patients who might consult us during hours as we felt justified in setting aside for this purpose." Committed though he was to academic medicine, Cushing even offered his resignation to Harvard president Lowell. But, as Cushing undoubtedly knew, Lowell considered the famous surgeon more important to Harvard's academic reputation than the $1.5 million endowment.[94]

Gates and Flexner continued to press for strict full-time commitments, turning down Harvard's proposals during several years of negotiations. In addition to their ideological commitment to full time, the GEB members had a pragmatic incentive for pushing it as quickly and widely as possible. Harvard and other schools that allowed their medical faculty to keep their consulting fees were raiding the faculties of schools that adhered to the GEB's policy. In 1921 David Edsall, dean of the Harvard medical school, tried to lure Charles Howland, the Johns Hopkins pediatrician, with the same salary he was getting at Hopkins *plus* consulting fees from private practice. Flexner had to help Hopkins upgrade their facilities as an inducement to keep Howland there.[95]

Harvard was able to resist the full-time plan because of its reputation as a leading scientific medical school and because its clinical faculty were too prominent in Boston's ruling social circles to be easily dismissed. Already by 1900 the Harvard medical faculty boasted that it controlled "probably more clinical material than any other one school in the country."[96] Such powerful medical figures were also physicians to the Boston upper class, and by virtue of their earnings, and many their births, they were themselves members of that very class-conscious city's upper crust. It took such Brahmins to refuse to surrender their consulting fees in the face of the GEB's compelling offer, particularly when the school's accounts were heavily in the red.

FEAR AND TREMBLING IN THE BOARD ROOM

Meanwhile, Charles Eliot, the illustrious former president of Harvard and a trustee of the GEB, carried the battle into the GEB's board room. Eliot argued that "great improvements in medical treatment have in recent years proceeded from men who were in private practice."[97] Eliot went on to argue not merely for Harvard's latest proposal but for a complete reversal of the full-time policy and the binding contracts imposed by the GEB on universities accepting its beneficence. How could the insistence of the GEB on full time be reconciled with the board's theoretical hands-off policy, he asked rhetorically. Eliot reminded the board that it had pledged itself not to interfere with the running of a recipient institution, "except as regards its prudential financial management." Yet the board was making its strict interpretation of full-time clinical organization the condition of a grant. "This condition does not seem to me consistent with what I have always believed the wise and generally acceptable policy of the board," Eliot diplomatically concluded.[98]

Eliot's arguments fell on receptive ears. The Rockefeller philanthropies were under fire from a range of groups, individuals, and newspapers spanning a considerable portion of the contemporary political spectrum. Ida Tarbell provided fuel for roasting John D. Rockefeller and his financial empire with her "History of the Standard Oil Company," published from 1902 to 1904 in *McClure's Magazine.* In the latter year, Theodore Roosevelt was elected President on a platform of vacuous promises to bring the trusts to heel. Encouraged by growing popular resentment against the "robber barons" and wishing to channel that resentment through stable political institutions, the Progressive movement won support from the courts as well as the Congress for small reforms and slaps on the wrists of the largest trusts. In 1907 federal Judge Kenesaw Mountain Landis struck Standard Oil of Indiana with an unprecedented $29 million fine for receiving rebates from the Chicago and Alton Railroad. Making its way through the courts was an unprecedented anti-trust suit. On May 15, 1911, the Supreme Court ordered the Standard Oil Trust, then controlling nearly 90 percent of oil refining and sales in the United States, broken up. Neither action slew the Standard Oil empire nor diminished the fortune of John D. Rockefeller and his family. But as part of a growing public attack on Rockefeller and on unrestricted capital accumulation, these attacks were taken seriously by the Rockefellers and their industrial, financial, and philanthropic organizations.

Hoping to calm the troubled waters of popular hostility and to fuel his engine of social transformation, the Standard Oil billionaire attempted to get a congressional charter for the new Rockefeller Foundation. The proposed charter sparked a veritable firestorm of protest from working-class and Progressive leaders and newspapers. *The Los Angeles Record* denounced the "gigantic philanthropy by which old Rockefeller expects to squeeze himself, his son, his stall-fed collegians and their camels, laden with tainted money, through 'the eye of the needle.'" Expressing a widespread suspicion of philanthropy, the paper argued that the "monopoly-ridden masses don't want charity under any guise, but justice." The charter bill foundered in Congress for three years and in the end failed to sweep aside the articulated public anger.[99]

The Rockefeller organization found a more receptive mood in Albany and was granted an unrestricted charter by the New York legislature in 1913. But even in New York, anti-Rockefeller Progressive sentiments continued to haunt both the man and his corporate philanthropies. In 1917 State Senator John Boylan introduced a bill to repeal the foundation's charter. Although this attack also failed to stop the Rockefeller philanthropy, it added flack to the assault. What most upset the Rockefeller group about this campaign were the testimony and speeches in support of the bill from Bird S. Coler, a respected Wall Street stockbroker cum-Progressive.[100]

Meanwhile, more specific attacks were being leveled against the Rockefeller and Carnegie foundation programs. The National Education Association (NEA), meeting in St. Paul in 1914, condemned the foundations' education programs for introducing undemocratic controls into the schools. Working-class and Progressive newspapers supported the NEA resolution. The radical organs understood the capitalist class character of the foundation programs in education. The Pittsburgh, Penn., *Leader* considered the foundation programs so effective "that it is difficult for genuine teachers to make any headway against the class concepts that hold their heads so high in school and college."[101]

The most thoroughgoing indictment, however, followed the "Ludlow Massacre" at the Rockefeller-controlled Colorado Fuel and Iron Company. When workers at the mining operation went on strike in 1914 for union recognition, an eight-hour day, and emancipation from the choking economic, political, and social control of the company over the Ludlow miners and their families, the company brought in armed guards. On April 20 the company's private army together with the state militia shot to death six workers and burned the tents in which the strikers' families were forced to live, cremating two women and eleven children inside them. The Ludlow Massacre shocked an already aroused public and focused anger against the Rockefellers. Labor unions, anarchists, socialists, and radicals organized demonstrations and demanded broad reforms to protect labor. Progressives joined the cry for action, and even conservative newspapers criticized the mining company.

Congress created, and President Wilson appointed, the Commission on Industrial Relations to investigate the Ludlow affair, relations between capital and labor, and the role of philanthropic foundations in general. The commission, headed by Frank Walsh, exposed much of capital's relations with the working class to examination and criticism and pointed to the important role of foundations in building a superstructure to extend capital's control throughout society. The Walsh Commission subpoenaed the senior and junior Rockefellers, Charles W. Eliot, and Jerome D. Greene to testify about the activities of the Rockefeller Foundation. The commission's final report noted that the Rockefeller and Carnegie foundations' policies are "colored, if not controlled, to conform to the policies" of the country's major corporations, which are themselves controlled by a "small number of wealthy and powerful financiers."[102]

The attacks on Standard Oil and on unrestricted capital accumulation, the hostility to foundations and the Rockefeller programs in particular, and the increased support for radical and socialist working-class movements greatly impressed the men of the Rockefeller philanthropies. Eugene Debs, a revolutionary socialist, rolled up nearly one million votes for President in 1912. In the Rockefeller offices and board rooms at 61 Broadway, the din outside must have sounded at times like the trumpets of Jericho.

General Education Board member George Foster Peabody, a New York banker, feared the rising tide would force the government to assume all support of educational institutions (robbing the foundations of their power and influence) and would also lead to "economic legislation which shall preclude the acquisition of surplus wealth" (the end of capitalism itself). Peabody preached caution in the face of such challenges.[103]

Charles Eliot feared the outcome of class conflicts, but he believed the best defense were the programs the foundation had already undertaken:

> We need not imagine that the process of accumulating great fortunes . . . is going to continue through the coming generations. . . . The evils which I look forward to with dread in the coming years of the Republic are injustice inflicted on those who have by those who have not, and corruption and extravagance in the expenditure of money raised by taxation. Against such evils I know no defense except universal education including the constant inculcation of justice and goodwill.[104]

Gates himself feared possible "confiscation" of wealth, but he had faith in the strength of capitalism to survive. "The recognition of the right to earn and hold surplus wealth marks the dawn of civilization," he noted to himself in 1911.[105]

Gates favored standing fast on the principle of private control of wealth and opposed any special defensive strategies. When Rockefeller Foundation president George Vincent drafted the annual report for 1917, Gates suggested removing a new self-limiting policy statement. Among other points, the new policy precluded the foundation from "supporting propaganda which seek to influence public opinion about the social order and political proposals." Vincent defended the statement on the ground that "the one thing that the opponents of foundations seem most to resent is that attempt to control public opinion."[106] It was hoped that the formal statement denying the charges would be accepted by the public as a verdict of innocence.

FEAR UNDERMINES THE FULL-TIME POLICY

Board members feared that the full-time contracts would be seen by the public as another example of private capitalist control of essentially public institutions. Visions of more public attacks and restrictive legislation undermined support for the full-time policy within the board. Anson Phelps Stokes, who succeeded Peabody on the board as the voice of caution, counseled against imposing the full-time policy through contracts. "It is not a question of whether we are right or wrong in our opinions," he explained. The full-time plan itself was not an issue. In fact, he thought it was a commendable program.

> But it is a question of whether or not we can . . . afford—in view of public opinion and our great wealth as a board—to be imposing, or at least requiring, detailed conditions regarding educational policy in medicine in elaborate contracts which can only be amended with our consent. . . . Personally, I think this policy unwise and fraught with serious dangers.[107]

The "elaborate contracts" were a policy brought by Gates from the American Baptist Education Society to the Rockefeller business dealings and philanthropies. Applied by the GEB to their grants to medical schools, contracts with the recipient universities uniformly included a clause specifying that if the full-time plan "shall, without the consent of the said General Education board, be abandoned, substantially modified or departed from, the said university will, upon demand of said board, return said securities or any securities representing their reinvestment."[108]

Stokes' fear that the contracts would become public knowledge was prophetic. While Eliot, Lowell, and the medical faculty at Harvard could be counted on to keep a gentlemanly silence about their conflict with the GEB, the more volatile president of Columbia, Nicholas Murray Butler, was not adverse to spilling the beans. Under Flexner's hard-nosed leadership, the GEB offered Columbia a substantial grant but only if the university took more decisive control of the medical school, booted out the reigning dean and clinical faculty while instituting the full-time policy, reduced the student enrollment in the medical school, and took more complete control of Presbyterian Hospital as a teaching facility.[109]

After lengthy negotiations between Butler, Flexner, and representatives of the Presbyterian Hospital trustees, Butler rejected the proposals as "so reactionary and so antagonistic to the best interests of the public, of medical education and of Columbia University, that they will not, under any circumstances, be approved by us."[110]

The Presbyterian Hospital trustees, led by philanthropists Edward S. Harkness, W. Sloan, and H. W. deForest, had favored creating a new medical center and had supported all the conditions the GEB was demanding. In 1911 Harkness had given

Presbyterian Hospital $1.3 million to encourage them to tighten their bonds with Columbia, giving the medical school exclusive teaching privileges in the hospital and control over Presbyterian's medical staff.[111] Angered at Butler's rejection of the proposals and his support for the existing practitioner faculty, the hospital trustees voted to sever all ties with the Columbia medical school.[112]

Negotiations continued, with Henry Pritchett and the Carnegie Foundation entering the fray in 1919. The Carnegie Foundation joined with the GEB and the Rockefeller Foundation to offer $1 million each toward building a new medical center for Columbia and endowing its faculty. Yet the GEB held out for complete fulfillment of their policy on full time.[113]

Pritchett could see no reason for such obstinacy. "It is quite true," he told Flexner, "that certain of the professors are allowed to take a small consulting practice. . . . That is not 100 percent fulfillment, but I should say that it was comparable to the claims of Ivory Soap to be 99.44 percent pure."[114]

Pritchett was not only uncommitted to complete subordination of the medical faculty through a strict full-time policy. He also, and perhaps more viscerally, feared attacks on the foundations and the recipient universities. "Such a contract binding a university to a fixed policy laid down by the giver of money seems to me a dangerous thing," he complained to Wallace Buttrick, president of the GEB. "If these contracts were made public, I am sure it would bring down on all educational foundations no less than on the universities themselves severe criticism. It seems to me a dangerous policy for those who administer trust funds to adopt."[115]

The standard response of the GEB officers to such criticisms of their full-time plan contracts was that "the policy was proposed to us by the trustees and medical faculty of the university and that the terms of the contract were such as they themselves asked for."[116] According to this fiction, it was Welch who proposed the full-time plan to the GEB. "We have never asked any institution to adopt the plan," Buttrick claimed. "The Hopkins proposal in all particulars came from Doctor Welch."[117] This self-serving posture was supported by carefully worded statements in letters, personal contacts, and even the contracts themselves. Flexner and others orally and confidentially made known the board's requirements, and they were always careful that any written proposals came from the institution. The painstaking, almost nit-picking negotiations with the Columbia medical school faculty, Columbia's president Butler, and trustees of the university belie the GEB's claims that it had "no fixed policy regarding medical education" and that they never attempted to influence the internal policies of universities.[118]

After continued resistance by Harvard and Columbia, public disclosure of the binding contracts, public criticism by the medical profession, and a long history of attacks on corporate philanthropy, the board in 1925 altered its contracts and thus its full-time policy. Eliot had continued his attacks within the board meetings right up to the time of his resignation in 1917, charging the GEB with interfering in the internal affairs of Harvard by demanding full-time organization as the price of an endowment grant. Board member Anson Phelps Stokes carried on the fight to do away with binding contracts and the GEB's narrow definition of full time.[119]

WINDOW DRESSING: GATES DEFEATED

Although the public clamor for abolition of foundations, or at least for their severe restriction, had abated with the demise of Progressivism, the entry of the United States in the Great War, and the repression of radical and socialist movements following the war, a majority of the GEB's trustees feared a resurgence of such attacks. "Some day the power of the 'dead hand' will again be the subject of political, if not popular, discussion," warned Thomas Debevoise, legal counsel to the board.[120]

Debevoise prepared the arguments to support the majority of the trustees in their fight with Flexner and Gates. First, it was important for the board not to *appear* to control recipient institutions. "It will hurt the reputation of the board if it attempts to direct the operation of the objects of its bounty," Debevoise argued. Second, binding contracts were *unnecessary* to keep the universities in line. "Most of the schools which receive money from the board come back at least a second time, and the possibility of their needing additional help should lend all the inducement necessary to make them follow the ideas of the board."[121]

On February 26, 1925, the board voted, with Gates adamantly dissenting, to authorize a contract with the University of Chicago that required full-time clinical faculty to receive no fees for patients seen in the university's teaching hospitals but allowed them to "continue to engage in the private practice of their professions outside of the university's hospitals." The contract also allowed the university's board of trustees to make "such modifications and changes by the university in future years as educational and scientific experience may . . . justify."[122]

The final defeat for Gates and Flexner came later that year. At the end of September the executive committee of the GEB voted to modify the original contracts with Johns Hopkins, Vanderbilt, Washington (at St. Louis), and Yale universities to allow the boards of trustees to compromise the full-time provision (if they desired). Gates specifically asked to have his negative vote recorded.[123] Gates took his defeat at age seventy-two as a personal attack and a political blunder. Actually, the policy change was a minor one, a question of tactics rather than of strategy.

The full-time plan was an entering wedge, the first thrust of a continuing struggle by corporate philanthropy to control medical education and medical care—to establish the principle that society's needs, as defined by the corporate class, would prevail over the medical profession's interests. It was the first attempt on a large scale to rationalize medical care in the United States. Gates saw clearly the potential value of academic medicine— doctors subordinated to the university, the university controlled by men and women of wealth, and academic physicians research- ing the causes of disease and eliminating those causes at their microbiological source. All these relationships and functions would assure that academic doctors, unlike their practitioner colleagues, would serve the needs set before them and not some competing professional interest.

But in 1925 Gates was a strategist from another era. Although a loyal manager himself, he was a product of early corporate capitalism's rugged individualism, who never adapted to corpo- rate liberalism's trust in the State and other bureaucratic organi- zations run by professionals and managers. He did not realize how fully academic medicine was *already* the instrument of foundation and capitalist interests.

Dependent on outside funding for its capital and operating expenses, medical education could be guided by whoever footed the bill. The GEB and Rockefeller Foundation efforts to institutionalize full-time clinical departments had their effect, even with the resistance and the final defeat of binding contracts. Of the $13 million in medical school operating expenses in 1926, the largest chunk—42 percent—went to salaries of full-time faculty. The Commission on Medical Education reported that in the twelve years since the GEB launched its program with Johns Hopkins, the largest single increase in budgets was "for salaries and other expenses in the clinical divisions, particularly in those schools which have placed the clinical departments on a university basis."[124]

Medical colleges were caught in a bind. Dependent on student fees, they had always been responsive to student demands. By the turn of the century, state licensing boards were requiring at least the rudiments of a scientific medical education. In 1907 the secretary of the Association of American Medical Colleges was able to report that students no longer sought merely the cheapest route to a medical degree. Guided by the demands of state boards, they wanted scientific medical education "and they are willing to pay for it." Every medical college that kept step with "the better schools" found "that the step taken was a profitable one in every way."[125]

The catch was that it took more than student fees to make those changes. Although tuition fees increased to pay for the changes—in 1910, 81 percent of the medical schools charged *less* than $150 per year whereas in 1925, 85 percent charged *more* than that in fees—they could not increase beyond the willingness of the middle class to pay them. Nevertheless, by 1927 more than one-third of the annual income of medical schools still came from tuition fees. Income from endowments was, by the mid-1920s, the second largest source of income and meant the difference, for most medical colleges, between making it as a class A school or not making it at all.[126] The influence of the General Education Board and the Rockefeller Foundation was profound.

STATE UNIVERSITIES: PROFESSIONALS, THE STATE, AND CORPORATE LIBERALISM

Between 1919 and 1921 Rockefeller, Jr., Flexner, and Gates persuaded the elder Rockefeller to give the General Education Board $45 million to be used for medical education. With the foundation's program of building up several elite private medical schools well underway, Flexner wanted to expand the program to the lesser but still "strategic" schools of the West and the South.

> In the East medical education is altogether in the hands of privately endowed institutions of learning. With the exception of some eight or ten schools, medical education in the West and South is in the hands of state universities. The board has found it practicable to cooperate with endowed institutions in developing their medical schools. It has had thus far no experience with state or municipal institutions in this field. It is evident, however, that if Mr. Rockefeller's benefaction is to be made generally effective, cooperation with state and municipal universities is necessary.[127]

It was not long before Flexner brought a concrete proposal to the board to help the University of Iowa build a modern medical center across the river from its small and outmoded facility. The state legislature had dramatically increased its support of the medical school from less than $70,000 in 1912–13 to more than $1 million in 1922–23. But generous though it was to the medical school, the legislature would not appropriate the whole $4.5 million needed to build a new medical center. Assured of continuing support by the governor and the legislature, Flexner proposed that the Rockefeller philanthropies donate $2.5 million, with the state agreeing to raise the remainder from the taxes of the people of Iowa.[128]

When Flexner brought the proposal before the board, Gates prepared an unusually long and passionate speech. The stormy meeting was held over two days at the Rockefeller funds' favorite retreat, Gedney Farms near White Plains. Gates orated for the first half day, his white hair falling in disarray over his forehead, and his necktie twisted out of place by his forceful gestures.[129]

Gates attacked the proposed grant to Iowa because: (1) it was a state university, (2) it was therefore "controlled by the taxpayers," (3) "the taxpayer is not intelligent on the needs and cost of first-class medical education," (4) no attempt was being made "to give Iowa the one supreme and simple thing Iowa needs—viz., illumination of the voter," (5) the indigenous Iowa leadership were incapable of carrying out their ideals of uplifting the medical school, and (6) the proposal was presented by Flexner, whom Gates had grown to despise as an upstart, one of the "bureaucratic officers, usurping the power of the board."[130]

Flexner followed Gates and presented his arguments in favor of supporting Iowa's medical school "in the mildest manner that I could possibly assume." He defended the plan as being practicable and necessary. "We are trying to aid in the development of a country-wide, high grade system of education in the United States. If we confine our cooperation to endowed institutions, we can practically operate only in the East." Flexner's brief, low-keyed presentation suggested the demeanor of a man assured of victory.[131]

That afternoon and the next day board members participated in the discussion. The vote was overwhelmingly in favor of funding the Iowa proposal.

Gates never forgave Flexner's opposition. "It is amazing," he angrily wrote Flexner. "How *could* you! You have never squarely met one of my arguments." The issue of not contributing to state universities was a sacred one to Gates.[132]

For Gates, the issue of the board's making gifts to state universities was bound up with his views on the relations between capital and the State and his attitude toward the people generally. Gates did not argue against the existence of state universities. "Indeed, not a few advantages must be conceded them arising out of the fact that they are tax-supported," Gates asserted. "Every taxpayer is told by his annual tax bills that the higher education is not less necessary for a democracy than the district school and the high school at his door; and that all three are equally the inheritance of his children; that the university is not a privilege reserved for religion or leisure or wealth, but belongs equally to every citizen."[133]

Gifts from private wealth, however, would violate the "principle" of taxpayer support for state universities. They are "needless and gratuitous" as well; in 1923 state medical schools received fifteen times more state funds than they got in 1900, a testimonial to the "pride which legislature and people alike take in their universities" as well as to the threefold increase in the states' wealth.[134]

Worse yet, gifts by the Rockefeller philanthropies to state universities would cooperate with the state and federal governments' inheritance taxes, "designed to confiscate between them

the whole of very large fortunes." Since the Rockefeller philanthropies were "the only part of the Rockefeller fortune certainly
safe," none of their funds should be "thrown into the swollen
maw of the confiscatory states."[135]

"ENDOW PRIVATE COLLEGES"

This attitude toward the states had been the official policy of
the GEB from 1906 until the 1919 policy statement on the need to
expand the medical education program to state-supported medical schools. The board was initially endowed by Rockefeller, Sr.,
with $1 million in 1902. In 1905 Gates and Junior persuaded the
old man to donate another $10 million to allow the board to
expand its program. Gates wrote Rockefeller's letter accompanying the gift, saying the funds were to be used "to promote a
comprehensive system of higher education in the United States."
As a member of the board, Gates proceeded to define what "the
founder" intended in "his" letter and gift. Gates emphasized the
necessity of forming a rationalized *system* of stable colleges and
universities, "comprehensively and efficiently distributed."[136]

Gates' plan was to build up private institutions in population
centers by providing them with substantial endowments. The
board should "cooperate with denominational agencies," which
then controlled most of the private colleges, but the colleges were
not to be aided so long as they remained creatures of any church.
All of the Rockefeller-funded colleges and universities, as with
the Carnegie Foundation's policy, were to be strictly nonsectarian
and nondenominational. In addition, Gates declared, "we must
seize the centers of wealth and population." Only they can assure
continuing support for universities and colleges, adequate student
enrollments, and a mutually supportive relationship between the
institution and the local business class. This relationship was
necessary "for influence, for usefulness, and for every form of
power."[137]

Finally, support by the foundation should usually take the
form of contributions to the institutions' endowments rather than
yearly appropriations for operating budgets. Gates and Rockefeller learned from their experience with the University of Chicago
that supporting a college's operating expenses could easily

become like quicksand, consuming the whole energy and fortunes of the foundation. Moreover, Gates laid out four strategic reasons for making endowments the prime work of the GEB.[138]

First, endowments will give universities and colleges financial stability, enabling them to attract a faculty of "great gifts and attainments" without having to pay them high salaries. High-calibre academicians are attracted "not for money but for security, for permanence and continuity of work, for freedom from distraction." The same argument, that people are drawn into academic careers for reasons of security and the undistracted pursuit of research, was applied a few years later to support the demand for full-time clinical faculty.[139]

Second, by providing endowments to carefully selected institutions, the foundation could "preserve and mass our income . . . on the strategic points in ever-increasing and cumulative power." It would not be dissipated in smaller amounts on the operating budgets of lesser programs. Third, general endowments given by the GEB would call forth other gifts and personal involvement by the local business class.[140]

Finally, the financial stability of the colleges, the involvement of local capitalists in them, and the continued power and wealth of foundations like the GEB would keep the colleges and universities out of the hands of the people. With sufficient endowments, "no clamor of the masses can embarrass the fearless pursuit and promulgation of truth." This truth, like the colleges themselves, was intended by Gates, as he quoted John Stuart Mill, "to rear up minds and aspirations and faculties above the herd [and] to educate the leisured classes."[141]

The failure of state universities is their financial dependence on the legislature and the populace. "That fact becomes a powerful reason for endowing the private institutions," Gates candidly argued to the board. "If the test should ever come, the power which will act most effectively to preserve the state institutions will be private and denominational colleges and universities amply endowed and holding and teaching truth whatever may be the passions of the hour, and ultimately directing popular opinion into right channels." And, Gates prophesied, guiding the universities will be private foundations, "everywhere numerous and free." They will "so enlighten and direct popular opinion at all times that there can never ensue a conflict between the democracy and its state universities."[142]

Thus, giving endowments to colleges in a system of higher education is like planting "apple trees" in the orchard of capitalism.

> I want to see a hundred colleges in this country so planted as to cover the whole land and leave no part destitute, each of them planted in a fruitful soil, each so planted that it shall not be overshadowed by others, each conducted under such auspices as will take care of it, see that it is watered, particularly in its earlier years, see that it is properly fertilized, see that the forces of destruction which always fasten themselves on institutions shall be pruned away.[143]

A NEW ROLE FOR THE STATE

During the period in which Gates' policy against giving to state universities was in force, the GEB, with Gates as chairman until 1917, often contributed to state programs. The board provided the salaries of professors of education at Southern state universities to tour their respective states to urge development of tax-supported high schools. The board paid the U.S. Department of Agriculture for the expenses of agricultural demonstration programs in the South. The campaign against the hookworm in the South and throughout the world was conducted by state and national health departments whose expenses were paid in part by Rockefeller money.[144] But there were two important differences between these programs and the issue of contributing to state university medical schools.

First, the Rockefeller organization directly controlled all these programs. The GEB named the professors of education and defined their duties. Each professor toured his state "as an officer of the university, laden with its wisdom and moral authority." The high schools that were built because of his efforts were paid for and supported by the state and local governments. Similarly, the GEB found and hired Seaman Knapp to develop the agricultural demonstration program. And, again, "the hookworm work is done in every state under the guise of the State Health Boards, while it is in fact minutely directed by Mr. Rockefeller's

staff and paid for with Mr. Rockefeller's money."[145] Clearly,
Gates and the Rockefeller philanthropies were willing to give
money to the State when the State provided legitimating cover for
their programs and when they were able to direct the operation.

Second, higher education differed from other programs. The
bulk of Rockefeller's fortune was being used to expand the
economic base of society—"employing labor, multiplying the
means of subsistence, and enlarging the national wealth." But
Gates recognized that other elements of civilization were equally
important if the base was to survive. While Rockefeller's industries were "enlarging the national wealth," his philanthropies
must stimulate "progress in government and law, in language
and literature, in philosophy and science, in art and refinement."
And all these "are best promoted by means of the higher
education."[146] Thus, the institutions that wrought progress in any
one sphere—agriculture, public schools, health—were not so
important as the institutions that promoted progress of the whole
of civilization.

Because they are so widely believed to be fundamental to
modern society, colleges and universities are more visible and
thus more difficult for a single, national private philanthropy to
control. Since the GEB and the Rockefeller Foundation could
not control the institutions directly, they had to rely on people
within each state. For Gates, it was tenuous enough to rely on
local business classes to control private colleges. It was unthink-
able to yield that control to the people, even through their
legislators. It became a sacrosanct principle for Gates not to
support state university programs that could not be directly
controlled by the foundation.

As public and governmental attacks on Rockefeller and his
philanthropies started to mount, Gates' confidence in the ability
of private colleges and foundations to protect private wealth
turned to bitter pessimism. "There are too many evidences for
my peace of mind," he wrote Rockefeller, Sr., following Judge
Landis' anti-trust decision in 1907, "that wherever the voice of
the people finds absolutely free expression, that voice is not the
voice of reason, of enlightenment, and least of all of a deep-
seated sense of right in public things." The people's voice is
merely "the voice of reckless greed to lay violent hands on other
people's property."[147]

Although all the political, legal, legislative, and public opinion attacks never seriously diminished Rockefeller's wealth,
they struck sufficient fear into members of the capitalist class to
make them somewhat circumspect in their actions. The GEB
members gave up binding contracts and their strict full-time plan.
But these "ominous" signs of the times made Gates all the more
rigid. He strongly opposed weakening the full-time conditions,
and he clung ever more fiercely to his view of the potential evils of
the state universities and the importance of "throwing around
them in every state a cordon of strong, free, privately endowed
colleges and universities."[148]

To Gates, then, the fight within the General Education Board
over the appropriation to the state University of Iowa's medical school was a struggle over fundamental principles. Would
Rockefeller's fortune be dissipated and, even worse, given over
to the enemy? The board answered by overturning the policy
established by Gates.

The GEB, including Rockefeller, Jr., and its newer officers
were not acting on impulse or out of fear in contributing to state
universities. They were impressed by the need to build a rationalized system of medical schools and realized that much of
the medical education in the country would necessarily fall to
state schools. Furthermore, they trusted the state universities
because they understood the strength of institutional structures
and the class ties of professionals as forces for "constructive" but
conservative social and technological change. Raymond Fosdick,
one of the new GEB members and later president of it and the
Rockefeller Foundation, explained the board's defeat of Gates'
policy: "Gates did not understand the progressive forces which,
even as he spoke, were converting the great state universities into
the social and scientific laboratories they have become."[149]

MODERNIZING THE GEB: GATES DEFEATED AGAIN

Soon after the board's decision to pursue and develop the
Iowa grant, Flexner brought in other requests to fund state-
supported medical schools. By the middle of 1921 the board
voted to aid four more taxpayer-supported medical schools—at
the universities of Cincinnati, Colorado, Georgia, and Oregon—

that had accepted the university arrangements that prevailed at Hopkins and the other elite private schools.[150]

After a couple of years of ad hoc decisions, Gates insisted his policy be respected or debated and voted on as *policy*. "Our funds, and our rules of policy," he declared to the board, "form our legacy to our successors." Exceptions "should be treated as exceptions. It is *vital* that these successive boards have written policies and the habit of them."[151]

At the end of 1924 the board voted to appointed a committee to recommend a policy on aid to state universities. The GEB committee consisted of Gates; Rockefeller, Jr.; George Vincent, president of the Rockefeller Foundation; James Angell, president of Yale University; Trevor Arnett, a vice-president of the University of Chicago; and Wickliffe Rose, the star director of the Rockefeller Foundation's International Health Commission. The committee met at least twice and presented its report at the end of May 1925.[152]

The two-page report, written by Vincent and Rose, tersely dispensed with Gates' old policy. It noted that the GEB, the Rockefeller Foundation's numerous divisions, the Laura Spelman Rockefeller Memorial Fund, and the International Education Board all had dealt with and financially aided taxpayer-supported universities and other institutions. The report politely acknowledged that in 1906 Gates' policy was "sound," but in 1925 it was clearly "unwise to adopt principles so rigid as to prevent occasional contributions to medical schools whose growth might be of importance in a national system of medical education." With Gates boycotting the meeting and Wallace Buttrick conveniently absenting himself so as not to have to vote against his friend, the board made the de jure policy coincide with the Rockefeller foundations' practice.[153]

The reversals of the full-time contracts and the policy on state universities were too much for Gates to accept. Still fuming in October, he resigned from the GEB executive committee.[154]

The same revision was underway at the Carnegie Foundation, which was unable to join the GEB and the Rockefeller Foundation in aiding the University of Iowa because of opposition from old-timers among its trustees, men like Elihu Root, a corporate lawyer and former Secretary of State.[155] The foundations and individual capitalists had lost their fear of State-run institutions. Indeed, many financiers and industrialists, adherents of the new corporate liberalism, saw great possibilities for stabilizing their markets and profits in cooperation with the State. Sufficient initiative in developing legislation and executive department agencies bore fruit in the creation of regulatory agencies that enabled the most powerful sectors of several industries to control and regulate their industry themselves. Capitalists, corporate managers, and professionals in America were coming to see the State in a new light. Corporate liberalism embraced the State as the guarantor of a stable, profitable economy.[156]

The state universities were no exception. In the years ahead, all the major foundations gladly developed programs at state universities as freely as they used private universities. As with physicians and medical education, the more expensive it became to operate universities, the more the universities—state and private alike—turned to any agency or organization offering money. If money was offered for developing computer sciences, there were long lines of university presidents at the foundation doors explaining how strong their mathematics, statistics, and electrical engineering departments were and how well they worked together in the campus' fledgling program in computer science. Just as with medical schools, a major foundation would fund a few key schools to develop model departments or programs. And soon thereafter other universities would be copying them or refining some problem area in a similar program, hoping to get on the bandwagon of money for research and to attract new faculty. The strategies developed in medical education were refined and applied by numerous foundations in a broad array of programs down through the years.

This willingness to use state universities and other state organizations came partly from the changed attitude of the business class toward the State, accepting the necessity and value of State intervention in the economy. But foundation officers and trustees had other reasons as well. State universities performed a valuable role by conducting foundation-designed programs at taxpayer expense. Just as the General Education Board had fostered the development of vocationally oriented secondary schools in the South, for which taxpayers picked up the major tab, its provisions for development grants in medical education and other fields committed a university to continue to support the new program once foundation funding was cut off. Gates had always supported this tactic for objectives outside the university, but to Gates the university was too essential an institution to be entrusted to "the people."

The decisive argument for including state universities in foundation programs, however, was necessity. In 1908 Andrew Carnegie dropped his opposition to including state university faculty in his foundation's retirement plan because in the Midwest and the West, state universities were the dominant institutions of higher education. The same understanding convinced John D. Rockefeller, Jr., and other members of the GEB to support state-run medical schools. If the foundations were to develop a *system* of higher education, it was necessary to include the predominant type of institution.

Finally, professionals as a group had demonstrated their value and loyalty to the objectives of the foundations. The foundations' own professional staffs had earned the trust and confidence of their employers—the financiers, industrialists, corporate lawyers, and university presidents who sat on the foundations' boards of trustees. Most staff officers felt trust in their fellow professionals in the field. Gates himself trusted professionals whom he hired and those who worked with his programs although at the end of his career he disagreed sharply with them. Rockefeller, Jr., voted with the board against Gates to rescind full-time binding contracts and to fund state university medical schools; he did so because he believed them important to the very goals of class domination that he shared with Gates. *The foundations were not captured by their officers,* as Gates asserted. *Rather it was the professionals who were captured by the foundations.* They did for the foundations what other members of the professional-managerial stratum had already been doing for the same people's industries and financial organizations.

Whether an economist or medical doctor teaching and doing research in a university or developing and implementing programs in foundations, professionals saw foundations supporting the development of their fields, providing for their livelihoods, promoting expanded opportunities, and rewarding excellence.

What could be wrong in cooperating with such foundations? Weren't they, after all, run by such esteemed men as university presidents, corporation directors, and other professionals?

These were the very relationships and attitudes encouraged by Gates and other self-conscious strategists who built the foundations and gave them purpose and direction. Like the medical schools in Gates' and Flexner's funding strategy, the leading foundations won the flattery of imitation by their weaker brothers and sisters. Gates was indeed the pillar of the General Education Board and the Rockefeller Foundation until his semi-retirement in 1917. Although his successors modified some of his policies and tactics, Gates' goals and strategies seemed inscribed in stone.

Corporate philanthropies continued to find their mission in making capitalist society work better. Sometimes they tried to make it work more justly, but even then it was because gross injustice leads to movements for radical change. Generally, they have followed the corporate liberal view developed in the Progressive era and later joined by Rockefeller, Jr. His son David, head of the Chase Manhattan Bank, recently summed up this perspective, still popular in business and dominant in foundations:

> In view of the emerging demands for revision of the social contract, a passive response on the part of the business community could be dangerous. . . . So it is up to businessmen to make common cause with other reformers—whether in government or on the campus or wherever—to prevent the unwise adoption of extreme and emotional remedies, but on the contrary to initiate necessary reforms that will make it possible for business to continue to function in a new climate. . . . [157]

If the foundations lost their fear of the State, it was not because they had turned aside the objectives or general strategies of people like Gates. They pursued the same goal of rationalizing higher education in general and medical education in particular to make them better serve capitalist society, and like the dominant view within the Rockefeller boards (but unlike Gates' personal view), they adopted corporate liberalism's perspective that the State is a necessary aid in rationalizing industries, markets, and social and educational institutions alike.

SUMMING UP

The reform of medical education led to a contest over who would control medicine and for what ends. At the end of the nineteenth century laboratory scientists and elite practitioners formed an alliance to promote scientific medicine, revamp the AMA, win licensing legislation, and begin reforming medical education. Abraham Flexner's report for the Carnegie Foundation capped the drive to eliminate proprietary medical schools, the pariahs of all proponents of scientific medicine. Proprietary schools, sensitive to the needs of the average general practitioner, had served the needs of most students going into family practice while their faculty enhanced their incomes with student fees and consultations referred by former students. These commercial schools, however, churned out "too many" doctors, resisted control by medical societies, and were completely inadequate to providing the scientific, research-oriented medical education that was desired by the profession's reform leaders and by capitalist philanthropies.

Focusing on "commercial" medical schools and their low standards, the Flexner report articulated criticisms of American medical education and a program for reform that unified elite practitioners, medical scientists, and philanthropists. With the rapid decline of proprietary schools in the 1910s, however, the basis of unity evaporated, and more fundamental conflicts emerged.

The organized medical profession, in particular the AMA, which represented practitioners, wanted to control entry into the profession, assure that the training of physicians upheld the newly established confidence of the public in doctors' technical ability, and ensure that medical schools provided material support and propaganda to continue the dominance of scientific, technological medicine.

The new academic medical men, especially laboratory scientists, saw the medical centers as their turf. They wanted a greater share of the money spent on medical care, and they wanted, through their medical centers, to control all health care services and facilities. It made sense, they argued, for those who were the source of medical science to direct the resources of the new scientific medical system.

Foundations, claiming objectivity from their position above interest group squabbles, wanted to *rationalize* medical care, to create an efficient and unified system that would contribute to the health of the people. To that end, the General Education Board and the Rockefeller Foundation together gave more than $100 million to transform medical education. Like the committed academicians, they believed medical schools were the pivot of an increasingly technological system of medicine.

The Carnegie Foundation stepped onto center stage before the conflicts between medical scientists and elite practitioners reemerged. Their support for the Council on Medical Education encouraged reform-minded practitioners and science-oriented academics vying for control Flexner's report supported practitioners' insistence on closing down medical colleges and raising the social class base of the profession, and academicians got support for channeling endowment and construction money into medical schools. The capitalist class was encouraged that a medical care system useful to and compatible with its interests was at last at hand. The Carnegie Foundation, under Henry Pritchett's personal guidance, lent its prestige and legitimacy to the profession's own strategy.

The General Education Board and the Rockefeller Foundation, under Frederick T. Gates' direction, jumped in with a different strategy. Rather than supporting the scheme of the profession's leadership, which sought unity among academics and practitioners, the Rockefeller philanthropies supported the dominance of the medical scientists. Practitioners espoused capitalist values in wanting to make a profit from their professional services qua small business. But Gates and other foundation leaders had in mind a more important political and economic role for medicine, a role that required that health care be organized along the most efficient and productive lines possible under leadership that had demonstrated its support for the interests of the greater capitalist society. Just as the AMA *Journal* had warned at the turn of the century, there were dangers in letting wealthy capitalists formulate their own philanthropic designs.[158] The GEB's full-time plan attacked the interests of clinicians and the organized profession's ties to the medical faculty.

The differences in the Carnegie and Rockefeller strategies can be traced to Pritchett and Gates. Pritchett, before organizing the foundation for Andrew Carnegie, had been president of MIT and before that an astronomer for the U.S. Coast and Geodesic Survey. He was a scientist and a professional, and he was concerned about developing and maintaining a sufficient supply of engineers and trained personnel for industrial and government needs. Gates was a former minister and, since the 1890s, a director of industry and finance. Gates' ministerial background probably contributed to his perception of the role of social institutions as an important superstructure for society. His daily experience with business affairs from his perch at the top of the capitalist class gave him a broad perspective on the needs of capital.

Though these two men were significant in shaping their foundations' policies, the differences between them were not personality differences. They differed on political questions—what will best serve the needs of capitalist society?—and their personal histories are merely sources for understanding how their differing political perspectives developed. Both men and both foundations supported rationalizing medical care. Gates foresaw the problems with the medical profession that Pritchett only later appreciated. Pritchett supported the profession's own plan of action for several years before he became piqued at the narrow concerns of the AMA and Bevan in particular.

Bevan and other clinicians leading the AMA resented the General Education Board's attack on clinicians' interests. The Rockefeller philanthropies had become "a disturbing influence by dictating the scheme of organization of our medical schools," Bevan wrote to Pritchett. "Their position has become a real menace to sound development." The GEB had been "badly advised by men who are laboratory workers and teachers of anatomy and pathology," he complained. These men regarded "the laboratory as representing the science of medicine, and they rather feel that clinical medicine is not scientific." Bevan argued that in the training of physicians "the controlling influence must lie with the teachers of clinical medicine."[159] But Pritchett had seen the results of leaving medical education to the practitioners' singular concern for their own interests and their disregard of the larger goal of rationalizing education in the society.

By 1920 the elite practitioners broke off their alliance with the medical academicians and other supporters of rationalized medical care. A plan for compulsory sickness insurance sponsored by the American Association for Labor Legislation—a corporate liberal organization of social reformers, enlightened capitalists, and a few labor leaders—had won the support of a few key men in the AMA beginning in 1915. From the perspective of the time, the efforts to rationalize medicine seemed to physicians and foundation people alike to be leading to the demise of the private practitioner. In 1915 Welch rather condescendingly urged that "every effort ought to be made to rescue this situation," to preserve the "fine" institution of the family doctor.[160] The dour prognosis for private practice medicine was definitely premature.

As local medical society leaders caught on to "the professional philanthropists" and their attempts to "put something over on us to our detriment," the Progressives within the AMA were denounced. The academics, like Welch who had been elected AMA president in 1909, were by then isolated. By 1920 at least 60 percent of the country's doctors were members of the AMA.[161] With so many physicians joining up to support practitioners' interests, with the academics out of leadership and the Progressives, like Alexander Lambert, in retreat, the conservative leadership of the practitioners prevailed, a reign uninterrupted to this day.[162]

By the time Gates resigned from the General Education Board's executive committee in 1925, the efforts to rationalize medical care had not gotten as far as Gates had hoped. The constraints on his program notwithstanding, Gates' position became the established foundation direction in medicine for half a century.

5 CHAPTER

Epilogue: A Half-Century of Medicine in Corporate Capitalist Society

A VIRTUAL revolution transformed American medicine from 1890 to 1925. The medical profession ascended from ignominy and frustrated ambition to prestige, power, and considerable wealth. Medical science was developed from a mere gleam in the profession's eye to an established and powerful force in society.

This American success story is attributable to several historical developments. First, industrial capitalism created a new role for science and its application. Science was elevated from a gentlemen's avocation to a vital element in the competition for increased productivity and decreased labor costs. Scientists seized the opportunity to be of service to the masters of this new economy, and they were in turn rewarded with money and facilities for their work and prestige for their achievements and themselves.

As the organization of production grew larger and as the financial and legal underpinnings of capital grew more complex, capitalists recognized the need for managers and professionals to run their factories, their banks, and the social institutions that serviced the society and held it together. Universities became the main vehicles for training this new stratum of managers, professionals, and scientists and for organizing scientific research.

Second, physicians who were dissatisfied with the state of their profession recognized the economic and political, as well as technical, advantages of applying science to their rather crude art. By embracing scientific medicine, leading practitioners bolstered their crusade for a monopoly over the practice of medicine. The forefathers of academic medicine chose "glory" over "gold" and advanced the cause of medical science. Working together, elite doctors and medical researchers adopted the analytic methods and rubrics of science and lodged the training of physicians in the university. They sought designation as the society's legitimate professionals in matters of health and illness. With this strategy, they won the political and financial support of the new corporate class.

Third, mobilizing the power of corporate wealth in the social sphere, foundations brought unprecedented aid to the promotion of scientific medicine and to the reform of medical education. As the guiding force for the reform and development of institutions to serve the scientific, educational, and cultural needs of capitalist society, foundations played the leading role in financing necessary changes in medicine. By providing the carrot of subsidy to capital-hungry medical schools, foundations secured a position of enormous power in medicine from 1910 to the 1930s. In this period, foundations gave some $300 million for medical education and research. Rosemary Stevens concluded, "Foundations were thus the most vital outside force in effecting changes in medical education after 1910."[1]

FREDERICK T. GATES AND THE ROCKEFELLER PHILANTHROPIES

Of all the foundations, the General Education Board was, in the boastful but true words of Abraham Flexner, "the leading influence in remodeling American medical schools on the Hopkins plan."[2] The more than $82 million they applied to medical education reform by 1930 had an enormous impact because they employed a carefully conceived and faithfully followed strategy in which they consciously analyzed the interests and goals they wished to further, mapped out a plan for achieving them, and imposed necessary financial and programmatic conditions on recipient schools. The GEB sought a rationalized medical care system, directed by medical schools that were committed to a scientific and technological type of medicine.

Frederick T. Gates and the General Education Board did not achieve everything they sought, but even by 1929, the year Gates died, they had firmly established three important strategies in the development of medicine in the United States. First, Gates and the GEB created an important role for foundations—to give direction to the development of American health care. They assumed the right to define what kind of health care their society needed, and they used their tremendous corporate wealth to realize that vision. In its early years, the GEB provided a leadership that was widely followed by other foundations and by wealthy individuals. *Gates and his associates achieved power over American medicine partly because of the wealth they wielded but, more fundamentally, because they articulated the interests of the corporate class in a strategy that won sufficient support to succeed.*

Second, as part of their strategy, Gates and the Rockefeller philanthropies promoted the dominance of scientific, *technological* medicine. Because of the ideological appeal of this new medicine and its presumed technical effectiveness, the philanthropies and many other groups in industrialized capitalist societies embraced the analytic theories and the research and development methodologies of medical science and advocated the organization of medical practice solely around technological medicine. By 1930 they had firmly established the importance of well-equipped medical centers for all medical practice and health care organizations as well as for training new medical professionals and for developing knowledge and technique.

Finally, Gates and his followers in and out of the GEB began the long struggle to *rationalize* medical care, that is, to coordinate and integrate the different elements of the system so that it performs its designated functions. One of the main obstacles in that struggle has been private practice physicians, whose desire to profit from other people's sickness and suffering evoked angry opposition and accusations of "commercialism" from Gates and his colleagues. Because the interests of the organized medical profession conflicted with the goals of disseminating the technical benefits and ideological influences of medicine as widely as possible, the Rockefeller philanthropies attacked the profession head-on. Although they did not succeed in vanquishing the medical profession, they did initiate the strategy that was continued and refined by foundations for decades to come.

The forces set in motion during Gates' time continued to develop over the next half-century, as the remainder of this chapter will make clear. Although foundations continued to provide leadership in medical affairs, the State soon took over from the foundations the dominant financial role in the reform and development of medical care. *The State continued foundation-developed strategies of rationalizing medical care and developing technological medicine.* This chapter will focus on two important developments that created conditions Gates and his contemporaries did not anticipate.

First, technological medicine created opportunities for the development of new medical industries that came to play powerful roles in medical politics as well as in the medical economy. Rationalization was simply applied to this private market sector, facilitating the expansion and control of capital-intensive medical industries but failing to correct the deficiencies inherent in market-distributed medicine.

Second, the State's continued emphasis on medical technology served the corporate class interest in its own legitimation and the interests of medical technology interest groups. But the explosively inflationary effects of medical technology in a market system eventually undermined support for its expansion and encouraged the partial substitution of other legitimizing ideologies. As we will also see, neither of these developments has produced a medical care system that meets the widely recognized needs of the population.

RATIONALIZING THE MEDICAL MARKET

THE COMMITTEE ON THE COSTS OF MEDICAL CARE

One of the milestones in foundation-led efforts to rationalize health care was the Committee on the Costs of Medical Care (CCMC). The committee was formed in 1927 and was provided with a million-dollar research and expense fund by eight foundations, including the Rockefeller, Rosenwald, Macy, Milbank, and Carnegie philanthropies. Over the next four years the CCMC's staff and consultants turned out twenty-six reports, and in 1932, the committee concluded with a final report that at the time seemed sweeping.[3]

The report documented the great disparity in medical care according to income. Middle- and upper-income families averaged substantially more physician visits per person each year than lower-income families. Hospitalization, dental care, preventive care, and eye care were likewise strongly related to family income. The committee's critical analysis implied an important principle: The sale of medical care as a commodity distributes that care to those who can pay for it rather than on the basis of need. That is, it is distributed according to the society's class structure.

The committee recommended reorganizing medical care into group practices and developing more hospitals rationally distributed where needed, voluntary insurance plans to spread the uneven financial risks of illness among the population, and coordination of health care by the government. The thrust of these recommendations was to reduce the runaway power of the medical profession over health care by weakening the fee-for-service system of private practitioners, strengthening the position of hospitals in the organization of health services, and organizing the callous market for medical services into a rationalized, regulated system.[4]

The report articulated and legitimized the perspective and goals of the medical care reform campaign, much as the Flexner report had done for the medical profession's campaign for medical education reform some twenty years before. The recommendations were supported by virtually all of the committee's thirty-eight public health officials, business leaders, foundation officers, medical school faculty members, social scientists, labor union officers, and government officials. Through the CCMC, they formed a loose coalition whose leaders included some foundation officers and staff members who had worked for or with Gates and the Rockefeller philanthropies. Over the years this coalition, soon joined by hospital administrators and some health insurance industry officers, led efforts to rationalize medical care.

Nine representatives of organized medicine on the committee dissented from the majority report, attacking the group practice and prepaid insurance proposals and supporting voluntary insurance only if it protected fee-for-service practice under local medical society control. Although the committee majority advocated a continuation of privately controlled medical care, their proposals for more publicly organized financing and increased coordination of care were taken as a declaration of war by private practitioners. The AMA *Journal* rose to the occasion with a classic in hyperbole:

> The alinement is clear—on the one side the forces representing the great foundations, public health officialdom, social theory—even socialism and communism—inciting to revolution; on the other side, the organized medical profession of this country urging an orderly evolution guided by controlled experimentation which will observe the principles that have been found through the centuries to be necessary to the sound practice of medicine.[5]

Efforts of this "revolutionary" coalition in the 1930s to develop some form of national health insurance met defeat at the hands of the AMA's well-funded lobbying machine. "The controversy between 'organized medicine' and many major interests in our society became intensified," I. S. Falk, research director for the CCMC, recently observed, "and a dichotomy of national proportions began to take shape."[6] The AMA, as an interest group, declared civil war against the corporate class-supported efforts to rationalize medical care. A long succession of national health insurance bills was submitted to Congress by the reform coalition, but they were defeated by the AMA wielding the medical profession's wealth and the resulting power to influence public opinion and legislators' votes.

DOCTORS AND THE CAPITAL-INTENSIVE COMMODITY SECTOR

In the long run, however, the medical profession's autonomy was undermined by the same economic forces that contributed to their seemingly irrepressible rise in power, wealth, and status. Just as outside capital was needed to finance the development of medical science and the reform of medical education, technological medical care requires a financial base that cannot depend on the fees paid by individual patients. The dependence of physicians on technological medicine and the requirements of technological medicine for large capital and operating expenditures eventually weakened the political autonomy of the profession.

Hospitals, for example, provided doctors with new diagnostic and treatment facilities that made physician care technically more sophisticated and enhanced the prestige of doctors' roles. But hospitals required increasing funds and a stable system of finance. Since physicians could not themselves provide the capital to build and equip hospitals, the hospitals had to depend on philanthropy, government, and commercial banks for their needed capital. As the demands for operational funds increased, hospitals had to look beyond the billing of individual patients to the resources of insurance companies and the government. Similarly, physicians depended on medical schools to produce advances that might be applied to medical practice, to train new members of the profession in science-based medical theories and techniques, and to socialize new members in norms that made the profession cohesive and powerful. They also depended on drug companies to produce their materia medica—the essential base of their practice since prescription drugs gave doctors new power by making the public see a physician in order to be allowed to obtain the fruits of medical research. Prescription drugs, hospital care, medical equipment and supplies, and health insurance all quickly became essential commodities of the medical kingdom over which physicians reigned.

Private practice medicine had been founded upon simple, or petty, commodities that the physician himself could produce and sell. But technological medicine made physicians dependent on capital-intensive commodities, ones that require substantial capital investments and a good deal of hired labor to produce.[7] For decades, this development redounded to the advantage of the profession. Medical technology enabled the profession and these new interest groups to further divide medical care into discrete service units and products that could be sold in the medical market. This intensive "commodification" of medical care enlarged the number of medical commodities that could be marketed. Physicians assumed a new role in this market as middlemen as well as more "productive" producers. They were able to control more and more of the increasingly lucrative medical market, claiming a monopoly of expertise and authority over health care and over the increasing numbers of health workers. But the profession's growing dependence on capital-intensive medicine contained the seeds of their political decline—the loss of their ability to protect the economic relations on which private practice was founded. This contradiction was focused especially in the hospital.

Hospitals, as the Committee on the Costs of Medical Care demonstrated, were inadequate in number and not rationally distributed according to need. In the 1930s, the Julius Rosenwald Fund gave the American Hospital Association (AHA) $100,000 and the loan of staff member Dr. C. Rufus Rorem (who had been a senior researcher for the CCMC) to help the AHA rationalize' hospital administration and organize Blue Cross associations.[8] The foundation and the AHA hoped the hospital insurance program would provide a stable income for hospitals hard hit by the depression, centralize and integrate local health services around hospitals, and further the cause of voluntary health insurance at least for hospital expenses.

Blue Cross plans were a phenomenal success and proved the value of "third-party" payment mechanisms. The risk of medical misfortune was spread among many individuals and families, enabling them to have access to more expensive kinds of care. The demands of labor unions for greater economic security and more benefits encouraged the spread of work-related group plans. By 1947, after several years of cost-plus government war contracts, Blue Cross enrollment reached 27 million members, 19 percent of the population. After the war commercial insurance companies, following the Blue Cross lead, pushed energetically into the health insurance market they had previously all but ignored. Blue Cross and commercial health insurance companies developed this new commodity into a major industry—totaling $39 billion in premium income in 1977–and strengthened hospitals' finances and their position in the medical delivery system.[9]

The groups that had coalesced around the Committee on the Costs of Medical Care pressed on with their campaign to reform medical care. Since these interest groups favored coordinating care under the leadership of medical schools with hospitals as the "logical center" of the system, hospitals became ardent advocates of reform and rationalization that expanded their roles and power. With the support of the AMA, the loose coalition won passage in 1946 of the Hospital Survey and Construction Act, better known as the Hill-Burton Act.[10] The Hill-Burton Act was another milestone, not merely because of the $5 billion it has since provided for hospital construction and modernization, but because it marked the entrance of the State as a principal power in the medical care system.

THE STATE: RATIONALIZING THE PRIVATE MARKET

After World War II, the State became the conduit for more funds to expand and rationalize health care, taking over from foundations the primary role of financing reforms in medical education and later providing the operating funds for medical schools and medical care itself. The State's intervention would not, of course, be neutral. The State's interests are larger than those of any interest group, whether in health or in the larger economy, but the State is only relatively autonomous. In developed capitalist countries, it shares a mutual dependence on and an interdependence with the dominant economic class. Top government officials come disproportionately from the corporate class. The government's tax revenues depend on the "health" of the capitalist economy. And the government promotes and protects the larger interests of the corporate class, particularly its dominant sectors. Though it might be to the disadvantage of any one company at a particular point in time, in the long run, government regulation benefits the dominant firms in an industry by permitting monopolistic concentrations of economic power but preventing those concentrations from turning into devastating wars of economic conquest. The State facilitates the process of capital accumulation and legitimizes the existing capitalist society. The explicit reliance of the corporate class on the State was articulated by corporate liberals in the Progressive era. Although the State's intervention in organizing production and social relations was initiated during that period, it matured rapidly during the Great Depression and became the ruling order during and following World War II. The State became as important to medicine as it is to the larger economy.[11]

While the commitment of the State to rationalizing medical care was clear, it was not clear whether it would rationalize it under existing private ownership and control or whether it would rationalize it under government ownership and control, as many Western European nations were doing. The consequences would be important.

Rationalizing health services under private ownership and

control would accelerate the transformation from simple commodity production to capital-intensive commodity production
while nationalization would begin to transform health services
from commodities into a public service function. The direction
was not decided as a matter of policy. It was shaped and
constrained by economic and political developments in medical
care and the larger society—in part by the AMA's opposition to
national health insurance and the lack of a sufficiently strong and
threatening working-class movement, in part by the growth of the
powerful capitalist commodity sector in medical care, and in part
by the role of the State in advanced capitalist countries.

In Europe national health insurance programs were established either by fairly conservative governments in response to
militant working-class revolt that threatened to overturn State
power and capitalism itself or by labor or social democratic
parties that won sufficient electoral victories. In 1883 Bismarck
established the Sickness Insurance Act to help stem the growing
support for socialism among the German working class. In
England Lloyd George and the Liberal party enacted the
National Health Insurance Act in 1911 to win the workingmen's
swing vote away from the socialistic Labor party. When the
Labor party finally came to power after the Second World War, it
nationalized the hospitals and the insurance system in the
National Health Service Act.

In the United States the closest the working class came to
threatening ruling powers was during the Progressive era when
the Socialist party won significant election victories and its
militant wing was gaining support for more revolutionary activity.
In 1916 the American Association for Labor Legislation
(AALL), an alliance of Progressive businessmen and reformers
and nonsocialist labor leaders, introduced its model compulsory
medical insurance bill into several state legislatures. Although
some Progressive AMA officials supported the bill, the proposal
was crushed by private practitioners who organized within and
outside the AMA to defeat this "attack"[12] and by the conservatism and political repression that swept the country following
America's entry into the war.

In the absence of a sufficiently independent and militant
working-class movement, national health insurance continued to
be defeated in the decades that followed. Throughout the 1930s

and 1940s the AMA carried on its vehement opposition to any federal intervention into the financing of medical care. Liberal reformers tried to get national health insurance included in the Social Security Act as part of the New Deal response to the Great Depression and the militant organizing among the unemployed and industrial workers. But the AMA was powerful enough to strike any mention of health care from the Social Security bill. In the 1940s the AMA waged well-funded, energetic, and successful campaigns against the Wagner-Murray-Dingell and Truman proposals for a nationalized health insurance system. The association even came around to supporting voluntary private health insurance as "the American way" to undercut the growing support for a government-run national health insurance program.[13] Finally accepting defeat, liberal proponents of medical care reform retreated to advocating proposals for government health insurance restricted to the beneficiaries of Social Security programs.

The depression and the Second World War firmly established the principle of federal economic intervention to organize and stimulate production and necessary social institutions and services. The Hill-Burton Act was an example of that principle extended to medical care. But the AMA continued its decades-old opposition to increasing the number of medical students and defeated proposals for direct aid to medical schools. Nevertheless, a back door was opened with medical research funds—which the AMA welcomed as furthering the development of medical technology—to help pay some of the overhead and salaries at medical schools. In the 1950s construction grants and traineeships for medical schools were finally approved by Congress because of the intensifying public concern about a growing doctor shortage. The AMA was learning the limits of its political power.[14]

In the mid-1960s the advocates of rationalization won a major legislative and programmatic victory over the AMA with the passage of the Medicare and Medicaid bills, fallback programs from earlier efforts to obtain comprehensive national health insurance. Medicare is a Social Security program that covers most hospital, physician, and related medical services for more than 95 percent of all Americans over sixty-five years of age. Medicaid, a welfare-linked federal and state program, helps pay the health care costs of people on welfare and other "medically indigent" persons. Bitterly and expensively fought by the medical societies, the passage of Medicare and Medicaid signaled the further decline of the medical profession's power and the growing dominance of forces committed to rationalizing medical care.

Like private health insurance, these State subsidies and "third-party" programs were parts of larger strategies to rationalize health services. Since attempts to *nationalize* even health insurance appeared blocked, proponents of rationalization seemed content with rationalizing the *private* medical market.

THE GROWTH OF
CAPITAL-INTENSIVE COMMODITIES

While private health insurance provided a stable cash flow on which hospitals could depend and expand, Medicare and Medicaid seemed a limitless largess. They fed the market competition between hospitals and the avariciousness of hospital administrators, construction companies, banks, the medical supply industry and others who could get their hands into the public till. Following the introduction of Medicare and Medicaid, hospital and physician fees rose each year at twice their previous rates of increase, and the cost of medical care in general rose twice as fast as inflation in the rest of the economy. Capital investment per hospital bed rose three times as fast in the five years after Medicare and Medicaid began as it did in the five years before, reaching $56,000 per bed in 1976. Medicare and Medicaid picked up an even bigger share of the medical care bill—$37 billion in 1977, a fourth of all personal health care expenditures from all sources.[15]

Medicare and Medicaid, together with private health insurance, effectively subsidized the rapid expansion of capital-intensive medical care. Hospitals felt assured that everything from automated blood-chemistry analysis machines (costing upwards of $100,000) to computerized axial tomography (CAT) scanners (costing $300,000 to $750,000) could be paid for. Expansion has resulted in as many as 100,000 excess hospital beds in the country, averaging about $20,000 per bed in annual operating costs.[16] Banks were among those who profited from this expansion by providing hospitals with profitable commercial loans, usually guaranteed by the government.[17] Clinical laboratories, hospital and medical supply, drug, and nursing home industries similarly boomed.

An increasing share of the medical commodities being produced were capital-intensive ones compared with physician services. The "average" person spent seven to eight times more on physician and dentist services in 1977 than in 1950, but he or she spent twelve times more on hospital care and forty-nine times more on nursing home care.[18] With the expansion of private health insurance and especially with the passage of Medicare and Medicaid, the power of physicians shrank relative to the increasing economic and political power of the capital-intensive medical sector. This sector has now surpassed the medical profession as the dominant political force in medical care, mainly because of the shared interests of three important groups.

THE "CORPORATE RATIONALIZERS"

Medicaid and Medicare are the offspring of the groups that articulated the majority position of the Committee on the Costs of Medical Care, helped the American Hospital Association develop and coordinate the role of the hospital as the "logical center" of the health care system, and secured passage of the Hill-Burton and other federal aid programs. They are what Robert Alford calls the "corporate rationalizers,"[19] favoring the coordination and organizational integration of the different parts of the medical care system, or as they refer to it, the "nonsystem."

In reality, there are three distinct groups that favor rationalization—two interest groups and a class. One interest group is composed of bureaucratic professionals—academic physicians and public health officialdom, advisers, planners, and consultants. They are the functionaries of bureaucratically organized medical care who staff the increasing layers of government units, medical schools, and health agencies and organizations of all types. Although the bureaucratic professionals generally maintain that the major goals of medical reform are equal access for the poor and racial minorities and more accessible primary care for everyone, they have a material interest in such reforms because they gain power and status with each new level of rationalization. They are the technicians and managers on whom foundations and government rely for planning and conducting the reforms that are proposed and implemented. Bureaucratic professionals are the least powerful of the three groups because their positions are dependent on those whom they serve.

The second interest group among the rationalizers are those industries with a direct economic stake in the medical market—the market rationalizers. The two most active industries in this group are hospitals and health insurance carriers. In 1976, voluntary hospitals, as privately owned nonprofit hospitals are called, claimed 70 percent of the beds, 72 percent of the average daily patient census, and 76 percent of the assets of nonfederal short-term hospitals.[20] And they took the lion's share of the more than $65 billion spent on hospital care in 1977, making them a major economic force in the health sector. While their existence does not depend on the medical commodity marketplace—that is, they would exist even in a nationalized health system—their autonomous power is greatly enhanced by this privately controlled market system. Like any corporation, hospitals have entrepreneurial power to capture what they can of the market,[21] accumulate a surplus of revenues above expenses, and allocate resources within the constraints of the market.

Similarly, Blue Cross and Blue Shield, though "not for profit," aggressively marketed about $19 billion of their insurance products in the medical market in 1977. Like the "Blues," profit-making insurance companies, which collected about $20 billion in health insurance premiums in that year, depend for their existence on the market system for medical care. The traditionally close ties of Blue Cross and Blue Shield to hospitals and medical societies, respectively, have weakened in recent years because of public pressure over rapid rate increases which brought stronger regulation and formal separation from their parent bodies. The Blues and commercial carriers now share increasingly similar interests in holding down medical costs to what the premium market will bear. Together with drug companies, banks, and other profit-making concerns, hospitals and insurance companies have a direct stake in the ascendance of an expanding commodity system in medical care, especially with the enormous State subsidies represented by Medicare and Medicaid or a national health insurance program. Their interest in rationalization is limited to expanding the market for their wares and protecting their respective places in the increasingly rationalized system they see as inevitable.

The third group of rationalizers is the corporate class, including those who own or manage the nation's corporate wealth and foundation trustees and officers who supervise the expenditure of that portion of the wealth that is devoted to managing social institutions. The contemporary corporate class includes the main shareholders and the top officers in the largest corporations. It certainly includes the one-half of one (0.5) percent of the nation's population who own one-fifth of all the nation's wealth, including half the net worth of all bonds and corporate stock.[22] Economic power is similarly concentrated among corporations, a minute fraction of which (0.06 percent, or 958 corporations) held a majority (53.2 percent) of all corporate assets in 1967. Similar concentrations are found in the separate economic sectors—manufacturing, banking, and insurance among them.[23]

Power is concentrated among foundations, too. Of the 2,818 foundations in the United States in 1976, the top eight (representing three-tenths of one percent of all foundations) held an average of $948 million in assets while three-fourths held less than $5 million each, and another fifth had assets of $5 million to $25 million.[24] The top eight—including such important ones in the health field as the Robert Wood Johnson, Rockefeller, Kresge, and Kellogg foundations—have an enormously disproportionate impact on educational, scientific, and cultural institutions. Although the members of this class do not think alike by any means, they share a common interest in maintaining the capitalist economic system and their collective positions of power and wealth in it.[25]

As my analysis of the involvement of earlier capitalists in medicine demonstrates, the corporate class has a compelling, but narrow interest, in the health of the people and the kind of medical care provided for them. But that interest extends only to assuring that the population maintains sufficient physical and mental health to provide an adequate work force and that medical care encourages dependence on technical and professional management of individual problems. Capitalists may be concerned about accessibility, as Gates was, because an inaccessible system cannot perform its designated functions. They may even favor the complete nationalization of medical care, as

Vicente Navarro points out,[26] to raise productivity or placate threatening movements and bolster the failing legitimacy of the system.

However, corporate owners and managers and foundation trustees and officers are ideologically reluctant to view private ownership and control as inherently problematic in providing for social needs. Members of the class who are associated with corporations obviously profit directly from the private control of capital accumulation while the influence of foundation members derives from their foundations' investments in corporate wealth. They thus share a material interest in ignoring any conflict between private control of resources and the stated goals of rationalizing medical care.

Bureaucratic professionals, medical industries, and the corporate class coalesced around their common interests—expanding capital-intensive medical care and bureaucratic organization as the main features of rationalization, being careful not to trample on private ownership and control. Faced with this corporate model of rationalization, how did the State respond?

THE STATE AND CAPITALIST MEDICINE

The State intervened with subsidy, incentive, and regulatory programs to readjust the market system, decrease the market economy's inequitable distribution of medical commodities, and restrain the unusually inflationary forces of the medical marketplace. Although it has provided "categorical" programs for those who could not afford essential medical services, the State has not tried to replace the commodity market with an equitably distributed public service. Because the power of the medical profession, in the absence of sufficient countervailing pressure, blocked efforts to nationalize the financing and delivery of medical care in this country, the privately owned and privately controlled system was simply expanded through direct subsidies and incentives. Expansion and subsidy favored the development of a capital-intensive commodity medical sector both because it was the economically dominant portion of the medical market and because it was consistent with the ideological perspectives and material interests of the corporate class.

Those corporation and foundation members who have no

investment in profit-making medical industries see the health care system as a support industry for the primary and secondary sectors of the economy. But by the 1950s the powerful finance sector of the economy, represented by insurance companies and banks, had developed a large stake in the subsidized medical market. Few members of the corporate class, even those without profit-making medical investments, railed against "commercialism" in medicine, as Rockefeller philanthropy officers had done in their drive against private practitioners early in the century. Even most bureaucratic professionals, who do not themselves have a financial stake in profit-making medical care, preferred to ignore the issue.[27]

The more the State intervened financially in the medical care system, the more likely it became that it would have to intervene politically to control the system in which it had developed a principal financial interest. Employers worried about the growing cost of health plan benefits they were paying. In 1976 General Motors spent more on Blue Cross and Blue Shield plans, about one billion dollars, than it did on purchases from U.S. Steel. Steel companies, banks, airlines, and most industries were unhappy about the 10 to 25 percent a year increase in the cost of employee health insurance benefits.[28] And unions were concerned because every increase in health insurance rates (paid for through fringe benefits) cuts into potential pay raises for their members. Other health services "consumer" groups also criticized the shrinking proportion of physicians and services devoted to primary care and the rising expenses that consumers had to pay out of their own pockets, in spite of increasing insurance coverage. Congress, the executive branch, and state governments were fearful of their impending fiscal crises in which expenditures were rapidly outstripping tax revenues; they wanted to restrain the rising costs of their medical care programs, which had increased from a fourth of total health expenditures before Medicare and Medicaid began to more than 42 percent in less than ten years.[29]

By the time market conditions and rising State subsidies necessitated rationalization, the only substantial profit-making medical sector without sufficient protective support in the corporate class or other powerful sectors of society was the *petty* commodity sector—private practitioners. The control and regulation of physician services seemed inevitable because doctors' orders for their patients' hospital stays and procedures were important elements in the meteoric rise in tax dollars being spent on Medicare and Medicaid as well as private expenditures for health services. Prepaid group practices, which originated in the 1920s and were strongly recommended by the Committee on the Costs of Medical Care, became a major part of the reorganization plans of rationalizers. Despite long-standing opposition from medical societies, the federal government promoted these pre-paid plans, called Health Maintenance Organizations (HMOs). HMOs have a built-in incentive to keep costs down because they convert high utilization by patients from an asset to the provider, as in fee-for-service practice, to a liability when a person gets all his or her care for a monthly fee paid in advance.[30] Bureaucratic organization seems destined to replace solo private practitioners.

In 1972, despite the AMA's enormous lobbying machine in Washington, the rationalizing forces won congressional approval of a bill to create Professional Standards Review Organizations (PSROs) that would establish utilization review over individ-ual practitioners' services to Medicare and Medicaid recipients. Some state and local medical societies, wanting nothing to do with outside review even if it were controlled by the profession, threatened to boycott the required program. But the AMA *Journal,* acknowledging the handwriting on the wall, soberly warned physicians: "If we stand as a rock against the current, our base will be eroded and we will be swept aside. Organized medicine must remain elastic and adapt to our time. To do less is to invite extinction in the manner of dinosaurs and dodos. . . . There are perilous times ahead but we must participate if we are to prevail."[31] As an example of their new realism, the AMA dropped its half-century-long opposition to any form of national health insurance and put forth its own "Medi-Credit" proposal to try to salvage for private practice physicians conditions that would permit their survival.

DIVIDED THEY STAND

Just as the unity among elite private practitioners and medical school faculty dissolved after their victory over traditional doctors and medical sectarianism early in this century, so is the unity among corporate rationalizers more fragile now that their victory over private practice medicine is in sight. Hospitals, though the centerpiece of rationalized health care, have become the *bête noire* to groups trying to contain rising health care expenditures. The state and local Comprehensive Health Planning agencies, mandated by Congress in the mid-1960s, failed to put a sufficient brake on hospital expansion and escalating costs. Their successors, a somewhat strengthened network of Health Systems Agencies (HSAs) created by the National Health Planning and Resources Development Act of 1974 (P.L. 93-641), are another attempt to bring order to the economic chaos of the unregulated medical market and to avert the fiscal bankruptcy of the government's medical care programs. While these agencies, in combination with state-run Certificate of Need programs, will probably slow expansion of hospitals and their acquisition of very expensive equipment, they are unlikely to bring the different medical interest groups to heel.[32]

Members of the corporate class, through business organizations and foundations, push for reform of medical care to improve its delivery of primary care services and to rationalize its organization and financing. The Committee for Economic Development (CED), a policy organization with representatives from nearly 200 major corporations, has urged the restructuring of medical care into HMOs, the development of national health insurance, and increased government planning and regulation of medical care providers.[33] Foundations similarly use their corporate wealth to encourage the coordination of care around hospitals and academic medical centers, with an emphasis on promoting "front-line" or primary medical care so badly neglected by the technology-oriented, medical market. The Robert Wood Johnson Foundation, with more than $1 billion in assets derived from the Johnson and Johnson band-aid empire, spends its funds entirely in the health field. The Rockefeller Foundation, with assets over $700 million, the Kellogg Foundation, with nearly $1 billion in assets, the Kresge Foundation, with more than $600 million in assets, and others all place great emphasis on reforming medical care.[34] Although their wealth is enormous, it is dwarfed by the health expenditures of the federal government each year. The foundations, therefore, concern themselves with developing model programs, which may then be taken over by the government, and with directly influencing policy in government as well as in medical care institutions.

The attempts of foundations and the State to rationalize health care have simply been superimposed over the market economy for health services. Despite their appealing rhetoric favoring coordination, integration, and planning, bureaucratic and corporate rationalizers are unable to control all the necessary factors in the production and provision of health services and products.[35] Doctors, hospitals, insurance companies, the Blues, drug and hospital supply and equipment companies, and medical schools all seek the commanding role in the health system—or at least the lion's share of its resources. Present rationalizing strategies conceal the disparity between stated goals and political and economic reality; they appeal to legislative and bureaucratic mechanisms to unify and integrate the system.

The failure of one mechanism is taken as evidence of the need for another patchwork mechanism. Endemic inflationary problems, caused in part by Medicare and Medicaid, were answered with Comprehensive Health Planning agencies, and their failure was the impetus for the creation of Health Systems Agencies (HSAs). Falk, the research director for the Committee on the Costs of Medical Care half a century ago, warned recently that the powerful interest groups in medical care will all be reluctant to let their interests be overridden by some higher social interest. But he is left with the strikingly naive hope that these "resistances will have to be overcome as far as possible by the *reasonableness* of the proposals and the *persuasiveness* of the explanations, and beyond that, by confrontations in the *legislative arena*."[36]

Such mechanical solutions, which dominate health planning, ignore the substantial political and economic power that simultaneously unites and divides the system's interests. The medical care system has evolved into a glut of interest groups, none of which has sufficient power to prevail by itself. Although the proponents of corporate rationalization have prevailed over the petty commodity sector, they do not share among themselves an interest in the coordination and integration of the entire system. However, their occasional bickering among themselves—for example, over who will be regulated and how much[37]—should not be mistaken for fundamental opposition. Corporate rationalizers and organized medicine share an overriding and unifying interest in the private ownership and private control of social resources. Each group is best able to promote its own survival, growth, and profits if it is not subordinate to either the State or any other interest group. Alford argues,

> Differences between dominant and challenging interests should not be overemphasized . . . because both professional monopoly and corporate rationalization are modes of organizing health care within the context of a market society. Both must avoid encroachments upon their respective positions of power and privilege which depend upon continuation of market institutions: the ownership and control of individual labor, facilities, and organizations (even nonprofit ones) by autonomous groups and individuals, with no meaningful mechanisms of public control.[38]

Thus the State has entered into the medical care arena very much as the foundations had. Whatever the intent of the supporters of specific legislative programs, federal and state programs have, in sum, furthered the transformation of medical care from simple commodities, produced and sold largely by private-practice physicians, to capital-intensive commodities, produced and sold by bureaucratic organizations that assemble large amounts of capital and hired labor and strive to accumulate a surplus of revenue over expenses.

State intervention to rationalize medical care thus benefited interest groups whose existence depends on technological medicine—especially hospitals, health insurance carriers, and medical technology industries—more than it helped the medical profession, although doctors gained financially, too. How did consumers fare in these developments? Did they also benefit from the State's rationalization of the private medical market?

UP AGAINST THE MEDICAL MARKET

The combination of private and public third-party payment programs has reduced the gross inequalities in utilization of medical care, but these programs have neither eliminated the inequities nor provided health care matched to the population's health needs. Rather than *need* determining the allocation and distribution of health services, which equity would require, we find that services became distributed according to their prevailing markets. The "commodification" of health services remains the major cause of the inaccessibility of health services to the poor and a major factor in the distortion of care to the entire society.

Over the last three decades private health insurance and public assistance programs have narrowed the gaps between the poor and nonpoor in their use of health services. Poor adults from eighteen to sixty-four years old now make slightly more visits to a physician on the average than do nonpoor adults. However, the poor at all ages receive less care relative to their *need* for medical care. The disparity between need and what's received is especially great for children.[39]

The reasons for these class differences are not difficult to find. First, many physicians do not accept Medicaid patients because Medicaid programs, which are administered by the states within federal guidelines, pay less than doctors are used to getting from their privately insured patients. In California, only about a third of the state's obstetricians and gynecologists participate in the Medicaid program, leaving nearly a third of the state's fifty-eight counties without a single obstetrician or gynecologist to serve Medicaid women.[40] Second, white physicians and dentists generally do not locate their offices in poor or minority communities.[41] Third, as of 1971 nearly half the country's 35.5 million people officially defined as poor had no Medicaid coverage.[42]

Health insurance itself is distributed in part according to the class structure. Today 90 percent of all Americans have some form of health insurance, three-fourths of them from private insurance plans. In general, however, the most comprehensive health insurance is available to persons in higher paying occupations and in the dominant sectors of the economy, which are more unionized and can more easily pass along the costs of health insurance to consumers. In 1974 some 60 percent of the employed poor had no health insurance at all, and fewer than 10 percent were insured for nonhospital services.[43]

While the growth of private health insurance and government third-party payment programs helped reduce the inequities, they do not cover all people or all health services equally well. In 1977 sixty-one cents of each dollar spent on personal health care services were paid by third-party payment plans, leaving consumers to pay thirty-nine cents of each dollar out of their own pockets. Third-party payers covered more than 90 percent of the cost of hospital care, but only 61 percent of physician fees and even less for drugs and other commodities.[44]

Thus, even with the government subsidizing medical care for the poor, the production and sale of medical care as commodities are still distributed according to the class structure of the society rather than on the basis of need. However, those at the bottom of the class structure have not been the only ones to suffer under this market economy.

The market system has also distorted the character and supply of medical care for most of the population. The relatively complete private and public third-party coverage of hospital care has encouraged hospitalization for diagnostic and therapeutic procedures that could be done more safely and inexpensively outside hospitals—or avoided altogether.

Most surgery in the United States is done on a fee-for-service basis. Doctors get paid high surgical fees for the operations they perform, not for those cases in which they decide surgery is unnecessary. As Dr. Charles Lewis has observed, "Patient admissions for surgery expand to fill beds, operating suites, and surgeons' time."[45] The United States has twice the ratio of full-time surgeons to its population as England and Wales—and twice as high rates of surgery.[46] A congressional report estimated that in 1974 approximately 2.4 million unnecessary operations were performed in this country, resulting in 11,900 *avoidable* deaths and a cost of $3.9 billion.[47]

Nationally, Medicaid patients have become a major source of revenue for "underemployed" surgeons and underutilized hospital facilities. Medicaid recipients undergo surgery at twice the rate of the general population and for some elective operations (that is, for conditions that are not life-threatening) the difference is even greater.[48] Many well-insured persons—whether they be privately insured members of the working class and middle class or government-subsidized members of the poor and near-poor strata—have been victimized by excessive care just as the poor have historically been victimized by being priced out of adequate medical care.

Physicians have concentrated themselves in specialties and locations where they can take best advantage of the market for their services. Because physicians have such a strong influence on the demand for their services, large numbers of doctors in even a relatively small but affluent area make an exceptionally fine living by ordering enormous numbers of diagnostic and therapeutic procedures which they either perform or evaluate. Their market in the past relied mainly on the middle and upper classes, and because of the financial and bureaucratic constraints of Medicaid, doctors are still attracted more to the shrinking but well-off areas of big cities and the expanding suburbs than to poor and working-class areas. While affluent areas of Chicago average 210 physicians per 100,000 persons, poverty areas have sixteen doctors per 100,000—one-eighth as many physicians to population. Similarly, Mississippi has only a third as many doctors as New York state's abundant average of 244 per 100,000.[49]

Physicians have also abandoned primary care practice for more lucrative and prestigious specialties. General practitioners, who in 1963 comprised nearly 28 percent of the country's nonfederal physicians, by 1973 represented less than 18 percent of the total. If we add to these GPs those specialists whose practices are mainly focused on primary care—those in internal medicine, pediatrics, gynecology, and family practice—still less than half of all U.S. physicians are involved in primary care. By contrast, prepaid group practices average 69 percent of their physicians in primary care and the British National Health Service includes 74 percent. This leaves the United States with only sixty primary care physicians per 100,000 population, far below the ratio of 133 such doctors per 100,000 persons recommended as necessary to provide adequate primary care.[50]

Since the turn of the century, the generalist and primary care have taken a back seat to specialized practice and sometimes even a career in medical research. The countryside, with its limited market for specialty services and its isolation from centers of technological medicine, cannot compete with more densely populated urban areas with their hospitals linked to research-oriented medical schools. Rural areas were of no interest to modern physicians, and the urban poor were of interest only when they served as research or teaching material. The technological imperative in medicine combined with the market organization of medical care to divert physicians from areas and types of services in which they were most needed to those that were most interesting, profitable, and professionally rewarding to them. In sum, the private medical market has remained a major contradiction in efforts to provide an accessible system of medicine geared to the needs of the population.

NATIONAL HEALTH INSURANCE:
MORE OF THE SAME

It can be stated as almost a certainty that national health insurance in the United States will continue to promote capital-intensive medical care in a market system. Each major medical interest group is represented by a bill in Congress. The AMA, the insurance industry, and the American Hospital Association have all submitted bills that would favor their members. The AFL-CIO and most bureaucratic professionals support the successive bills sponsored by Senator Edward Kennedy. The Kennedy bills would go farther than other national health insurance bills in providing comprehensive and accessible care. Some versions of the bill would even eliminate any administrative or third-party role for insurance companies. All versions include an incentive payment system to encourage physicians to join prepaid group practices. While the Kennedy proposals would weaken the financial base of fee-for-service medicine, none of them would eliminate it nor would they eliminate the professional control of hospitals and medical schools.

Only one proposal now under consideration would radically alter the commodity system of medical care. The Health Service Act, a bill sponsored by Representative Ronald Dellums, would create a national health *service* that would employ physicians and all other personnel on a salaried basis, take over the nation's hospitals, control the production of health workers in medical schools and other training programs, eliminate insurance companies from health care, and reduce the hierarchy of power among health workers by subordinating all policy to community-based boards. The Dellums bill would effectively transform the commodity production of medical care into noncommodity "social production." Were the Dellums proposal implemented, it would give the United States one of the most advanced health care systems in the world, surpassing the most progressive systems in Western Europe and perhaps equaling the organizational rationality and public service character of health care in many socialist countries. The Dellums bill is supported by a small proportion of bureaucratic professionals, some of whom are leaders of the American Public Health Association, and by left-of-center political groups. So thoroughly does it assault every vested interest in health care and the ideological tenets of capitalist society that it is a virtual certainty that the Dellums bill will not see the light of legislative victory in the near future. Nevertheless, it may serve as a model for those who want to reform the U.S. medical care system.

The more far-reaching of the Kennedy bills are also unlikely to win congressional approval. Their attacks on the interests of the AMA, the best-financed lobby in the country, and the insurance industry, not only a powerful lobby but a controlling force in the nation's economy as well, make their legislative future very dim. The other bills submitted by medical interest groups will also fail because they too narrowly support the interests of one sector of the industry. Instead, an administration-sponsored bill will become the foundation of national health legislation, with amendments and revisions made to accommodate the more powerful interest groups that have entered the fray.

The legislation that emerges from this process will undoubtedly favor the medical market and enhance the capital-intensive sector of the system. It is likely that whatever plan is adopted will convert additional services that are now provided by the government into commodities that can be bought and sold on the private market.[51] The insurance system will organize the collection and payment of private funds into this commodity system with federal tax dollars subsidizing only those who are priced out of the medical market, thereby increasing the access of those groups to medical care. While national health insurance will probably encourage a slight redistribution of physicians, geographically and between specialties and primary care, it will *not* break up the power of interest groups and their manipulation of the medical market to their advantages. It is likely that national health insurance will push doctors toward prepaid group practice at a slightly faster rate, and it will strengthen the control of most dominant interest groups—especially the hospitals, medical schools, insurance companies, and drug and medical supply industries. More regulation will be developed to restrain inflationary forces, somewhat protecting the interests of the State, and to prevent the competitive interests of each segment from destroying the medical care system they share. In other words, through national health insurance, the State will intensify the capital-intensive commodity production of medical care and rationalize the medical system in ways that further the common interests of the system's dominant members. If this sounds familiar, it should. National health insurance essentially promises to give us more of the same.

Given the present size and importance of the medical commodity sector and the absence of militant demands from the underclasses, the State will continue to develop the role it has increasingly taken over from foundations since World War II. It will protect and promote a medical care system that is compatible with corporate capitalist society's economic and political organization—not only in the organization of medical care, but in its content as well.

TECHNOLOGICAL MEDICINE

After World War II, the State rapidly replaced foundations as the major source of financial support and direction in medical research and education, just as it did in medical care. As the remainder of this chapter will demonstrate, the State, like foundations and wealthy individuals before it, continued to promote and develop a narrowly technical and ideologically conservative type of medicine—despite the overwhelming evidence that broad factors in the physical and social environment have at least as great an impact on health status as the microbiological factors that receive most of the attention.

SCIENTIFIC MEDICINE: BELIEFS AND REALITY

Nearly all of us turn to medicine when we are sick. Whether the healer is called a shaman, a witchdoctor, a priest, a feldsher, or a physician, we all seek someone in whom to place our confidence, someone we believe will make us well. Early in the nineteenth century, most Americans relied on lay healers. By the middle or latter part of that century, most Americans turned to physicians, who were being prodigiously produced in mush-rooming medical schools throughout the land. At the time, one could choose the particular medical theory one wanted in a physician—from homeopathy to orthodox or "allopathic" medicine—or the particular type of healer—from herbal traditions to Christian Science. Not until the last two decades of the last century were there any significant number of physicians who practiced what they called "scientific" medicine, meaning a medical practice based on principles continuously being developed and refined by the analytic biological and physical sciences.

Today most of us look to doctors and hospitals and surgery and drugs to cure us of every ill. We want solace, and, therefore, we expect it. The medical profession has, of course, encouraged such beliefs through its campaigns to increase the confidence of the populace (described in Chapter 2). Other medical interest groups, like the American Cancer Society and the National Cancer Institute, have joined in the campaign for public confidence, frequently hosting briefing sessions for newspapers' science and medical writers to learn about the "latest advances" in cancer treatment. We have come to credit scientific, technological medicine with having reduced the enormously high death rates of past centuries and with being effective against most disease and suffering in our time.[52] Yet such past successes and current prowess are greatly exaggerated.

LIFE, DEATH, AND MEDICINE

THE HISTORICAL RECORD

Historical epidemiological evidence overwhelmingly supports the conclusion that medical science has played a relatively *small* role in reducing morbidity and mortality. Thomas McKeown[53] argues very convincingly that improved health and the great decline in Western Europe's total death rate from the eighteenth century to the present were due to four factors. First, nutrition improved because food supplies increased from the early eighteenth century, due initially to the reorganization of agriculture rather than improved chemical or mechanical technology. Second, environmental sanitation measures—cleaning up the accumulated filth of the cities, assuring uncontaminated water supplies, and so forth—instituted by the late nineteenth century added to improved nutrition and further reduced mortality, particularly of children. These measures were well underway by the middle of the century, before either the concept of specific causes of disease or the germ theory was widely accepted. Third, these improvements in the standard of living caused a substantial increase in population, which would have overrun the gains in health if birth rates and family size had not soon sharply declined. Finally, specific preventive and therapeutic medical measures gradually introduced in the twentieth century slightly accelerated the already substantial decline in mortality and also improved physical health. While science greatly extended the original nontechnological advances in agriculture, hygiene, and birth control, the contribution of medical science to the overall reduction in death rates and improved health was relatively quite small.

In the great majority of cases the toll of the major killing diseases of the nineteenth century declined dramatically *before* the discovery of medical cures and even immunization. Tuberculosis, the Great White Plague, was one of the dread diseases of the nineteenth century, killing 500 people per 100,000 population at midcentury and 200 people per 100,000 in 1900. By 1967 the U.S. rate had dropped to three deaths per 100,000. This tremendous decline was only slightly affected by the introduction of collapse therapy in the 1930s and chemotherapy in the 1950s.[54] Similarly, for England and Wales John Powles shows that overall mortality declined over the last hundred years well in advance of specific immunizations and therapies.[55]

René Dubos, the microbiologist formerly with the Rockefeller Institute, succinctly summed up the historical record. "The tide of infectious and nutritional diseases was rapidly receding when the laboratory scientist moved into action at the end of the past century," Dubos wrote in *Mirage of Health*. "In reality," he observed, "the monstrous specter of infection had become but an enfeebled shadow of its former self by the time serums, vaccines, and drugs became available to combat microbes."[56]

Improvements in general living and working conditions as well as sanitation, all brought about by labor struggles and social reform movements, are most responsible for improved health status. Improved housing, working conditions, and nutrition—not medical science—reduced TB's fearsome death toll. Responding to riots and insurrections as well as the pitiable living conditions of the poor and working classes in Western Europe and North America, nineteenth-century reformers brought dramatic declines in mortality without the benefit of even the germ theory.[57]

Children have benefited the most from these changes. The average baby born in 1900 could have expected to live only forty-seven years. A baby born in 1973 can expect to live more than seventy-one years. Most of this increased life expectancy at birth has been due to a sharp decline in infants' and young children's deaths from infectious diseases. At the turn of the century young children succumbed to influenza, pneumonia, diarrhea, scarlet fever, diphtheria, whooping cough, and measles. By 1975 the infant death rate had fallen to sixteen per 1,000 live births—less than one-ninth the rate in 1900. And the death rates of young children have similarly declined.[58] Improved housing, nutrition, water supplies and waste disposal, pasteurization of milk, and the virtual elimination of child labor (except for migrant farm workers) drastically cut the spread of infectious diseases and enabled children's bodies to resist them.

LIFE, DEATH, AND MEDICINE TODAY

The physical and social environments are just as important in determining disease and death rates today as they were historically, despite the fact that "degenerative" diseases, such as heart disease, cancer, and stroke, have replaced most of the infectious diseases as leading causes of death.

Infant death rates are still strongly influenced by environmental factors. Twelve countries—Sweden, East Germany, and England among them—have lower infant death rates than the United States. Within the United States an infant born to a black mother with eight years of schooling or less is three times as likely to die before its first birthday as a baby born to a white college-educated mother. Although white and black infant death rates have decreased in parallel through most of this century, the death rate for black infants has remained consistently about twice the rate for white babies. And a baby born into a poor family, white or black, is much more likely to die than if he or she were born into a nonpoor family.[59]

Indeed, a person who is poor or nonwhite is more likely to die at *every* age. Nonwhite children die at twice the rate of white children. Up to the age of sixty-five, nonwhite male death rates exceed white male death rates by 40 to 95 percent, and nonwhite females die at more than twice the rate of white females in most age groups.[60] The probability of being disabled (temporarily or permanently) is negatively related to income and education, but positively related to being black.[61] The more privileged your class, race, education, and occupation, the less likely you are to get sick or die at each age.[62] As epidemiologist Warren Winkelstein put it, poverty "remains among the most powerful determinants of altered health status and clinical disease today. It may well be that elimination of poverty in and of itself would drastically alter the health status of the population in a favorable direction."[63]

Environmental and occupational pollutants are also major determinants of disease and death rates. Even "normal" levels of air pollution have been associated with increased rates of disease. Air pollution causes temporary deterioration of lung function and increased frequency of lower respiratory tract infections in children, in whom smoking and occupational dust exposures are assumed to be minimal. Air pollution is also associated with lung, stomach, and other forms of cancer, as well as chronic bronchitis and asthma.[64]

More than 14,000 workers are killed each year in work accidents, and between 2.5 million and 5.6 million workers suffer temporarily or permanently disabling injuries on the job. Occupation-related diseases are estimated to kill well over 100,000 persons each year.[65] Even the president of the Blue Cross Association has estimated that "31 percent of workers' health problems are caused by factors in their environment."[66]

Social relations—the patterned ways in which individuals relate to one another in society—also have a broad and dramatic impact on how healthy people are and how long they live. Hypertension, or high blood pressure, is associated with the stresses of moving to or living in industrialized, urban society; it is also related to working at high-pressure jobs and to being poor or black.[67] The poor and racial minorities have higher rates of alcoholism, mental illness, and homicide, and nonwhites at every age die at rates 40 to 100 percent higher than those of whites. From birth to old age, males have higher rates of death than females, including death from many stress-related diseases, such as heart attacks and strokes, and from many nondisease causes of death, such as auto accidents, work accidents, homicides, and suicides.[68] Even whether labor is alienated or satisfying is related to life expectancy. A Department of Health, Education, and Welfare task force reported that "in an impressive 15-year study of aging, the strongest predictor of longevity was work satisfaction."[69] Clearly, people's social roles and their positions in the social structure have a major impact on their health.

Health and disease are thus determined by a combination of factors. Genetic inheritance is one conditioning factor, and the social, economic, and physical environment into which people are born and in which they must live are other critical factors. These factors determine the person's receptivity to disease as an unwitting "host." Whether a person remains healthy or gets sick is determined by inheritance, environment, and external "insults" to the person—bacteria and viruses, chemical and physical assaults on the body, social and emotional assaults.

Technological intervention in this process is very limited. Robert Haggerty, a nationally respected pediatrician, recounts some of the limitations of children's medicine in the 1970s:

> We do not know how to prevent or treat effectively most of the major killing disorders of childhood in the United States. . . . The state of knowledge about acute and chronic conditions that usually do not kill but impair function for short or long periods is not much better. There is little we can now do to prevent or treat specifically most acute respiratory infections or chronic handicapping conditions.[70]

Efforts to improve medical care in very poor communities have had only a slight impact on people's health. A well-known project that brought advanced primary care to a Navajo community succeeded in reducing the recurrence of active tuberculosis and the prevalence of infections of the middle ear but had little or no effect on the pneumonia-diarrhea complex which continued as the biggest single cause of illness and death as it had throughout the country up to half a century ago. By the end of the experiment the infant mortality rate for the community remained about three times the national average.[71] Other experiments in the United States and underdeveloped countries have had similar results.[72]

These sobering observations of the limits of medicine and the importance of the environment should reduce our enthusiasm for turning to medical science and physicians to cure all our ills. But we need not become "therapeutic nihilists"[73] in the process. While we reject the popular mythology that cloaks medicine in robes of omniscience, while we reject the unquestioning assumption that technology can solve all our health problems, we must recognize the advances and considerable value of modern medicine. Until the 1930s all but a few drugs were palliatives, at best relieving the symptoms of a disease. Sulfonamides were developed in the 1930s, penicillin in the 1940s, and other antibiotics in the 1950s. All were major additions to the arsenal of physicians in the long-anticipated "war against disease." The most rapid development of technical advances in medicine occurred from the late 1930s, accelerated during and after the war in the 1940s, and peaked in the 1950s.

Only some medical care, however, has had a significant positive impact on the health status of the population. Campaigns to immunize the population with polio vaccines, introduced in the 1950s, have reduced one of the most dread childhood diseases from 18,000 cases in 1954 to only six in 1975. Rubella (or "German measles"), which in pregnant women can cause devastating congenital defects in their offspring, was reduced from an average of more than 47,000 cases a year before widespread use of the vaccine to 16,343 cases in 1975, following even limited immunization of the population.[74]

Good maternal health services—including prenatal and maternal medical care *and* coordinated social services—provided to the entire population could materially reduce infant mortality rates. David Kessner and other researchers, who carefully studied New York City births in 1968, concluded that adequate maternal health services provided to all women in the city would have reduced infant mortality there by one-third. The percentage of low-birth-weight infants and infant deaths both decreased as the adequacy of maternal health services increased, within each racial, socioeconomic, social-risk, and medical-risk group. Among college-educated mothers, the infants of those with inadequate care were twice as likely to die as the babies of those with adequate care. Among black college-educated mothers, the infant death rate for those with inadequate maternal care was six times as great as the rate for those with adequate care.[75] As valuable as good maternal care is, however, one-quarter of the substantial decline in the infant mortality rate in the late 1960s is accounted for by women giving birth at lower risk ages (mainly in their twenties) and having fewer children.[76]

Thus, comprehensive health services can have a limited but positive impact on health status. Some vaccines have substantially reduced infectious disease and death rates, although historically most have simply accelerated already falling rates. Antibiotics and sulfa drugs have also reduced disability and death from infectious diseases. Recently developed antibiotics have greatly reduced the isolation and convalescence of TB patients. Adequate maternal care can lower infant mortality rates although most of the decline has been and is still due to improvements in environmental conditions and patterns of child-bearing. In general, comprehensive primary medical care can help limit the progress of disease and help restore a sick or injured child or adult to healthy development and functioning. When distributed throughout the population, such care can contribute to improving the general health status of that population. *When combined with social reforms—particularly ones that would eliminate the inequities of class, the brutality of racism, and the destruction of the physical environment—good technological medical care and supportive personal and social services can reduce the burden of disease an individual, a family, or a society must bear.* From the Progressive era to the present, however, foundation- and government-sponsored medical research and medical care have been narrowly technological and ideologically conservative.

TAPPING THE STATE TREASURY

Up to World War II foundations were the leading force, besides the medical profession, shaping the direction of medical education and research and, ultimately, medical theory and practice. By 1940 the Rockefeller philanthropies alone had contributed more than $161 million to medical education and medical research.[77]

Until World War II the federal government's support for medical research and education was minor. In 1938 the Public Health Service's research budget amounted to only $2.8 million. In order to develop and apply medical research to the country's war needs, however, the Committee on Medical Research was set up in 1941 in the new Office of Scientific Research and Development. By 1944 the committee had received $15 million to allocate to medical research activities.[78]

After the war federal support for medical education and research blossomed. The AMA's opposition to direct financial aid for medical education was circumvented by channeling Hill-Burton funds to teaching hospitals and turning on the spigot of federal support for medical research, both of which the AMA approved. The National Institutes of Health became the major single source of medical research money. Its research budget doubled from $28 million in 1950 to $60 million in 1955, and doubled again every two or three years up to 1963. By 1975 total federal health research expenditures reached $2.8 billion, sixty cents out of every dollar spent by all sources on health research. While the federal government's expenditures increased more than thirty-six times in this period, philanthropy's contributions increased only six times.[79]

What was responsible for this astronomical increase in State support for technological medicine? Three sets of interests benefited from this emphasis on and funding of technological medicine—the academic medical profession, the corporate class as a whole, and corporate and medical interests that profit from medical technology. It was largely these groups that opened and sustained the pipeline from the federal treasury to medical research and technological development.

A "SUPERACADEMIC GENERAL STAFF"

First, an influential medical research elite has grown up around medical schools, universities, private research laboratories, and teaching hospitals and clinics. Medical schools, however, have been the main beneficiaries of the foundation and government largess for research, receiving the largest share of the money and having the greatest influence in the direction and organization of medical research. Since World War II medical school research funds have increased faster than operating income. By 1953, research grants accounted for more than a fourth of total U.S. medical school income. Federal support for medical school operating and research expenses continued to grow, topping $1.4 billion in 1973, most of it in research subsidies. By the late seventies about sixty cents of every dollar spent by medical schools were provided by the federal government, three times its share in 1950.[80]

The ranks of full-time researchers and teachers among physicians swelled to match the availability of funds. The government, like the Rockefeller philanthropies under Frederick T. Gates, encouraged the expansion of full-time clinical faculty—from 2,200 in 1950 to 24,000 in 1973, a 1,100 percent increase! Doctors engaged full-time in medical teaching or research increased from less than 2 percent of all physicians in 1950 to nearly 5 percent in 1973.[81]

The bonanza of federal dollars bestowed on medical schools since World War II fragmented them into collections of virtually autonomous departments. Departments and institutes of full-time faculty and researchers grew like mushrooms in response to one or another funding program. Empires were built by prominent faculty members who seemed to have a direct line to the National Institutes of Health. Medical school and teaching hospital administrators, wanting to expand their own domains of facilities and staff, courted foundation and government officials responsible for doling out research funds as well as the faculty who attract the grants and contracts. Faculty members who excelled at grantsmanship, rather than those who were the best teachers, were favored with money and prestige, and became models for medical students.[82] The situation remains unchanged today.

Prominent members of this academic medical elite not only control the considerable sums of research money that they receive from outside, or extramural, sources; they also have a major role in determining who else will receive such funds. Moving easily among medical schools, institutes, foundations, and government agencies, this national academic elite has become a formidable interest group. Even by 1927 Hans Zinsser complained that the "guidance of medical education is to a considerable extent passing out of the hands of the universities" and into those of a "superacademic general staff."[83]

Following the dictates of their training, their intellectual and practical competence, and their material interests, this academic medical lobby has promoted technological and curative medical research that has focused largely on hospital and medical school clinic patients. They encourage the appropriation of money for health research, and they shape the specific research directions and programs for which money is given.

But they and their institutions are dependent on outside sources for both capital and operating expenses, and they tend to be very responsive to agencies that foot their bills. They have been supported by the larger medical profession which benefits from the production of knowledge and technique (some of the commodities of medical practice), but more fundamental support comes from outside the health professions. That support depends on the interests and programs of this dependent group coinciding with the interests and strategies of economically and politically more powerful groups. At first, foundations and then the federal government provided that financial support and exercised the control that goes with it, just as the AMA's *Journal* had feared and warned the profession against as early as 1901.[84]

THE CORPORATE CLASS

As in the organization of medical care, foundation and government programs in medical research represent the interests of the corporate sector of society. From the founding of the Rockefeller Institute for Medical Research in 1901 to the present time, substantial sums of corporate wealth have supported medical science and its technological applications. In 1975 foundations contributed $64 million, mainly income from their corporate investments, to health research while private industry itself spent $1,322 million on medical research and development.[85] Even more important has been the strong political support by foundation and corporate leaders for increasing appropriations from the vast federal treasury. Private wealth accounts for only a third of national health research expenditures, but it has been influential in generating the other two-thirds from the State.

The reasons for this support include the same considerations that led to the founding of the Rockefeller Institute. As we found in Chapter 3, Gates and other members of the corporate class embraced scientific medicine because it supported their political and economic struggles. Technological medicine provides the corporate class with a compatible world view, an effective technique, a supportive cultural tool, and a focus on the disease process *within* the body that provides a convenient diversion from the health-damaging conditions in which people live and work.

Continuing its earlier policies, the Rockefeller Foundation spearheaded efforts in the 1930s to develop a scientific biological perspective in medicine and to integrate chemistry and physics with biology. The Rockefeller, Macy, Milbank, and Ford philanthropies also generously supported the development of research into mental illness, almost exclusively focused on physiological factors with a little behavioral research.[86]

Like the foundations and individual capitalists earlier in the century, federal health research has focused on the narrowly technical components of disease and death rather than on the broader economic and physical environments so central to the population's health status. Cancer research is a prominent but typical example. Throughout its existence since 1937, the National Cancer Institute (NCI) has sought the key to understanding the etiology, cure, and prevention of cancer largely in microbiological research. In 1971 the Nixon administration launched a grand "war on cancer," the second leading cause of death, and gave the NCI a hefty 62 percent boost in its appropriations for the next year, the biggest since a 90 percent increase it received in 1957. By 1977 the NCI's annual budget had grown to $815 million—three and a half times the pre-"war" level.[87]

Neither the National Cancer Institute nor the American Cancer Society has shown much interest in investigating the environmental contribution to cancer. A committee of the NCI's National Advisory Cancer Board expressed its "astonishment" that the National Cancer Program allocated only 10 percent of its budget to this area. In 1975 the NCI expanded its environmental carcinogens program to $100 million, an impressive sum except that it is only 17 percent of the NCI's budget for the year. This miserly proportion devoted to environmental causes of cancer seems especially ironic because NCI director Frank J. Rauscher, Jr., publicly stated on several occasions the widely substantiated view that up to 90 percent of all cancers originate in the environment. According to federal health officials, epidemiological evidence demonstrates that at least 20 percent—and perhaps 40 percent—of all cancer cases are caused by occupational carcinogens, the most neglected area of environmental cancer research.[88]

The more dominant lines of research focus on possible viral causes, hereditary factors, and immunological defenses in the etiology of cancer. The so far unproductive search for a viral origin for human cancer cost three-quarters of a billion dollars by 1977. This and other lines of microbiological research have contributed only marginally to improving survival rates for most cancer victims. Rausher boasted in 1974, "The 5-year survival rate for cancer patients in the 1930s was about 1 in 5. Today, the figure is 1 in 3." However, Daniel Greenberg notes, "virtually all of this improvement was achieved prior to 1955, which, ironically, was when federal spending for cancer research began to accelerate to its present level." Greenberg chalks up much of the improvement in survival rates through the midfifties to the postwar introduction of antibiotics and blood transfusions that reduced the death toll due to cancer surgery. "It wasn't that more patients were surviving *cancer*," Greenberg asserts, "rather, they were surviving cancer *operations* that previously killed them." In Greenberg's view the contributions of chemotherapy, radiation therapy, and new surgical techniques have been negligible.[89]

Typified by the federal cancer research program, lavish funds are available for microbiological investigations of many diseases, but relatively scant support is provided for research on occupational and other environmental causes. At most, one-sixth of all federal health research dollars in 1977 were spent on environmental factors. One out of every five working coal miners in the United States is a victim of black lung disease (which kills 4,000 miners each year), and on the average one miner is killed every other day in mine accidents. Yet the amount of money per miner spent in the United States for studying ways to improve miners' occupational health and safety is only one-twentieth of that spent in the majority of European countries.[90]

This neglect of occupational and environmental bases of disease and death is *not* primarily due to conspiracy. The medical profession is, as we have seen in previous chapters, tied to the corporate class. Office-based physicians' median incomes reached $63,000 in 1976, placing them in the top few percentiles of the society's income structure.[91] Physicians in private practice earn their money from a market system of medical commodities, encouraging a conservative "free enterprise" political perspective and a sympathy for other entrepreneurs in the capitalist system.

Medical researchers may be free of the influence of the medical commodity marketplace, but to win fame and fortune they must obey the rules of the medical research funds "market." Their dependence on foundation and government funding agencies restricts the range of problems and methods they may investigate and constrains their creative intellectual processes as well. The malignant neglect of occupational and environmental, social, and economic factors in medical research is thus due to the lopsided financial support provided for narrow microbiological investigations, the financial and class interests of the medical profession, mechanistic and reductionist medical theory, and the correspondingly narrow technical training of physicians.

Underlying these largely institutional and class factors, however, are the deliberate policies of major corporate and political institutions. Foundations, corporations, and government agencies differ among themselves and over time in their financial and political support for social versus technical perspectives in medicine. But in the long run and at any time they overwhelmingly support technical perspectives that separate health problems from their social and political contexts. Their policies reflect a general corporate *class* concern that any excess sickness and death not be attributed to the admitted inequalities of capitalist society or to the organization of production that places profits before environmental protection and workers' health. In addition to this broad class interest in legitimation, however, a growing interest group within the corporate class has a direct financial stake in the dominance of technological medicine.

THE MEDICAL-INDUSTRIAL COMPLEX

The interests of doctors, hospitals, research scientists, and medical industrial corporations all coincide in the promotion of expensive medical technology. They have built a profitable symbiotic relationship based on the commodity system of medical care and society's cultural affinity and ideological support for technological medicine.

A recent report of the congressional Office of Technology Assessment showed how the introduction of new medical technologies creates or expands a market. Most of the risk capital is supplied by the government although the profits derived from the products of this research are taken by private industry. In 1975 the federal government provided about $2.8 billion out of a total of $4.6 billion spent on health research and development. State and local governments picked up about 5 percent of the total, and private nonprofit agencies gave another 5 percent. These public and private funding agencies provided almost all the funds for basic research, the fundamental laboratory and clinical science work that develops new knowledge in medicine. The $1.3 billion spent by private industry, together with a healthy chunk of government money, went mainly for product development, applying knowledge gained from basic research to the creation of technologies that can be used in medical care.[92]

Private industry not only controls the fourth of all this research and development money it spends; it also determines whether the knowledge generated by basic research will be made available as new medical products. Since both kinds of decisions are based on the expected profitability of any investment rather than on the basis of medical need and safety, it is not surprising that drugs and equipment of questionable usefulness and often significant danger are produced and that other medically useful products fail to be developed.[93]

Once a product or service is developed, the major medical interest groups determine its market. The commodity's producers extol its advantages and push for acceptance and sales. If the drug, instrument, or procedure increases the technical effectiveness of physicians, it is likely to be ordered by them. If it increases the status or incomes of physicians, it is also likely to be used. If its availability in a hospital is likely to attract physicians or otherwise produce income, hospitals will want to buy it. If third-party payers will foot the bill, it is a certain winner. The growth of clinical laboratory testing illustrates the effectiveness of these market forces.

Automated blood analyzers, first introduced in the 1950s and perfected in the years since, make it possible to perform many "extra" tests on a single sample of blood, at a low unit cost but at a high aggregate cost. Physicians order increasing numbers of tests which were previously considered unnecessary and which are, to many analysts, not necessary "for even the most rigorous medical practice." Physicians frequently fail to use the results of tests they have ordered. As fears of malpractice suits increased, doctors began expanding the limits of "defensive medicine," ordering ever larger numbers of tests to protect themselves against "litigious" patients. The growth of third-party payment programs facilitated increased use of clinical laboratories, and hospitals found it economically desirable to expand their laboratory capacities. Between the added fees doctors could charge, the economic "necessity" that hospitals felt, the facilitation of third-party payments, and the advertising of equipment and supply companies, the number of clinical laboratory tests reached 5 billion in 1975 (an average of twenty-three tests for every woman, man, and child in the country) and is increasing by 11 percent a year. Although automated laboratory equipment is expensive—for example, the latest automated blood chemistry analyzer (the SMAC 60) costs more than $250,000—it represents only a minute fraction of the costs generated by clinical laboratory technology. The $375 million spent on laboratory instruments in 1975 was only 2.5 percent of the $15 billion bill for clinical laboratory testing, most of which went for space, supplies, maintenance, personnel, and profits for the laboratories and physicians.[94]

The cost of this and other medical technology in a commodity medical care system is enormous and rising at essentially geometric rates. Medical technology is estimated to account for *half* the increase in costs of hospital care from 1965 to 1974, a period in which hospital expenditures tripled.[95]

In the days when Frederick T. Gates dreamed of medical research laboratories unlocking nature's secrets, medical technology was a fledgling business. Today the "medical-industrial complex" is a huge business that sops up an increasing share of national health expenditures for products and services that return a handsome profit to manufacturing and sales companies, researchers, hospitals, laboratories, and doctors. However, the economic return to these interest groups and the political value of technological medicine to the corporate class were not enough to overcome the serious economic problems caused by medical technology in a subsidized market economy.

TECHNOLOGY IN CRISIS

As hospitals increased their charges at more than twice the rate of inflation in the rest of the economy, as health expenditures took a bigger and bigger bite of national resources and the federal budget, as medical fringe benefits consumed more corporate income and medical expenses cut into more and more of workers' incomes; government, corporate, union, and consumer leaders grew critical of the endless expansion of capital-intensive medicine. Besides demanding regulation of hospital expansion and the imposition of cost controls, these groups' political support for the expansion of medical technology fell off sharply. The market system's tendency to produce and absorb an inordinately expensive medical technology forced an examination of the value of that technology.

Dr. David Rogers, president of the giant Johnson Foundation, whose wealth emanates from the medical supply business, called for "technologic restraint."[96] Anne Somers, usually an advocate of the hospitals' interests, succinctly summarized the case against unlimited expansion of technological medicine: "The more advanced and the more effective the technology, the greater the overall costs of health care."[97]

By the midsixties support for continued growth of technological medicine began to wither. Rapidly increasing health expenditures and the well-documented role of medical technology in pushing up those costs darkened the previously bright future for medical research and its applications. The war in Vietnam was competing for federal tax dollars while the anti-war movement and the rapidly growing movement to protect what was left of the environment undermined political support for indiscriminate technological development. The virtual war in American cities in the midsixties, whose demands were articulated by the civil rights and black liberation movement, forced increasing appropriations for improving inner city services, including medical care. The combination of all these factors reduced political support for technological medicine—and cut into medical research's share of health expenditures. Federal appropriations for health research, which had increased 745 percent between 1955 and 1965, increased less than a fifth that much in the next ten years.[98]

Foundations and the government increased their support for the study of medical care delivery problems. They supported experiments and reforms that would either lower the costs of medical care or improve access to low-technology primary care. They also gave new life and prominence to an old medical

ideology—one that justified clamping down on medical care
expenditures and provided a substitute for the legitimizing
functions performed by the increasingly discredited medical
technology.

BLAMING THE VICTIM: NEW PROMINENCE
FOR AN OLD IDEOLOGY

At first the criticisms of technological medicine focused on the
many systemic factors that increased its use. Medical economist
Victor Fuchs criticized the "technological imperative" in medicine, the attitude that if something technological *can* be done for
a patient, it *should* be done.[99] Fuchs attributed this accelerator
tendency to the training of physicians, the reimbursement
insurance system that encourages the use of costly services, drug
and medical supply companies pushing their products, and
pressure from patients.

Disenchantment with medicine's technical effectiveness, or
rather its ineffectiveness and its dangers, reinforced the attack on
medical technology that began with medicine's fiscal problems.
Doubts about all this emphasis on medical technology spread
from a small coterie of academic critics in the 1950s to the highest
policy circles of government and foundations in the 1970s. In the
latter half of the fifties, René Dubos[100] and a handful of other
observers were pointing out the futility of relying on medicine to
cure the ills created by social and physical environments. In the
seventies Jesuit priest and social philosopher Ivan Illich,[101]
Canadian Health and Welfare Minister Marc Lalonde,[102] and
others[103] criticized medicine for the disease it breeds, for its
relatively small positive impact on health status and disease rates,
and for extending its domain of control to more and more of our
social and personal relations.

One outcome of this criticism was the belief that what doctors
and medical technology were doing badly, we could do better for
ourselves. Critics of medicine advocated individual "self-help" as
a source of liberation from professional and technological
control. Many of them, however, extended this position to
identify individuals as the greatest dangers to their own health. A
large-scale study of health behavior in California supported the
view that a person's "lifestyle" is a powerful determinant of his or

her health status.[104] Fuchs, ignoring contrary epidemiological evidence, asserts that "the greatest potential for reducing coronary disease, cancer, and the other major killers still lies in altering personal behavior."[105] A host of other academic health researchers and writers and members of the growing "holistic" health movement fastened on the individual as the core of health problems.[106] Perhaps the ultimate absurdity of this position blames lead poisoning of young children in low-income neighborhoods on maternal deprivation[107] and "permissive socialization of oral behavior"[108]—instead of on landlords who fail to remove the lead-based paint peeling from walls of their rental units and to repaint with lead-free paint now required by law.

These arguments quickly caught the attention of major health policy makers. Walter McNerney, president of the Blue Cross Association, argues,

> We must stop throwing an array of technological processes and systems at lifestyle problems and stop equating more health services with better health. . . . people must have the capability and the will to take greater responsibility for their own health.[109]

Technological medicine is becoming prohibitively expensive, but victim blaming is cost-effective. "The cost of sloth, gluttony, alcoholic intemperance, reckless driving, sexual frenzy, and smoking have now become a national, not an individual, responsibility, all justified as individual freedom," asserts Dr. John Knowles, the influential president of the Rockefeller Foundation. "But one man's or woman's freedom in health is now another man's shackle in taxes and insurance premiums." Knowles sternly warns that "the cost of individual irresponsibility in health has become prohibitive."[110] Fuchs attacks what he sees as "a 'resolute refusal' to admit that individuals have any responsibility for their own distress."[111] And Leon Kass, denying that health or health care is a *right,* proclaims that "health is a *duty,* that one has an obligation to preserve one's own good health." Kass, a professor of medicine and bioethics, goes on to condemn "excessive preoccupations with health" such as "when cancer phobia leads to government regulations that unreasonably restrict industrial activity or personal freedom."[112]

Individual failure has long been used to explain why the poor and racial minorities use many physician and dental health services, especially preventive ones, less than more affluent groups do. Health professionals and their academic colleagues often conclude that low utilization reflects inadequate knowledge of the importance of preventive and early illness care and insufficient motivation to use them.[113] "Under-utilization" and disapproved lifestyles are, in this view, individual failings which can perhaps be remedied by educational programs—an opportunity for professional intervention to teach the poor "correct" health habits and the importance of health services.

Attitudes do influence health behavior, but there is substantial evidence that when racial minorities and the poor have accessible and comprehensive medical services, their utilization rates are similar to those of the general population.[114] This evidence supports the argument that the lower use of such health services is the result of structural and functional problems in the services themselves rather than disfunctions in the potential users.

Victim blaming has been used not only to explain lower utilization by the poor but as a way of *decreasing* the use of health services by Medicaid recipients. In order to cut the escalating costs of Medicaid programs, the Nixon administration and conservative governors created barriers to the use of services. Setting limits on physician and dentist visits, especially for preventive care, and setting up bureaucratic delays for hospitalization (such as requiring physicians to obtain prior authorization before admitting a Medicaid patient to the hospital), the State made the "beneficiaries" of its programs pay for the market system's fiscal problems.[115] Similarly, Medicare patients have been forced to pay higher deductibles and copayments in order to encourage them to spend less on their care. With the recent campaign of putting increasing responsibility on the individual, the working and middle classes, as well as the poor, are being blamed for getting sick in the first place.

The prospects of national health insurance raised fears that further socializing the costs of medical care would only escalate the "technological imperative." Rather than question the decades-old policy of rationalizing the private medical market, health policy makers focus instead on the individuals who dare to succumb to the hazards of life in our society. Paying little more than lip service to the need to do something about the physical environment and social and economic conditions that are known to breed disease, they settle on an ideological position that is less threatening to the capitalist society of which they are important members. Technological medicine was proving a costly hardware system whose legitimacy has been undermined. Victim blaming is a cheap and ideologically safe software alternative.

However, the victim-blaming strategy is generating opposition. Some public health officials have spoken out against this perspective. "For the vast majority of people in our society," argued C. Arden Miller as president of the American Public Health Association, "the life circumstances leading to poor health are not adopted as a matter of personal choice, but are thrust upon people by the social and economic circumstances into which they are born."[116] Opposition is also developing in the labor movement to screening workers for at-risk health habits and "sensitivity" or "susceptibility" to occupational carcinogens, and to the barring of fertile women from hazardous jobs in the lead and chemical industries instead of eliminating the hazards from the workplace.[117]

An alternative to victim blaming and narrowly technological approaches to environmentally generated disease is an "ecological" strategy. In this model, health workers analyze the different factors that contribute to a health problem and, then, with the people affected develop social and political, as well as medical-technical, strategies for changing them.[118] Individually oriented curative medicine is obviously needed because human beings are not perfectly adapted to any physical or social environment. But health care should do more than apply a band-aid to the wounds created by disharmony between people and environment. Much of this disharmony is the result of exploitation of the physical and social environment for profit, a process in which cancer caused by occupational and environmental pollution, high blood pressure due to stress, and excessively high death rates related to poverty and racism are considered "social costs" of production. However, political pressure can be developed to change these conditions and, ultimately, to reorganize production around social needs rather than the private accumulation of capital.

CONCLUSION

American society is faced with a health system that is at once expensive and incapable of serving the important health needs of the population. Despite many decades of efforts to make medicine more effective and improve its accessibility, the system seems to remain impervious to fundamental change. The reform efforts, however, are themselves fundamentally flawed.

From the early Rockefeller medical philanthropies to the opening of the federal treasury to the health sector, the major strategy for making medicine more effective has been biomedical research and the development of technological medicine. Technical advances have been very great, but the results have not been distributed equitably, coordinated rationally with needed primary care, or matched with support for improvements in the physical and social environments. Technique has also increasingly re-placed personal caring and emotional support in doctor-patient relationships. As we have seen, these emphases have had only a limited positive impact on the health of the population. The persistence of such narrowly technical approaches is due to their usefulness to powerful classes and interest groups. For members of the corporate class, technological medicine has legitimized their economic and political dominance by diverting attention from the consequences of their control—that is, from such "social costs" as class inequalities, domination based on race or sex, occupational hazards, and environmental degradation. For the medical profession, the knowledge generated by medical science and the techniques of medical technology provided the basis for physicians' claims to a monopoly of authority over the practice of medicine. Over the last few decades medical technology has been the foundation of a whole new industry, an interest group that directly profits from the emphasis on technical approaches to health problems. Technological medicine has benefited all these groups, and they have, in turn, supported its expansion.

The Rockefeller philanthropies also began the long process of rationalizing medical care. This campaign has been joined by groups in and outside the health sector and has been increasingly supported by the State over the last several decades. The political power of the medical profession was strong enough to block early efforts at subordinating all elements of the system into a hierarchy of organizational authority. So pieces of the rationaliz-ing strategy were implemented where there was least resistance. Voluntary health insurance programs—private and later public ones—were developed mainly around hospital care, financing the expansion of high technology medicine with the hospital at its center. The rationalizing of the private medical market helped the growth of the capital-intensive medical commodity sector, which has a major stake in technological medicine. The private control of this market, the emphasis on medical technology, and the socializing of costs by third-party payers combined to make expenditures soar, compounding government fiscal problems and draining ever-increasing amounts of money from the economy.

Medicine's upper-class reformers, from Gates and his foundation colleagues to present-day officials of the State, have been unwilling to oppose the private market in its entirety, producing a profound contradiction in their struggles to rationalize medicine. They favored the development of the private market with legislative and financial support in lieu of nationalizing medical care. The present crisis is a result of this political-economic process. It was an inevitable outcome only in that those who shaped the system believed in, or at least accepted, the needs and constraints of capitalist economic and social relations. If Gates and subsequent foundation and government leaders in the field of medicine had been committed to making health care serve the needs of the majority population rather than the needs of capitalism and the interests of the corporate class, a different course would have been followed. Even today a comprehensive, centrally planned nationalized health service could effectively control cost and provide equal care for the whole population. Health care could be more effective in improving health if its research and action were directed at environmental conditions in about the same proportion that those conditions contribute to sickness and death.

But health policy makers cannot be counted on to make these fundamental changes. As members of the corporate class or identified with its interests, they believe, to paraphrase Charles Wilson's audacious aphorism, "what's good for business is good for America." Furthermore, the capitalist sector of medicine has grown rich and powerful, bringing the economic and political influence of insurance companies, banks, and industrial corporations into active support for retaining the private medical market. National health insurance is supported because it will further socialize the costs of medicine, but nationalizing medicine in a national health service is unacceptable to the powerful private market forces and therefore is ignored by health policy makers. Instead of overhauling the medical system, they put the burden of controlling costs on people who have been afflicted with disease by restricting their access to services and demanding that they improve their health by changing their behavior.

However, even a national health service would not necessarily end medicine's role of legitimizing corporate capitalist society. It would, if anything, enable these ideological functions to compete less with the needs of the marketplace. Without the access problems that remain in the present market system, the "healing ministration," as Gates called medicine, could bring individual-focused, technical perspectives and methods to the health problems of the entire population.

Health care, potentially, has a great deal to offer. We rightfully expect it to prevent sickness, diagnose our ills, relieve our pains, and, when we are sick, return us to at least our usual level of functioning. If it were not distorted by its character as a commodity and by the ideological functions demanded of it, health care might well be developed as we wish it would. It is possible to make a health care system that effectively serves the health needs of the majority classes rather than the economic and political interests of its providers and the upper classes. It is doubtful, however, that such a health care system can be realized in a capitalist society, committed as it must be to maintaining the primacy of capital accumulation. Nevertheless, the struggle for that new health system may contribute to the larger struggle for a new, more just economic and social order.

Notes

The *Journal of the American Medical Association* is abbreviated throughout as *JAMA.*

INTRODUCTION

1. *New York Times,* April 26, 1977.
2. Ivan Illich, *Medical Nemesis, The Expropriation of Health* (New York: Pantheon, 1976).
3. See, for example, René Dubos, *Mirage of Health* (Garden City, N.Y.: Anchor Books, 1959); Marc Lalonde, *A New Perspective on the Health of Canadians* (Ottawa: Government of Canada, 1974); A. L. Cochrane, *Effectiveness and Efficiency: Random Reflections on Health Services* (London: Nuffield Provincial Hospital Trust, 1972); Rick J. Carlson, *The End of Medicine* (New York: John Wiley, 1975); Howard B. Waitzkin and Barbara Waterman, *The Exploitation of Illness in Capitalist Society* (Indianapolis, Ind.: Bobbs-Merrill, 1974); and John Ehrenreich, ed., *The Cultural Crisis of Modern Medicine* (New York: Monthly Review Press, 1978).
4. David Mechanic, *The Growth of Bureaucratic Medicine* (New York: John Wiley, 1976), p. 42; and his *Politics, Medicine, and Social Science* (New York: John Wiley, 1974), chap. 3.
5. Illich, *Medical Nemesis,* p. 211.
6. See the excellent critique of industrialism and technological determinism in Robin Blackburn, "A Brief Guide to Bourgeois Ideology," in A. Cockburn and R. Blackburn, eds., *Student Power* (Baltimore: Penguin, 1969), pp. 163–213; the brief discussion in David Noble's illuminating book, *America by Design—Science, Technology, and the Rise of Corporate Capitalism* (New York: Knopf, 1977), especially the introduction; and Vicente Navarro's critique of industrialism in his review of Illich's work, in Navarro, *Medicine Under Capitalism* (New York: Prodist, 1976), pp. 103–31.
7. William Weinfield, "Income of Physicians, 1929–1949," *Survey of Current Business,* 31 (July 1951), 11; and Maurice Leven, *The Incomes of Physicians: An Economic and Statistical Analysis,* Committee on the Costs of Medical Care, Publication no. 24 (Chicago: University of Chicago Press, 1932), p. 88.
8. Zachary Y. Dyckman, *A Study of Physicians' Fees* (Washington, D.C.: President's Council on Wage and Price Stability, March 1978), pp. 74–75; Harris polls reported in *Newsweek,* Dec. 10, 1973, p. 45, and *New York Times,* June 12, 1977, p. 55. See also Navarro, *Medicine Under Capitalism,* pp. 135–69.
9. On physician dominance, see Victor R. Fuchs, *Who Shall Live? Health,*

Economics, and Social Choice (New York: Basic Books, 1974), chap. 3; Eliot Freidson, *Profession of Medicine: A Study of the Sociology of Applied Knowledge* (New York: Dodd, Mead and Co., 1970); and Barbara Ehrenreichand John Ehrenreich, "Medicine and Social Control." in J. Ehrenreich, ed., *Cultural Crisis*, pp. 39–79.

10. Herman M. Somers and Anne R. Somers, *Doctors, Patients, and Health Institutions: The Organization and Financing of Medical Care* (Washington, D.C.: Brookings Institution, 1961), p. 42; *Physician Distribution and Medical Licensure in the United States, 1974* (Chicago: AMA, 1975), p. 66; and Harry T. Paxon, "Why Wesley Hall Ripped into the AMA Hierarchy," *Medical Economics*, Jan. 3, 1972, pp. 25–42, 101.

11. Robert Alford, *Health Care Politics: Ideological and Interest Group Barriers to Reform* (Chicago: University of Chicago Press, 1975).

12. Anne R. Somers, *Health Care in Transition* (Chicago: Hospital Research and Educational Trust, 1971), chap. 3, presents the AHA point of view.

CHAPTER 1

1. The best biography of Carnegie is Joseph Frazier Wall, *Andrew Carnegie* (New York: Oxford University Press, 1970).

2. Of the numerous biographies of Rockefeller, I have relied mainly on Allan Nevins, *John D. Rockefeller: The Heroic Age of American Enterprise*, 2 vols. (New York: Charles Scribner's Sons, 1940); and Peter Collier and David Horowitz, *The Rockefellers: An American Dynasty* (New York: Holt, Rinehart and Winston, 1976), pp. 1–73. The former book is the most detailed, but the latter puts his life into perspective and examines it somewhat critically.

3. On the changing class structure resulting from industrialization during the nineteenth century, see William Appleman Williams, *The Contours of American History* (Cleveland: World Publishing Co., 1961); and Robert H. Wiebe, *The Search for Order, 1877–1920* (New York: Hill and Wang, 1967).

4. Williams, *Contours*, pp. 315, 333. See also Richard O. Boyer and Herbert M. Morais, *Labor's Untold Story*, 3rd ed. (New York: United Electrical, Radio, and Machine Workers of America, 1972).

5. John D. Rockefeller, *Random Reminiscences of Men and Events* (New York: Doubleday, Page and Co., 1909), pp. 141–42.

6. Ibid., p. 158.

7. Quoted in Edward Chase Kirkland, *Dream and Thought in the Business Community, 1860–1900* (Chicago: Quadrangle Books, 1964; originally published 1956), p. 165.

8. Hanna quote from M. A. Hanna to J. D. Rockefeller, Sept. 8, 1885, Rockefeller Family Archives, record group 1. On Hanna's role in building political capitalism, see Williams, pp. 349, 360–62, 381. On the development of close ties between the executive branch and private industry and finance, see Gabriel Kolko, *The Triumph of Conservatism: A Reinterpretation of American History, 1900–1916* (Chicago: Quadrangle Books, 1967; originally published 1963); and on the further development of this corporate liberal program of reforming government to serve the needs of monopolistic industry, see James Weinstein, *The Corporate Ideal in the Liberal State, 1900–1918* (Boston: Beacon Press, 1968).

9. Correspondence between Hanna and Rockefeller, 1885 to 1892, Rockefeller Family Archives, record group 1.

10. For a brief view of how the wealthiest Americans lived in this period and complaints and defenses regarding their ostentation, see Kirkland, *Dream and Thought,* chap. 2.

11. For an uncritical historical survey of philanthropy in the United States, see Robert H. Bremner, *American Philanthropy* (Chicago: University of Chicago Press, 1960); the Mather and Franklin quotes are from pp. 12–17.

12. Ibid., pp. 96–99.

13. Richard Hofstadter, *Social Darwinism in American Thought* (Boston: Beacon Press, 1955); quote from Spencer on p. 41.

14. See, for example, any of the *Proceedings of the National Conference of Charities and Correction* for this period; Amos G. Warner, *American Charities,* rev. ed. (New York: Thomas Y. Crowell, 1919; originally published 1894); and Frank D. Watson, *The Charity Organization Movement in the United States: A Study in American Philanthropy* (New York: Macmillan, 1922)—all representative of this movement.

15. Edward T. Devine, "The Dominant Note of the Modern Philanthropy," *Proceedings of the National Conference of Charities and Correction* (1906), p. 3.

16. Warner, *American Charities,* pp. 28, 46–47.

17. Anthony Platt, *The Child Savers: The Invention of Delinquency* (Chicago: University of Chicago Press, 1969), pp. 35–36.

18. Quoted in Howard S. Miller, *Dollars for Research: Science and Its Patrons in Nineteenth-Century America* (Seattle: University of Washington Press, 1970), pp. 159–60.

19. Jane Addams, *Twenty Years at Hull-House* (New York: Signet/Macmillan, 1961; originally published 1910), p. 299; quoted in Platt, *Child Savers,* pp. 96–97.

20. On the development of public schools, see Michael B. Katz, *Class, Bureaucracy, and Schools—The Illusion of Educational Change in America* (New York: Praeger Publishers, 1971); and Joel H. Spring, *Education and the Rise of the Corporate State* (Boston: Beacon Press, 1972).

21. Hamilton A. Hill, *Memoir of Abbott Lawrence* (Boston: "Printed for Private Distribution," 1883); p. 108.

22. Ibid., p. 109.

23. See Harry Braverman, *Labor and Monopoly Capital: The Degradation of Work in the Twentieth Century* (New York: Monthly Review Press, 1974), pp. 125–37.

24. Miller, *Dollars for Research,* p. 7.

25. Ibid., pp. 3–8.

26. Merle Curti and Roderick Nash, *Philanthropy in the Shaping of American Higher Education* (New Brunswick, N.J.: Rutgers University Press, 1965), pp. 70–72.

27. Ibid., pp. 69–70. See also Frederick Rudolph, *The American College and University: A History* (New York: Vintage Books, 1965), pp. 222–31.

28. Curti and Nash, *Philanthropy,* pp. 64–65.

29. Elbert Vaughan Wills, *The Growth of American Higher Education—Liberal, Professional, and Technical* (Phila.: Dorrance and Co., 1936), p. 147.

30. Curti and Nash, *Philanthropy,* p. 135.

31. Ibid., pp. 64–65, 112–14.

32. "Wealth," *North American Review,* 148 (June 1889), 653–64; and 149 (Dec. 1889), 682–98; reprinted in Andrew Carnegie, *Gospel of Wealth and Other Timely Essays* (Cambridge, Mass.: Harvard University Press, 1962), pp. 14–49.

33. Quoted in Wall, *Carnegie,* pp. 812–13.

34. For gifts given by Carnegie in his lifetime and bequeathed by him at his death, see *A Manual of the Public Benefactions of Andrew Carnegie* (Washington, D.C.: Carnegie Endowment for International Peace, 1919).

35. Wall, *Carnegie,* pp. 806–12.

36. *Manual of the Public Benefactions.*

37. The account of Rockefeller's life is taken from Nevins, *Rockefeller;* and Collier and Horowitz, *Rockefellers,* pp. 1–73.

38. Quoted in Nevins, *Rockefeller,* II, 177.

39. Quoted in Collier and Horowitz, *Rockefellers,* p. 48.

40. A detailed and readable account of the development of the University of Chicago is found in Nevins, *Rockefeller,* II, 191–227.

41. Ibid., 213–14.

42. Ibid., 213–14, 627, 266.

43. Ibid., 269, 427; and Collier and Horowitz, *Rockefellers,* pp. 45–47.

44. Gates describes the meeting with Rockefeller in his Autobiography. At the time this book was researched and written, Gates' autobiography was an unpublished typescript in the Rockefeller Foundation Archives. It has since been published as *Chapters in My Life* (New York: Free Press, 1977). I continue to use the citation "Gates, Autobiography," referring to the typescript pages. Gates' meeting with Rockefeller is also recounted in detail in Nevins, *Rockefeller,* II, 266–69.

45. Gates, Autobiography, p. 342; and quoted in Nevins, *Rockefeller,* II, 268.

46. Nevins, *Rockefeller,* II, 268.

47. Gates, Autobiography, pp. 342–45.

48. Rockefeller, *Random Reminiscences,* p. 116; Allan Nevins, *A Study in Power: John D. Rockefeller, Industrialist and Philanthropist* (New York: Charles Scribner's Sons, 1953), II, 197; and Gates, Autobiography, p. 366.

49. Nevins, *Rockefeller,* II, 274–81; and Rockefeller, *Random Reminiscences,* p. 117.

50. Nevins, *Rockefeller,* II, 279–81.

51. Ibid., 274; and Gates, Autobiography.

52. The only account of Gates' early life is in his Autobiography; it is summarized with quotes in Nevins, *Rockefeller,* II, 269–72.

53. Nevins, *Rockefeller,* II, 272–73.

54. Memo, April 20, 1891, GEB files, Rockefeller Foundation Archives.

55. Nevins, *Rockefeller,* II, 282–85; and Gates, Autobiography, p. 375.

56. Gates, Autobiography, pp. 310–15; F. T. Gates to J. D. Rockefeller, June 12, 1916, and E. N. Cary to J. D. Rockefeller, May 4, 1909, both in Rockefeller Family Archives, record group 2.

57. Quoted in B. C. Forbes, "How John D. Rockefeller Became America's Foremost Organizer and Richest Man," *Leslie's,* Sept. 29, 1917. See also Rockefeller, *Random Reminiscences,* p. 117.

58. Details of Junior's life are available in Collier and Horowitz, *Rockefellers,* pp. 75–178. The period of his entry to his father's office is described on pp. 87–92.

59. Gates, Autobiography, pp. 517–18; Nevins, *Rockefeller,* II, 289.

60. Raymond Fosdick, *John D. Rockefeller, Jr., A Portrait* (New York: Harper and Bros., 1956), p. 111; Nevins, *Rockefeller,* II, 290.

61. Raymond Fosdick, *The Story of the Rockefeller Foundation* (New York: Harper and Bros., 1952), p. 2.

62. For the authorized and largely uncritical histories of the Rockefeller philanthropies, see Fosdick's history of the Rockefeller Foundation, cited above, and his *Adventure in Giving: The Story of the General Education Board* (New York: Harper and Row, 1962); George W. Corner, *A History of the Rockefeller*

Institute—1901–1953 (New York: Rockefeller Institute Press, 1964); and Greer Williams, *The Plague Killers* (New York: Charles Scribner's Sons, 1969), about the worldwide public health programs. For more critical views, see Harry Cleaver, Jr., "The Origins of the Green Revolution," unpublished doctoral dissertation, Stanford University, 1975; E. Richard Brown, "Public Health in Imperialism: Early Rockefeller Programs at Home and Abroad," *American Journal of Public Health*, 66 (1976), 897–903; Collier and Horowitz, *Rockefellers;* and the following chapters in this book.

63. Quoted in Nevins, *Rockefeller*, II, 291.

64. Rockefeller, *Random Reminiscences*, pp. 159–60.

65. See F. Emerson Andrews, *Philanthropic Giving* (New York: Russell Sage Foundation, 1950); Warren Weaver, *U.S. Philanthropic Foundations—Their History, Structure, Management, and Record* (New York: Harper and Row, 1967); and Bremner, *American Philanthropy*.

66. See Franklin Parker, *George Peabody, A Biography* (Nashville: Vanderbilt University Press, 1971), pp. 160–67, on the founding of the Peabody Fund; and see Jessie Pearl Rice, *J. L. M. Curry—Southerner, Statesman, and Educator* (New York: Columbia University Press, 1949), pp. 159–75, on Curry's role in Southern education funds.

67. Louis R. Harlan, *Separate and Unequal: Public School Campaigns and Racism in the Southern Seaboard States, 1901–1915* (Chapel Hill: University of North Carolina Press, 1958), discusses the Southern Education Board, pp. 75–101. Some of the important contributions to the board's total income, $400,000 in the thirteen years of its existence, came from George Foster Peabody, Andrew Carnegie, Rockefeller's General Education Board, Frank R. Chambers of New York, the Russell Sage Foundation, and Robert C. Ogden.

68. Hugh C. Bailey, *Liberalism in the New South—Southern Social Reformers and the Progressive Movement* (Coral Gables, Fla.: University of Miami Press, 1969), p. 138.

69. Harlan, *Separate and Unequal*, pp. 75–101; Bailey, *Liberalism*, pp. 75–76; Lawrence A. Cremin, *The Transformation of the School—Progressivism in American Education, 1876–1957* (New York: Knopf, 1961), pp. 23–57. Washington was financially supported by Northern businessmen and Southern liberals; he was hired as an agent of the SEB though he was never allowed to attend a board meeting. More assertive black leaders denounced the Hampton model of industrial schooling for blacks. W. E. B. DuBois pointed out that exclusive support of industrial schooling emphasized blacks' duties and put their rights into the background. "Take the eyes of these millions off the stars and fasten them in the soil," he mockingly told a Hampton audience, and let their dreams be of "corn bread and molasses." DuBois, *The Education of Black People*, ed. H. Aptheker (Amherst: University of Massachusetts Press, 1973), p. 9.

70. Quoted in Cleaver, "Origins of the Green Revolution."

71. Fosdick, *Adventure in Giving*, pp. 10–11. SEB member William H. Baldwin, president of the Long Island Railroad, argued that blacks "will willingly fill the more menial positions, and do the heavy work, at less wages," leaving to whites "the more expert labor," Harlan, *Separate and Unequal*, p. 78, 75–101.

72. Fosdick, *Rockefeller, Jr.*, pp. 117–18.

73. Memorandum in Rockefeller Family Archives, record group 2.

74. Copy of press release in Rockefeller Family Archives, record group 2.

75. Harlan, *Separate and Unequal*, pp. 75–101; Frissell quoted on p. 86.

76. Fosdick, *Adventure in Giving*, pp. 10–11; Buttrick to Gates, Oct. 14, 1904; confidential report of Jerome D. Greene, Wallace Buttrick, and Abraham

Flexner, Oct. 22, 1914; Raymond B. Fosdick, Wickliffe Rose, and James Dillard, report of special committee on programs and policies, Oct. 6, 1922, all in GEB files, Rockefeller Foundation Archives. The GEB greatly influenced several other foundations that worked in the Southern education movement; e.g., see Abraham Flexner, *Abraham Flexner: An Autobiography* (New York: Simon and Schuster, 1960), p. 274; this is a revision of his autobiography published in 1940 as *I Remember*.

77. Gates, Autobiography, pp. 460–64; Gates to Wickliffe Rose, Aug. 21, 1914, Rockefeller Sanitary Commission files; R. B. Fosdick, W. Rose, and J. Dillard, report of special committee on programs and policies, Oct. 6, 1922, GEB files; *Annual Report of the General Education Board, 1921–1922,* pp. 42, 65.

78. See Brown, "Public Health in Imperialism."

79. Gates, Autobiography, p. 460.

80. Gates to Rockefeller, June 3, 1905, Gates papers, Rockefeller Foundation Archives.

81. Gates, Autobiography, pp. 440–42.

82. *Current Literature,* 42 (1909), 253–54; Gates to Rockefeller, Aug. 9, 1907, Gates papers.

83. Gates, "Some Reflections on Questions of Policy," memo to the board, Jan. 23, 1906, GEB files, Rockefeller Foundation Archives.

84. William S. Vickery, "One Economist's View of Philanthropy," in F. G. Dickerson, ed., *Philanthropy and Public Policy* (New York: National Bureau of Economic Research, 1962), p. 31.

85. Wall, *Carnegie,* p. 828.

86. The origins and early years of the Carnegie Foundation are described in Burton J. Hendrick, *The Life of Andrew Carnegie* (Garden City, N.Y.: Doubleday, Doran, and Co., 1932), vol. 2, 263–64; and Wall, *Carnegie,* pp. 869–79.

87. Henry S. Pritchett, "Introduction" to Abraham Flexner, *Medical Education in the United States and Canada,* Bulletin no. 4 (New York: Carnegie Foundation for the Advancement of Teaching, 1910), p. vii. See also A. Flexner, *Henry S. Pritchett, A Biography* (New York: Columbia University Press, 1943), p. 96.

88. Phone conversation quoted in Buttrick to Gates, March 30, 1906; see also Buttrick to Pritchett, March 31, 1906, and April 16, 1906; and Pritchett to Buttrick, April 5, 1906, and Jan. 4, 1909, all in GEB files, Rockefeller Foundation Archives. See also Pritchett to Buttrick, Feb. 3, 1911, Feb. 6, 1911, Nov. 12, 1915, and Nov. 24, 1916; and Buttrick to Pritchett, Feb. 8, 1911, and Dec. 1, 1916; and Pritchett to Gates, Nov. 12, 1915, all in Carnegie Foundation files.

89. Gates to Rockefeller, June 6, 1905, Rockefeller Family Archives, record group 2.

90. W. Buttrick to H. S. Pritchett, May 29, 1917, Carnegie Foundation files; A. Flexner, "Supplement to the Gedney-Farm Memorandum," March 31, 1924, GEB files, Rockefeller Foundation Archives. A. Flexner, *Autobiography,* pp. 127, 129.

91. Fosdick, *Rockefeller, Jr.,* pp. 143–87; and Collier and Horowitz, *Rockefellers,* pp. 109–34.

92. Charles P. Howland to Raymond B. Fosdick, Jan. 28, 1927, Rockefeller Foundation files; A. Flexner to W. Buttrick, Aug. 3, 1925, GEB files; A. P. Stokes to W. Rose, May 2, 1928, and Edwin R. Embree to George Vincent, May 7, 1928, GEB files; memos by Edwin Embree about 1932, Edwin Embree papers—all Rockefeller Foundation Archives.

93. Gates, memo to himself, Nov. 20, 1911, Rockefeller Family Archives, record group 2.

94. Rockefeller, Jr., to Rockefeller, Dec. 31, 1906, Rockefeller Family Archives, record group 2.
95. Gates, memo to GEB, Nov. 1911, Rockefeller Family Archives, record group 2.
96. University of Chicago relationship described and letter quoted in Nevins, *Rockefeller,* II, 230–31, 246, 263–64, 627.
97. Gates to George Foster Peabody, March 20, 1912, Rockefeller Family Archives, record group 2; *Annual Report of the General Education Board, 1924–1925,* p. 5; A. Flexner, *Autobiography,* p. 209.
98. Williams, *Contours,* pp. 352–53. An illustration of the profitable use of managers comes from Carnegie's career. In 1873 Carnegie hired Captain William Jones to run his steel mill, and it was largely Jones who kept the company's costs below and its profits above those of its competitors. Jones introduced technical innovations that he personally designed, and he maintained relatively stable relations with his workers despite the intolerably exploitative wages and working conditions he and the company imposed on them. He worked the men under him twelve hours a day, seven days a week in mills where temperatures frequently topped 100°, but he also understood the necessity of setting some floor below which wages would not be pushed in order to keep his workers—a position that Carnegie had difficulty accepting. On Jones' role, see Wall, *Carnegie,* pp. 314–16, 328–29, 344–45.
99. A. Flexner, *Autobiography,* p. 109.

CHAPTER 2

1. Joseph E. Kett, *The Formation of the American Medical Profession—The Role of Institutions, 1780–1860* (New Haven: Yale University Press, 1968), pp. 9–10.
2. William G. Rothstein, *American Physicians in the Nineteenth Century* (Baltimore: Johns Hopkins University Press, 1972), pp. 35–36.
3. A Maryland physician named Alexander Hamilton complained of the empirics he found in his travels through the colonies in 1744. "A great many of them take the care of a family for the value of a Dutch dollar a year, which makes the practice of physick a mean thing, and unworthy of the application of a gentleman." Quoted in Rothstein, *American Physicians,* p. 35.
4. L. H. Butterfield, ed., *Letters of Benjamin Rush* (Princeton: Princeton University Press, 1951), vol. 2, 661.
5. On lay healers, see Barbara Ehrenreich and Deirdre English, *Witches, Midwives, and Nurses: A History of Women Healers* (Old Westbury, N.Y.: The Feminist Press, 1973); and Kett, *Formation.*
6. For a detailed description and discussion of regular medical practice in the first half of the nineteenth century, see Rothstein, *American Physicians,* pp. 41–62.
7. On the Popular Health Movement and some of its component groups, see Richard H. Shryock, "Sylvester Graham and the Popular Health Movement, 1830–1870," in Shryock, *Medicine in America, Historical Essays* (Baltimore: Johns Hopkins Press, 1966), pp. 111–25; and Ehrenreich and English, *Witches,* pp. 22–25. On licensing, see Shryock, *Medical Licensing in America, 1650–1965* (Baltimore: Johns Hopkins Press, 1967).
8. See Rothstein, *American Physicians,* pp. 152–74; and Harris L. Coulter, *Divided Legacy,* 3 vols. (Washington, D.C.: McGrath Publishing Co., 1973).
9. Rosemary Stevens, *American Medicine and the Public Interest* (New Haven: Yale University Press, 1971), p. 24.
10. Rothstein, *American Physicians,* p. 95.
11. "Medical Education in the United States," *JAMA,* 79 (1922), 629–37.
12. Kett, *Formation,* p. 179.

13. Dr. S. E. Chaillé, quoted in Gerald E. Markowitz and David K. Rosner, "Doctors in Crisis: A Study of the Use of Medical Education Reform to Establish Modern Professional Elitism in Medicine," *American Quarterly,* 25 (1973), 90.
14. Rothstein, *American Physicians,* pp. 120–21.
15. *The Three Ethical Codes* (Detroit: Illustrated Medical Journal Co., 1888), p. 31. This publication includes codes of ethics of the AMA, the American Institute of Homeopathy, and the National Eclectic Medical Society.
16. Donald E. Konold, *A History of American Medical Ethics, 1847–1912* (Madison: State Historical Society of Wisconsin for the Department of History, University of Wisconsin, 1962), pp. 1–24. Regarding the internal and external functions of codes of ethics in the medical profession, see Jeffrey L. Berlant, *Profession and Monopoly* (Berkeley: University of California Press, 1975), chap. 3.
17. Abraham Flexner, *Medical Education in the United States and Canada,* Bulletin no. 4 (New York: Carnegie Foundation for the Advancement of Teaching, 1910), p. 14.
18. A. M. Carr-Saunders, "Professionalization in Historical Perspective," in H. M. Vollmer and D. L. Mills, eds., *Professionalization* (Englewood Cliffs, N.J.: Prentice-Hall, 1966), pp. 3–4.
19. William J. Goode, "Encroachment, Charlatanism, and the Emerging Professions: Psychology, Medicine, and Sociology," *American Sociological Review,* 25 (1960), 902–14.
20. Ernest Greenwood, "Attributes of a Profession," *Social Work,* 2 (1957), 44–55.
21. Eliot Freidson, *Profession of Medicine: A Study of the Sociology of Applied Knowledge* (New York: Dodd, Mead and Co., 1970), p. 80.
22. Harold L. Wilensky, "The Professionalization of Everyone?" *American Journal of Sociology,* 70 (1964), 137–58.
23. Freidson, *Profession,* p. 81.
24. Carr-Saunders, "Professionalization," p. 6.
25. Everett C. Hughes, "Professions," in Kenneth S. Lynn, ed., *The Professions in America* (Boston: Houghton Mifflin Co., for American Academy of Arts and Sciences, 1965), pp. 2, 3, 9.
26. Freidson, *Profession,* pp. 79, 80 (emphasis added).
27. Henry E. Sigerist, *American Medicine* (New York: W. W. Norton and Co., 1934), pp. 267–73.
28. George W. Corner, *A History of the Rockefeller Institute—1901–1953* (New York: Rockefeller Institute Press, 1964), pp. 7–8.
29. Stevens, *American Medicine,* p. 40.
30. Sigerist, *American Medicine,* pp. 273–74.
31. See, for example, William Allen Pusey, *A Doctor of the 1870s and 1880s* (Springfield, Ill.: Charles C. Thomas, 1932).
32. Rothstein, *American Physicians,* p. 209.
33. For an illuminating analysis of scientific management, see Harry Braverman, *Labor and Monopoly Capital—The Degradation of Work in the Twentieth Century* (New York: Monthly Review Press, 1974), pp. 70–138.
34. John Powles, "On the Limitations of Modern Medicine," *Science, Medicine, and Man,* 1 (1973), 15.
35. Markowitz and Rosner, "Doctors," 92.
36. Erwin H. Ackerknecht, *A Short History of Medicine* (New York: Ronald Press, 1955), pp. 130–31.
37. Charles E. Rosenberg, *The Cholera Years—The United States in 1832, 1849, and 1866* (Chicago: University of Chicago Press, 1962).

38. Corner, *Rockefeller Institute*, p. 4. See also Edward H. Kass, "Infectious Diseases and Social Change," *Journal of Infectious Diseases*, 123 (1971), 110–14.

39. Richard H. Shryock, *American Medical Research, Past and Present* (New York: Commonwealth Fund, 1947), pp. 43–44. See also Corner, *Rockefeller Institute*, pp. 8–9, on rising public interest in and expectations from medical science.

40. Leonard Keene Hirshberg, "Popular Medical Fallacies," *American Magazine*, 62 (1906), 655–60; Harvey Cushing, "Triumphs of Modern Medicine," *Education Review*, 47 (1914), 86–95; and C.-E. A. Winslow, "The War Against Disease," *Atlantic Monthly*, 91 (Jan. 1903), 43–52. The *New York Times* (Feb. 19, 1911) reported on a lecture by Dr. Harvey Wiley, then chief chemist with the U.S. Department of Agriculture and later first head of the Food and Drug Administration, in which he asserted that in fifty years chemistry will have practically eliminated all forms of disease.

41. See, for example, Charles A. L. Reed, "President's Address," *JAMA*, 36 (1901), 1599–1606.

42. William H. Welch, "Medical Advancement," *American Magazine*, 6 (1903), 675; quoted in Markowitz and Rosner, "Doctors," 92.

43. Elizabeth Bisland, "The Tyranny of the Pill," *North American Review*, 190 (1909), 819–25.

44. Pusey, *Doctor*.

45. Fielding H. Garrison, *John Shaw Billings, A Memoir* (New York: G. P. Putnam's Sons, 1915), pp. 256–57.

46. Richard H. Shryock, *The Unique Influence of the Johns Hopkins University on American Medicine* (Copenhagen: Ejnar Munksgaard, Ltd., 1953), p. 19.

47. Donald Fleming, *William H. Welch and the Rise of Modern Medicine* (Boston: Little, Brown and Co., 1954), especially p. 21. Welch's letter to his sister is quoted in Simon Flexner and James Thomas Flexner, *William Henry Welch and the Heroic Age of American Medicine* (New York: Viking Press, 1941), pp. 75–76.

48. Konold, *Ethics*, pp. 33–35.

49. Ibid., p. 58.

50. Rothstein, *American Physicians*, pp. 292–94.

51. C. A. L. Reed, "President's Address," *JAMA*, 36 (1901), 1605.

52. A. Flexner, *Medical Education*, pp. 10–11. See also Rothstein, *American Physicians*, p. 19.

53. "Medical Education in the United States," *JAMA*, 79 (1922), 629–37.

54. W. J. Reader, *Professional Men—The Rise of the Professional Classes in Nineteenth-Century England* (New York: Basic Books, 1966), pp. 10–17.

55. Richard Hofstadter, "The Age of the College," in R. Hofstadter and W. P. Metzger, *The Development of Academic Freedom in the United States* (New York: Columbia University Press, 1955), p. 228.

56. Daniel Drake, *Practical Essays on Medical Education and the Medical Profession in the United States* (Cincinnati: Roff and Young, 1832; reprinted by Johns Hopkins Press, 1952), p. 11.

57. William H. Welch, from an article in *Science,* quoted in Markowitz and Rosner, "Doctors," 95.

58. Inez C. Philbrick, "Medical Colleges and Professional Standards," *JAMA*, 36 (1901), 1700.

59. Frank Billings, "Medical Education in the United States," President's Address, *JAMA*, 40 (1903), 1271–76.

60. Quoted in James J. Walsh, *History of the Medical Society of the State of New York* (New York: The Medical Society, 1907), p. 173.

61. Bryan, it should be noted, argued not from the needs of the working class nor even humanitarian grounds. An early advocate of what has become known as the "equal opportunity" doctrine, his argument for including the poorer classes in medicine came from his belief that "it is certain the only hope of this country for salvation from anarchy is in keeping the doors of higher opportunity open to the poorest." From Association of American Medical Colleges, *Proceedings of the 18th Annual Meeting,* Cleveland, March 16–17, 1908, p. 37.

62. F. C. Shattuck and J. L. Bremer, "The Medical School, 1869–1929," in S. E. Morison, ed., *The Development of Harvard University, 1869–1929* (Cambridge, Mass.: Harvard University Press, 1930), p. 581.

63. Quoted in Garrison, *Billings,* p. 256.

64. Philbrick, "Medical Colleges," 1700–02.

65. Rothstein, *American Physicians,* pp. 230–34.

66. Kett, *Formation,* pp. 135–38.

67. Walter L. Burrage, *A History of the Massachusetts Medical Society, 1781–1922.* (Norwood, Mass.: Plimpton Press, 1923), pp. 426–27; and Konold, *Ethics,* pp. 22–26.

68. Quoted in Rothstein, *American Physicians,* p. 245 (emphasis added).

69. Ibid., p. 307. See also, Richard Shryock, *Medical Licensing in America, 1650–1965* (Baltimore: Johns Hopkins Press, 1967), pp. 51–52.

70. Shryock, *Medical Licensing,* pp. 53–54; Robert C. Derbyshire, *Medical Licensure and Discipline in the United States* (Baltimore: Johns Hopkins Press, 1969), p. 7; Stevens, *American Medicine,* p. 43; and Berlant, *Profession and Monopoly,* chap. 5.

71. Rothstein, *American Physicians,* pp. 307–09.

72. Reed, "President's Address," 1605.

73. "Report of the Committee on Medical Ethics," *JAMA,* 40 (1903), 1379–81.

74. Reed, "President's Address," 1605.

75. Rothstein, *American Physicians,* p. 23.

76. See, for example, T. McKeown, "A Conceptual Background for Research and Development in Medicine," *International Journal of Health Services,* 3 (1973), 17–28; and Powles, "Limitations."

77. Stevens, *American Medicine,* p. 40.

78. Edgar Allen Forbes, "Is the Doctor a Shylock?" *World's Work,* 14 (1907), 8892–96.

79. B. Ehrenreich and D. English, *Complaints and Disorders: The Sexual Politics of Sickness* (Old Westbury, N.Y.: The Feminist Press, 1973). See also their *For Her Own Good: 150 Years of the Experts' Advice to Women* (Garden City, N.Y.: Anchor Press/Doubleday, 1978).

80. H. Bigelow, "The Conservation of Energy and Conservative Gynaecology," *JAMA,* 4 (1885), 311.

81. Quoted in Stevens, *American Medicine,* p. 50.

82. Konold, *Ethics,* pp. 35–37; and "Report of the Committee on Specialties, and on the Propriety of Specialists Advertising," *Transactions of the AMA,* 20 (1869), 111–13.

83. Konold, *Ethics,* pp. 38–40.

84. Stevens, *American Medicine,* p. 50.

85. Figures based on Rothstein's estimate (*American Physicians,* p. 344) of the number of physicians in the United States in 1900 less 5 percent who may have been full-time specialists, while the current figure is from Cambridge Research Institute, *Trends Affecting the U.S. Health Care System* (Washington, D.C.: Government Printing Office, 1976), pp. 357–66.

86. Stevens, *American Medicine,* pp. 85–88, 92.
87. Maurice D. Clarke, "Therapeutic Nihilism," quoted in Rothstein, *American Physicians,* pp. 184–85.
88. Rothstein, *American Physicians,* p. 324.
89. Stevens, *American Medicine,* p. 134.
90. On the successful campaign to get rid of midwives, see Frances E. Kobrin, "The American Midwife Controversy: A Crisis of Professionalization," *Bulletin of the History of Medicine,* 40 (1966), 350–63.
91. Morris Fishbein, *The New Medical Follies* (New York: Boni and Liveright, 1927), p. 231.

CHAPTER 3

1. Sander Kelman describes the contradiction that technological medicine posed for private practice physicians in their attempt to control the profession in "Toward the Political Economy of Medical Care," *Inquiry,* 8 (Sept. 1971), 30–37.
2. Rosemary Stevens, *American Medicine and the Public Interest* (New Haven: Yale University Press, 1971), pp. 78, 52. On the cost of hospital construction, see C. Rufus Rorem, *The Public's Investment in Hospitals* (Chicago: University of Chicago Press, 1930), especially pp. 124–25.
3. Stevens, *American Medicine,* p. 145.
4. Richard Hofstadter, *The Age of Reform* (New York: Vintage Books, 1955), pp. 137–38.
5. *JAMA,* 35 (1900), 1353.
6. Simon Flexner and James Thomas Flexner, *William Henry Welch and the Heroic Age of American Medicine* (New York: Viking Press, 1941), pp. 111–17.
7. Ibid., pp. 130–34.
8. Donald Fleming, *William H. Welch and the Rise of Modern Medicine* (Boston: Little, Brown and Co., 1954), conveys the impression that Welch was driven by competition. See also S. Flexner and J. T. Flexner, *Welch,* p. 138.
9. Fleming, *Welch,* pp. 65–70; and Flexner and Flexner, *Welch,* pp. 136, 154, 171.
10. The account is printed in full as "Recollections of Frederick T. Gates on the Origins of the Institute," in George W. Corner's official *A History of the Rockefeller Institute—1901–1953* (New York: Rockefeller Institute Press, 1964), pp. 575–84. It is extensively relied on by Corner and by Allan Nevins, *John D. Rockefeller, The Heroic Age of American Enterprise* (New York: Charles Scribner's Sons, 1940), vol. 2, 466–70; and Flexner and Flexner, *Welch,* 269–71. I have also quoted and referred to Gates' memo in the following pages.
11. Corner, *Rockefeller Institute,* p. 30; and a letter from L. Emmett Holt, quoted in T. Mitchell Prudden's unpublished history of the Rockefeller Institute.
12. Corner, *Rockefeller Institute,* pp. 30–31.
13. Ibid., pp. 51–52.
14. Frederick T. Gates, Autobiography, unpublished ms., 1928, pp. 387–88, Gates collection, Rockefeller Foundation Archives; and Corner, *Rockefeller Institute,* p. 49.
15. Corner, *Rockefeller Institute,* p. 68.
16. Ibid., pp. 39–40.
17. Ibid., pp. 40–41.
18. John D. Rockefeller to Starr J. Murphy, Dec. 29, 1916, Rockefeller Family Archives, record group 2.

19. John D. Rockefeller to Starr J. Murphy, July 1, 1919, Rockefeller Family Archives, record group 2.
20. Starr J. Murphy to John D. Rockefeller, July 8, 1919, Rockefeller Family Archives, record group 2.
21. Frederick T. Gates to John D. Rockefeller, Jan. 20, 1911, Gates collection, Rockefeller Foundation Archives.
22. John D. Rockefeller, Jr., to Starr J. Murphy, July 5, 1919, Rockefeller Family Archives, record group 2.
23. Starr J. Murphy to John D. Rockefeller, Jan. 2, 1917, Rockefeller Family Archives, record group 2.
24. William G. Rothstein, *American Physicians in the Nineteenth Century* (Baltimore: Johns Hopkins University Press, 1972), pp. 159–60, 234–39.
25. Quoted in Raymond B. Fosdick, *John D. Rockefeller, Jr., A Portrait* (New York: Harper and Bros., 1956), pp. 111–12.
26. The McGill appeal is related in Corner, *Rockefeller Institute,* pp. 70–71.
27. Gates, "Philanthropy and Civilization," 1923, Gates collection, Rockefeller Foundation Archives.
28. Gates, "Some Elements of an Effective System of Scientific Medicine in the United States" (n.d.), Gates collection, Rockefeller Foundation Archives.
29. Gates, "Concerning Private Gifts to States and a Medical Policy," Memo to the General Education Board, Feb. 26, 1925, Gates collection, Rockefeller Foundation Archives.
30. Gates, "Philanthropy and Civilization."
31. Gates, "Private Gifts."
32. Walter Fisher, "Physicians and Slavery in the Ante-bellum Southern Medical Journal," *Journal of the History of Medicine and Allied Sciences,* 23 (1968), 36–49.
33. Ibid., 37.
34. Quoted in George M. Frederickson, *The Inner Civil War: Northern Intellectuals and the Crisis of the Union* (New York: Harper and Row, 1965), pp. 102–04. My thanks to Michael Cohen for calling my attention to this chapter.
35. Carnegie quotes himself in *Autobiography of Andrew Carnegie* (Boston: Houghton Mifflin Co., 1920), p. 231.
36. Quoted in David Brody's excellent study of working conditions, labor organizing, and employers, *Steelworkers in America: The Nonunion Era* (New York: Harper and Row, 1969; originally published, 1960), p. 178. See also Stuart D. Brandes, *American Welfare Capitalism, 1880–1940* (Chicago: University of Chicago Press, 1976).
37. Frederick T. Gates to John D. Rockefeller, Dec. 12, 1910, Rockefeller Family Archives, record group 2. See also E. Richard Brown, "Public Health in Imperialism: Early Rockefeller Programs at Home and Abroad," *American Journal of Public Health,* 66 (1976), 897–903; Greer Williams, *The Plague Killers* (New York: Charles Scribner's Sons, 1969); Mary Boccaccio, "Ground Itch and Dew Poison: The Rockefeller Sanitary Commission, 1909–1914," *Journal of the History of Medicine and Allied Sciences,* 27 (1972), 30–53; and James H. Cassedy, "The 'Germ of Laziness' in the South, 1900–1915: Charles Wardell Stiles and the Progressive Paradox," *Bulletin of the History of Medicine,* 45 (1971), 159–69.
38. May quoted in *Tropical Health—A Report on a Study of Needs and Resources* (Washington, D.C.: National Academy of Sciences, National Research Council, Publication no. 996, 1962), pp. vii–viii. See also Brown, "Public Health in Imperialism," and Williams, *Plague Killers.*

39. Quoted in "Recent American Opinion in Favor of Health Insurance," *American Labor Legislation Review,* 6 (1916), 347.

40. Quoted in ibid., 345.

41. On the history of European sickness insurance programs, see Matthew J. Lynch and Stanley S. Raphael, *Medicine and the State* (Springfield, Ill.: Charles C. Thomas, 1963). On the social reforms of Progressivism, see James Weinstein, *The Corporate Ideal in the Liberal State, 1900–1918* (Boston: Beacon Press, 1968).

42. C. W. Hopkins, "The Hospital Organization of Railway Systems," in *Medicine, An Aid to Commerce,* paper from 40th Annual Meeting of the American Academy of Medicine, San Francisco, June 25–28, 1915 (Easton, Pa.: American Academy of Medicine, 1916), pp. 149–52.

43. Charles W. Eliot, "The Qualities of the Scientific Investigator," in *Addresses Delivered at the Opening of the Laboratories in New York City, May 11, 1906* (New York: Rockefeller Institute for Medical Research, 1906), p. 49.

44. W. H. Welch, "The Benefits of the Endowment of Medical Research," in *Addresses* (Rockefeller Institute), p. 32.

45. Gates, "Notes on Homeopathy, No. 3," written as a memo to Rockefeller, Sr., and circulated approvingly within the Rockefeller philanthropies about 1911, Gates collection, Rockefeller Foundation Archives. Gates' quotes on the next few pages are taken from this memo.

46. Gates, "Address on the Tenth Anniversary of the Rockefeller Institute," 1911, Gates collection, Rockefeller Foundation Archives.

47. F. T. Gates to J. D. Rockefeller, Jan. 31, 1905, Letterbook no. 350, Rockefeller Family Archives, record group 1.

48. J. A. Hobson, *Imperialism* (London: George Allen & Unwin, 1938; originally published 1902).

49. Described and quoted in a newsletter published for a short time by the foundation, "Hospital Ship for the Sulu Archipelago," *The Rockefeller Foundation,* Aug. 15, 1916, pp. 1, 14.

50. George E. Vincent, *The Rockefeller Foundation—A Review of Its War Work, Public Health Activities, and Medical Education Projects in 1917* (New York: Rockefeller Foundation, 1918), pp. 31–32.

51. For a history of class conflicts over the reform of public schools, see Joel H. Spring, *Education and the Rise of the Corporate State* (Boston: Beacon Press, 1972); and Michael B. Katz, *Class, Bureaucracy, and Schools—The Illusion of Educational Change in America* (New York: Praeger Publishers, 1971).

52. New London (Conn.) *Day,* July 10, 1914.

53. Autobiography, p. 281.

54. Gates, "Address." Gates had grown very ecumenical indeed: "Rev. Simon Flexner, D.D." was Jewish.

55. Speech reprinted in John B. Roberts, *The Doctor's Duty to the State: Essays on the Public Relations of Physicians* (Chicago: American Medical Association, 1908), especially p. 20. Roberts was also a member of the AMA Committee on Legislation, one of the profession's powerful lobbying units.

56. Jürgen Habermas, "Technology and Science as 'Ideology,' " in Habermas, *Toward a Rational Society—Student Protest, Science, and Politics* (Boston: Beacon Press, 1971), p. 105. See also Herbert Marcuse, *One-Dimensional Man* (Boston: Beacon Press, 1964).

57. See Samuel Haber, *Efficiency and Uplift: Scientific Management in the Progressive Era, 1890–1920* (Chicago: University of Chicago, 1964); and Harry Braverman's excellent study, *Labor and Monopoly Capital—The Degradation of*

Work in the Twentieth Century (New York and London: Monthly Review Press, 1974).

58. Quoted in Haber, *Efficiency and Uplift,* p. 20.

59. A writer of the period quoted in ibid., p. 62.

60. Nicholas Murray Butler, "Scientific Research and Material Progress," in *Addresses* (Rockefeller Institute), p. 40.

61. Ibid., p. 39.

62. Quoted in George Rosen, "The Evolution of Social Medicine," in H. E. Freeman, S. Levine, and L. G. Reeder, eds. *Handbook of Medical Sociology,* 2nd ed. (Englewood Cliffs, N.J.: Prentice-Hall, 1972), p. 39.

63. René J. Dubos, "The Gold-Headed Cane in the Laboratory," in *Annual Lectures, 1953* (Washington, D.C.: National Institutes of Health, 1953), pp. 89–102.

64. Gates to Rockefeller, Sr., Oct. 8, 1910, Rockefeller Family Archives, record group 2.

65. Gates, "Philanthropy and Civilization."

66. Gates, Autobiography, p. 395.

67. See, for example, *Studies from the Rockefeller Institute for Medical Research, Index for Volumes I–XV* (New York: Rockefeller Institute, 1912).

68. See Corner's *Rockefeller Institute,* which describes the lines of research pursued at the institute from 1901 to 1953.

69. Shryock notes the "heavy emphasis and reliance on the basic sciences" at the new Johns Hopkins School of Hygiene and Public Health in his *The Unique Influence of the Johns Hopkins University on American Medicine* (Copenhagen: Ejnar Munksgaard, Ltd., 1953), pp. 49–50.

70. C. W. Stiles, "Soil Pollution: The Chain Gang as a Possible Disseminator of Intestinal Parasites and Infections," *Public Health Reports,* 28 (1913), 985–86.

71. Gates, "Capital and Labor," memorandum (n.d., but probably 1916), Gates collection, Rockefeller Foundation Archives. Quotes on pages 130–131 are from this memo.

72. Quotes in this paragraph taken from two similar passages in Gates' "Address," and Autobiography, pp. 396–97.

73. "Address."

74. Ibid.

75. "Philanthropy and Civilization."

76. Quotes in this paragraph are taken from similar passages in Gates, "Address," and Gates, Autobiography, pp. 399–400.

CHAPTER 4

1. Quoted in Gerald E. Markowitz and David K. Rosner, "Doctors in Crisis: A Study of the Use of Medical Education Reform to Establish Modern Professional Elitism in Medicine," *American Quarterly,* 25 (1973), 88.

2. *JAMA,* 37 (1901), 270.

3. Richard H. Shryock, *Medical Licensing in America, 1650–1965* (Baltimore: Johns Hopkins Press, 1967), pp. 53–54.

4. Rosemary Stevens, *American Medicine and the Public Interest* (New Haven: Yale University Press, 1971), p. 24.

5. Markowitz and Rosner, "Doctors," 87.

6. Morris Fishbein, *A History of the American Medical Association, 1847 to 1947* (Phila.: W. B. Saunders Co., 1947), pp. 206–13; William G. Rothstein,

American Physicians in the Nineteenth Century (Baltimore: Johns Hopkins University Press, 1972), pp. 69–70, 317–18; Stevens, *American Medicine,* p. 29; and James G. Burrow, *AMA, Voice of American Medicine* (Baltimore: Johns Hopkins Press, 1963), pp. 27–32.

7. Quoted in Fishbein, *History,* p. 211.

8. One physician, unhappy with the new leadership, criticized the AMA for being self-proclaimed politicians of the profession, for representing only about 8 percent of the country's doctors, and for being controlled by merely "a half dozen men." See B. M. Jackson, "The Medical Profession: Its Politics and Politicians," *Pacific Medical Journal,* 47 (1904), 456–61.

9. On the coalition of university medical school physicians and private practitioners, their interests, strategy, and effect, see the excellent article by Markowitz and Rosner, "Doctors."

10. Arthur D. Bevan, "Cooperation in Medical Education and Medical Service," *JAMA,* 90 (1928), 1173.

11. "Council on Medical Education of the AMA," *JAMA,* 48 (1907), 1702.

12. Stevens, *American Medicine,* pp. 65–66. Today, in half the fifty states the state medical society has a direct hand in selecting the licensing board, according to Robert C. Derbyshire, *Medical Licensure and Discipline in the United States* (Baltimore: Johns Hopkins Press, 1969), p. 33.

13. "Council," *JAMA,* 48 (1907), 1702–05.

14. Bevan, "Cooperation," 1174–75; and "Medical Education in the United States," *JAMA,* 79 (1922), 629–37.

15. See, for example, George M. Kober's presidential address in Association of American Medical Colleges, *Proceedings of the 17th Annual Meeting,* Washington, D.C., May 6, 1907, pp. 31–32.

16. "Council," 1703.

17. *JAMA,* 35 (1900), 1353.

18. "Council," 1703.

19. *JAMA,* 37 (1901), 200–01.

20. "Council," 1703.

21. "Council on Medical Education of the AMA," *JAMA,* 44 (1905), 1471.

22. Abraham Flexner, *Henry S. Pritchett: A Biography* (New York: Columbia University Press, 1943), p. 108.

23. Howard J. Savage, *Fruit of an Impulse, 45 Years of the Carnegie Foundation, 1905–1950* (New York: Harcourt, Brace and Co., 1953), pp. 30, 54–55, 73–78; and A. Flexner, *Pritchett,* p. 97.

24. Information on precisely how Abraham Flexner's name was suggested to Pritchett is not readily available. But this scenario seems most consistent with available accounts and information. See Savage, *Fruit,* p. 105.

25. Abraham Flexner, *Abraham Flexner: An Autobiography* (New York: Simon and Schuster, 1960), pp. 45, 70–71.

26. Regarding Pritchett's views on the relationship of the medical study to the foundation's general program, see Pritchett's "Introduction," in Abraham Flexner, *Medical Education in the United States and Canada,* Bulletin no. 4 (New York: Carnegie Foundation for the Advancement of Teaching, 1910), p. xi.

27. Ibid., p. viii.

28. A. Flexner, *Autobiography,* p. 74.

29. Ibid., p. 85.

30. Ibid., p. 74; Stevens, *American Medicine,* pp. 66–67. Five medical schools had closed between the Council on Medical Education's survey in 1906 and Flexner's survey in 1909.

31. A. Flexner, *Pritchett*, p. 110.
32. Pritchett, "Introduction," in A. Flexner, *Medical Education*, p. ix.
33. Henry S. Pritchett to Jerome D. Greene, Pritchett to Cyrus Adler, and Pritchett to Dr. William T. Councilman, Jan. 22, 1909; Councilman to Pritchett, Jan. 26, 1909. Pritchett papers, Library of Congress.
34. A. Flexner, *Medical Education*, pp. 24–26.
35. Pritchett, "Introduction," in ibid., p. xiv.
36. Flexner, *Medical Education*, pp. 14–18 (emphasis added).
37. Ibid., pp. 7–8.
38. Ibid., p. 19.
39. Ibid., pp. 18–19, 48; Pritchett, "Introduction," in ibid., p. x.
40. National Center for Education Statistics, *Digest of Educational Statistics, 1974* (Washington, D.C.: Government Printing Office, 1975), pp. 33, 76.
41. A. Flexner, *Medical Education*, pp. 180–81.
42. Ibid., pp. 178–80; and Flexner, *Autobiography*, p. 207. See also Barbara Ehrenreich and Deirdre English, *Complaints and Disorders: The Sexual Politics of Sickness* (Old Westbury, N.Y.: The Feminist Press, 1973).
43. A. Flexner, *Medical Education*, pp. 26, 28–30.
44. Ibid., pp. 52–89.
45. Ibid., p. 16.
46. G. Frank Lydston, "Medicine as a Business Proposition," *JAMA*, 34 (1900), 1320.
47. *JAMA*, 37 (1901), 1119.
48. "Council," *JAMA*, 44 (1905), 1471.
49. For further evidence of medical reformers' views on reducing output and raising the profession's class base, see Chapter 2.
50. "Council," *JAMA*, 44 (1905), 1471.
51. Frederick C. Shattuck and J. Lewis Bremer, "The Medical School, 1869–1929," in S. E. Morison, ed., *The Development of Harvard University Since the Inauguration of President Eliot, 1869–1929* (Cambridge, Mass.: Harvard University Press, 1930), pp. 558–62. See also Frank Billings, "Medical Education in the United States," President's Address, *JAMA*, 40 (1903), 1271–76, for a brief summary of the organization's position on this and other planks in the reform platform.
52. Pritchett to Bevan, Nov. 4, 1909, correspondence with AMA, Carnegie Foundation files.
53. Pritchett to Bevan, June 18, 1910, and Bevan to Pritchett, Dec. 17, 1910, correspondence with AMA, Carnegie Foundation files. The reviews of Flexner's report were mixed. The *New York Times* (June 12, 1910) praised the report but called it "slightly contentious and unnecessarily irritating." The *Chicago Daily Tribune* (June 6 and 7, 1910) observed that schools that were given favorable evaluations by Flexner praised his report while those that were condemned by Flexner denied the validity of his report. The same paper noted that "the recommendations lean toward depriving the poor man of an education." *American Medicine* [5 (1910), 441–42] criticized the report for saying little that was not already known in the medical profession and for disregarding "the very evident progress of the past ten to fifteen years." The journal wishfully asserted that "the day of the small, comparatively inconsequential medical college is by no means passed." The *New York State Journal of Medicine* [10 (1910), 483–84] criticized the Carnegie Foundation for meddling in the internal affairs of universities and colleges and attacked the Flexner report's "wholesale and intemperate criticisms" of American medical schools. The homeopathic medical sect, of course, joined the chorus of criticism from

wounded professional interests; see the *Homeopathic Recorder*, 25 (1910), 241–43, 337–39, 413, 416; and 26 (1911), 15–16. The *JAMA* [54 (1910), 1949] equally predictably praised the report and voiced the leadership's fervent hope that "this report will call the attention of men of wealth to the need of endowments for medical education."

54. Pritchett to N. P. Colwell, Dec. 29, 1913, correspondence with AMA, Carnegie Foundation files.

55. Pritchett accused the council of giving greater leniency to Baylor University's medical school than to Meharry. Pritchett to Colwell, April 3, 1918, and May 2, 1921, and other letters between Pritchett and Bevan from 1918 to 1922, correspondence with AMA, Carnegie Foundation files. By 1917 Pritchett was so disenchanted with the council, and presumably ashamed of his own gullibility a decade earlier, that he rejected out of hand a request by Bevan that the foundation undertake a new study designed to discredit "medical cults." Bevan included in this term "everything that masquerades as branches or cults in the art of healing outside of regular scientific medicine." Bevan to Pritchett, March 23, 1917; Pritchett to Bevan, April 3, 1917; and Clyde Furst, secretary of the Carnegie Foundation, to N. P. Colwell, Dec. 1, 1917; all in correspondence with AMA, Carnegie Foundation files.

56. A. Flexner, *Autobiography*, p. 165; Saul Jarcho, "Medical Education in the United States, 1910–1956," *Journal of the Mount Sinai Hospital*, 26 (1959), 339–40.

57. A. Flexner, *Medical Education*, pp. 10–11.

58. On the impact of the Flexner report see Stevens, *American Medicine*, pp. 68–69; Rothstein, *American Physicians*, pp. 292–94; Markowitz and Rosner, "Doctors," 101; Robert P. Hudson, "Abraham Flexner in Perspective: American Medical Education, 1865–1910," *Bulletin of the History of Medicine*, 46 (1972), 545–61; H. David Banta, "Abraham Flexner—A Reappraisal," *Social Science and Medicine*, 5 (1971), 655–61; and Carleton B. Chapman, *"The Flexner Report* by Abraham Flexner," *Daedalus*, 103 (Winter 1974), 105–17. For a thorough discussion of the Flexner report in its historical context, see Howard S. Berliner, "A Larger Perspective on the Flexner Report," *International Journal of Health Services*, 5 (1975), 573–92.

59. Herbert M. Morais, *The History of the Negro in Medicine* (New York: Publishers Co., for Association for the Study of Negro Life and History, 1967), pp. 86, 100. De facto segregation is still the reality in the North as well as in the South. Black physicians serve a nearly all-black clientele while few white doctors locate their offices in poor or racial minority areas. Cf. Lois C. Gray, "The Geographic and Functional Distribution of Black Physicians: Some Research and Policy Considerations," *American Journal of Public Health*, 67 (1977), 519–26; and Eva J. Salber et al., "Access to Health Care in a Southern Rural Community," *Medical Care*, 14 (1976), 971–86.

60. Quoted in John F. Fulton, *Harvey Cushing, A Biography* (Springfield, Ill.: Charles C. Thomas, 1946), p. 379. Bevan's memory did not serve him well (or perhaps it served him better than it served truth). He remembered there being twenty-two homeopathic schools and twelve eclectic schools "running at the time." The council's own figures indicate that there were twenty-two homeopathic schools in 1900 and never more than nine eclectic schools at any one time (although a total of thirty-two had been started during the previous century).

61. "Medical Education in the United States," *JAMA*, 79 (1922), 629–37.

62. *Annual Report of the General Education Board, 1919–1920* and *1928–1929;* and Stevens, *American Medicine*, p. 69.

63. "The Art of Endowing Medical Colleges," *JAMA*, 37 (1901), 201.

64. A. Flexner, *Autobiography*, pp. 109–10; R. B. Fosdick, *Adventure in Giving, The Story of the General Education Board* (New York: Harper and Row, 1962), pp. 154–55; and A. Flexner to F. T. Gates, June 24, 1911, GEB files, Rockefeller Foundation Archives.

65. A. Flexner, *Autobiography*, pp. 110–11.

66. Ibid., pp. 112–13; Fosdick, *Adventure*, p. 157; A. Flexner, "From the Report on the Johns Hopkins Medical School," GEB files, Rockefeller Foundation Archives.

67. See George W. Corner, *A History of the Rockefeller Institute, 1901–1953* (New York: Rockefeller Institute Press, 1964), p. 94; and S. Flexner and J. T. Flexner, *William Henry Welch and the Heroic Age of American Medicine* (New York: Viking Press, 1941), p. 304. The policy was established before the hospital opened in 1910.

68. F. T. Gates, "Concerning Private Gifts to States and a Medical Policy," Memo to the General Education Board, Feb. 26, 1925, Gates collection, Rockefeller Foundation Archives.

69. J. D. Greene to Dr. Henry A. Christian, Nov. 30, 1914, GEB files, Rockefeller Foundation Archives.

70. Gates, "Private Gifts."

71. For descriptive history of full-time plan's origins, see Flexner and Flexner, *Welch*, pp. 297–314, 320–28.

72. Richard H. Shryock, *The Unique Influence of the Johns Hopkins University on American Medicine* (Copenhagen: Ejnar Munksgaard, Ltd., 1953), p. 19.

73. Donald Fleming, *William H. Welch and the Rise of Modern Medicine* (Boston: Little, Brown and Co., 1954), especially p. 21; S. Flexner and J. T. Flexner, *Welch*, pp. 71–72.

74. Quotes and information about Mall are from Florence R. Sabin, *Franklin Paine Mall, The Story of a Mind* (Baltimore: Johns Hopkins Press, 1934), especially pp. 29, 127–33, 203, 261, 264.

75. *JAMA*, 35 (1900), 501.

76. Victor C. Vaughan, "Reorganization of Clinical Teaching," *JAMA*, 64 (1915), 785–90.

77. Quoted in Sabin, *Mall*, p. 270.

78. Fosdick, *Adventure*, p. 160.

79. Stevens, *American Medicine*, p. 96.

80. Arthur D. Bevan, "Report of the Council on Medical Education," *JAMA*, 65 (1915), 110–11.

81. Benjamin Moore, "The Value of Research in the Development of National Health," *Popular Science Monthly*, 85 (1914), 366.

82. Quoted in Ilza Veith and Franklin C. McLean, *Medicine at the University of Chicago, 1927–1952* (Chicago: University of Chicago Press, 1952), p. 22.

83. William H. Welch, "Report on the Endowment of University Medical Education," 1911, copy in GEB files, Rockefeller Foundation Archives.

84. A. Flexner, *Autobiography*, pp. 114–15.

85. Welch's letter to GEB, quoted in Fosdick, *Adventure*, p. 158.

86. Ibid., p. 159.

87. William H. Welch to Simon Flexner, Dec. 5, 1915, GEB files, Rockefeller Foundation Archives.

88. Quoted in S. Flexner and J. T. Flexner, *Welch*, p. 326. Janeway's article was "Outside Professional Engagements by Members of Professional Faculties," published in Nicholas Murray Butler's journal, *Educational Review*, 55 (1918), 207–19.

89. Quoted in S. Flexner and J. T. Flexner, *Welch*, pp. 326–27.

90. A. Flexner to H. S. Pritchett, March 27, 1919, correspondence with GEB, Carnegie Foundation files.

91. Fosdick, *Adventure*, p. 328.

92. Ibid., p. 180.

93. Fulton, *Cushing*, pp. 383–84; and Fosdick, *Adventure*, p. 163.

94. Fosdick, *Adventure*, p. 163; and Fulton, *Cushing*, pp. 377–84.

95. A. Flexner to W. Buttrick, May 7, 1921, GEB files, Rockefeller Foundation Archives.

96. "Reasons Why the Harvard Medical School Offers the Best Opportunities for Surgical Scientific Work," by "Members of the Surgical Department," attached to letter from H. P. Bowditch (?) to John D. Rockefeller, Jr., Oct. 31, 1900, Rockefeller Family Archives, record group 2.

97. Eliot quoted in Fosdick, *Adventure*, p. 163.

98. Ibid., p. 164.

99. Los Angeles *Record*, May 14, 1912; quoted in Catherine Lewerth, "Source Book for a History of the Rockefeller Foundation" (typewritten ms., bound in 21 vols., Rockefeller Foundation Archives, c. 1949), p. 23.

100. Bird S. Coler to Starr J. Murphy, April 19, 1917, and clipping from Brooklyn *Standard Union*, April 12, 1917, Rockefeller Family Archives, record group 2. Coler had strong Progressive leanings. He believed the foundation was driving "an artificial line of division between the more fortunate minority and the less fortunate majority of our people." In this respect he was clearly wrong since the foundation was attempting to cover up the class divisions in the society.

101. Pittsburgh (Pa.) *Leader*, July 10, 1914, clipping enclosed in letter from Starr J. Murphy to F. T. Gates, July 21, 1914, Rockefeller Family Archives, record group 2.

102. Commission on Industrial Relations, Final Report (Washington, D.C.: Barnard and Miller Print, 1915), pp. 116–19. See also James Weinstein, *The Corporate Ideal in the Liberal State, 1900–1918* (Boston: Beacon Press, 1968), pp. 172–213.

103. G. F. Peabody to F. T. Gates, Nov. 5, 1911, Rockefeller Family Archives, record group 2.

104. C. W. Eliot to F. T. Gates, March 27, 1914, Gates collection, Rockefeller Foundation Archives.

105. F. T. Gates, memo to himself or the board (n.d., but apparently Nov. 1911), Rockefeller Family Archives, record group 2.

106. George E. Vincent, *The Rockefeller Foundation, A Review for 1917* (New York: Rockefeller Foundation, 1918), p. 8; F. T. Gates to G. E. Vincent, March 20, 1918, and G. E. Vincent to F. T. Gates, March 25, 1918, Program and Policy File, Rockefeller Foundation Archives, record group 1.

107. Fosdick, *Adventure*, p. 164.

108. Ibid., p. 164.

109. Lewerth, "Source Book," pp. 5116, 5119–21.

110. Quoted in ibid., p. 5115.

111. *Annual Report of the General Education Board, 1920–1921* (New York: GEB, 1922), p. 22.

112. Lewerth, "Source Book," pp. 5115–16.

113. H. S. Pritchett to Wallace Buttrick, Feb. 11 and 24, 1919, correspondence with GEB, Carnegie Foundation files.

114. Pritchett to Flexner, June 10, 1925, correspondence with GEB, Carnegie Foundation files.

115. H. S. Pritchett to Wallace Buttrick, Nov. 11, 1919, correspondence with GEB, Carnegie Foundation files.

116. W. Buttrick to H. S. Pritchett, Nov. 21, 1919, correspondence with GEB, Carnegie Foundation files.

117. W. Buttrick to Harry Pratt Judson, president of University of Chicago, Dec. 26, 1914, GEB files, Rockefeller Foundation Archives.

118. Correspondence regarding Columbia University medical school, 1917–1920, GEB files, Rockefeller Foundation Archives; and W. Buttrick to H. S. Pritchett, Nov. 21, 1919, correspondence with GEB, Carnegie Foundation files.

119. C. W. Eliot to W. Buttrick, April 24, 1917, GEB files, Rockefeller Foundation Archives; and A. P. Stokes to A. Flexner, March 10, 1925, GEB files, Rockefeller Foundation Archives. Stokes was always wary of public criticism that the GEB was attempting to control educational institutions with its grants (cf. A. P. Stokes to W. Buttrick, Jan. 29, 1917, GEB files, Rockefeller Foundation Archives).

120. T. M. Debevoise to F. T. Gates, Oct. 7, 1925, GEB files, Rockefeller Foundation Archives.

121. Ibid.

122. Minutes of the GEB, Feb. 26, 1925, GEB files, Rockefeller Foundation Archives.

123. Minutes of the GEB Executive Committee, Sept. 30, 1925, GEB files, Rockefeller Foundation Archives.

124. Commission on Medical Education, *Supplement to the Third Report* (New Haven: Office of the Director of the Study, May 1929), p. 58.

125. Association of American Medical Colleges, *Proceedings of the 17th Annual Meeting,* Washington, D.C., May 6, 1907, p. 17.

126. Commission on Medical Education, *Supplement,* pp. 58–59.

127. Memorandum, Dec. 1919, quoted in Fosdick, *Adventure,* p. 166.

128. *Annual Report of the GEB, 1922–1923,* pp. 17–19.

129. Fosdick, *Adventure,* pp. 166–67.

130. F. T. Gates to A. Flexner, Dec. 2, 1922; quoted in Lewerth, "Source Book," pp. 5230–31; and Gates memo, quoted in Fosdick, *Adventure,* p. 167.

131. A. Flexner, *Autobiography,* p. 189; A. Flexner to H. S. Pritchett, Nov. 1, 1922; quoted in Fosdick, *Adventure,* p. 167.

132. Lewerth, "Source Book," p. 5231.

133. Gates, "Private Gifts."

134. Ibid.

135. Ibid.

136. Gates, Autobiography, unpublished ms., 1928, Gates collection, Rockefeller Foundation Archives, p. 463; Gates, "Some Reflections on Questions of Policy," memo to the board, Jan. 23, 1906, Gates collection, Rockefeller Foundation Archives.

137. Ibid.

138. Ibid.

139. Ibid.

140. Ibid.

141. Ibid.

142. Ibid.

143. Gates, memo "written for the sake of clarifying my own thought" concerning conflicts he was having with board member Charles W. Eliot over GEB funding policies. Eliot favored using some funds to support current expenses of colleges as opposed to Gates' insistence on permanent endowments. He criticized Eliot's conception of the board's mission as much too "humble." "Dr. Eliot's plan is to buy [apples] at a dollar a bushel and distribute them. My plan is to plant apple trees." Memo, Feb. 28, 1910, Rockefeller Family Archives, record group 2.

144. See E. Richard Brown, "Public Health in Imperialism: Early Rockefeller Programs at Home and Abroad," *American Journal of Public Health*, 66 (1976), 897–903.

145. Gates, Autobiography, pp. 456–57, 463–64.

146. Gates, "Fundamental Principles of Mr. Rockefeller's Philanthropy," Oct. 7, 1908, Gates collection, Rockefeller Foundation Archives.

147. Gates to Rockefeller, Sr., Aug. 9, 1907, Gates collection, Rockefeller Foundation Archives.

148. Gates, "Thoughts on the Rockefeller Public and Private Benefactions," Dec. 31, 1926, Gates collection, Rockefeller Foundation Archives.

149. Fosdick, *The Story of the Rockefeller Foundation* (London: Odhams Press, Ltd., 1952), p. 117.

150. *Annual Report of the GEB, 1920–1921*, pp. 30–34.

151. Gates, "Private Gifts."

152. Minutes of the GEB, Nov. 1924 through March 1925; and W. Buttrick to J. D. Rockefeller, Jr., Dec. 29, 1924, GEB files, Rockefeller Foundation Archives.

153. Minutes of the board, May 28, 1925; and Document of Record no. 474, GEB files, Rockefeller Foundation Archives.

154. Minutes of the GEB Executive Committee, Nov. 9, 1925, GEB files, Rockefeller Foundation Archives.

155. Lewerth, "Source Book," p. 5240, based on correspondence between Iowa officers, Rockefeller and GEB officers, and Pritchett at Carnegie Foundation.

156. On the development of monopoly control through intervention by the State, see Gabriel Kolko, *The Triumph of Conservatism—A Reinterpretation of American History, 1900–1916* (Chicago: Quadrangle Books, 1967); and Weinstein, *The Corporate Ideal.*

157. David Rockefeller quote from *Wall Street Journal*, Dec. 21, 1971, p. 10.

158. *JAMA*, 37 (1901), 200–01.

159. A. D. Bevan to H. S. Pritchett, Oct. 5, 1921, correspondence with AMA, Carnegie Foundation files.

160. W. H. Welch, "Duties of a Hospital to the Public Health," *Proceedings of the National Conference of Charities and Correction*, 42nd Annual Meeting, Baltimore, May 12–19, 1915, p. 215.

161. Markowitz and Rosner, "Doctors," 87.

162. The history of the AMA's involvement with social insurance from 1915 to 1920 is developed in Elton Rayack, *Professional Power and American Medicine* (New York: World Publishing Co., 1967), pp. 136–46; and Burrow, *AMA*, pp. 132–51. Other views of the ascendancy of the conservatives in the AMA in 1920 can be found in Shryock, *Licensing*, pp. 91–94; and in Stevens, *American Medicine.*

CHAPTER 5

1. Rosemary Stevens, *American Medicine and the Public Interest* (New Haven: Yale University Press, 1971), pp. 68–69; and Richard H. Shryock, *American Medical Research, Past, and Present* (New York: Commonwealth Fund, 1947), pp. 96–97.

2. Abraham Flexner, *Abraham Flexner: An Autobiography* (New York: Simon and Schuster, 1960), p. 37.

3. Committee on the Costs of Medical Care, *Medical Care for the American People: The Final Report of the Committee on the Costs of Medical Care* (Chicago: University of Chicago Press, 1932).

4. Although one-third of the committee's membership was private practitioners, two-thirds were persons generally committed to rationalizing medical care, including Secretary of the Interior Ray Lyman Wilbur and Winthrop W. Aldrich, president of the Chase National Bank and brother-in-law of John D. Rockefeller, Jr. For other discussions of the CCMC, see Odin W. Anderson, *The Uneasy Equilibrium: Private and Public Financing of Health Services in the United States, 1875–1965* (New Haven: College and University Press, 1968), pp. 91–103; and Elton Rayack, *Professional Power and American Medicine: The Economics of the American Medical Association* (Cleveland: World Publishing Co., 1967), pp. 146–55.

5. *JAMA*, 99 (1932), 1950–52. See also Rayack, noted above.

6. I. S. Falk, "Medical Care in the U.S.A.: 1932–1972. Problems, Proposals, and Programs from the Committee on the Costs of Medical Care to the Committee for National Health Insurance," *Health and Society, Milbank Memorial Fund Quarterly*, 51 (Winter 1973), 6, 15.

7. Leonard Rodberg and Gelvin Stevenson, "The Health Care Industry in Advanced Capitalism," *Review of Radical Political Economics*, 9 (Spring 1977), 104–15.

8. Edwin R. Embree and Julia Waxman, *Investment in People: The Story of the Julius Rosenwald Fund* (New York: Harper and Bros., 1949), pp. 128–31.

9. For a thorough examination of Blue Cross, see Sylvia Law, *Blue Cross: What Went Wrong?* (New Haven: Yale University Press, 1974). For a brief history of Blue Cross, Blue Shield, and insurance company involvement in commercial health insurance, see Herman M. Somers and Anne R. Somers, *Doctors, Patients, and Health Insurance—The Organization and Financing of Medical Care* (Washington, D.C.: Brookings Institution, 1961), pp. 249–340. For later data on premium income, see Robert M. Gibson and Charles R. Fisher, "National Health Expenditures, Fiscal Year 1977," *Social Security Bulletin*, 41 (July 1978), 3–20.

10. For a summary of information on the Hill-Burton program, see Cambridge Research Institute, *Trends Affecting the U.S. Health Care System* (Washington, D.C.: Government Printing Office, 1976), pp. 91–95.

11. See, for example, G. William Domhoff, *The Higher Circles: The Governing Class in America* (New York: Vintage Books, 1971); Ralph Miliband, *The State in Capitalist Society* (New York: Basic Books, 1969); Claus Offe, "Political Authority and Class Structures: An Analysis of State Capitalist Societies," *International Journal of Sociology*, 2 (1972), 73–108; and James O'Connor, *The Fiscal Crisis of the State* (New York: St. Martin's Press, 1973). For analyses of the State and health care under capitalism, see Marc Renaud, "On the Structural Constraints to State Intervention in Health," *International Journal of Health Services*, 5 (1975), 559–71; and Vincente Navarro, *Medicine Under Capitalism* (New York: Prodist, 1976), pp. 183–228.

12. See Rayack, *Professional Power*, chap. 5; and James G. Burrow, *AMA, Voice of American Medicine* (Baltimore: Johns Hopkins Press, 1963), chap. 7.

13. Rayack, *Professional Power*, chap. 5; and Burrow, *AMA*, pp. 194–251, 293–301, 340–71.

14. Rayack, *Professional Power*, chap. 3.

15. Gibson and Fisher, "National Health Expenditures"; and *Hospital Statistics*, 1977 ed. (Chicago: American Hospital Association, 1977).

16. See, for example, Barry Ensminger, "The $8-Billion Hospital Bed Overrun: A Consumer's Guide to Stopping Wasteful Construction" (Washington, D.C.:

Public Citizen's Health Research Group, 1975); and Institute of Medicine, *Controlling the Supply of Hospital Beds* (Washington, D.C.: National Academy of Sciences, 1976).

17. Cambridge Research Institute, *Trends,* p. 180.
18. Gibson and Fisher, "National Health Expenditures."
19. Robert Alford, *Health Care Politics: Ideological and Interest Group Barriers to Reform* (Chicago: University of Chicago Press, 1975), especially pp. 190–217.
20. *Hospital Statistics,* pp. 4–5.
21. See, for example, Douglass J. Seaver, "Hospital Revises Role, Reaches Out to Cultivate and Capture Markets," *Hospitals,* 51 (June 1, 1977), 59–63; David D. Karr, "Increasing a Hospital's Market Share," in same issue, 64–66; and Warren C. Falberg and Shirley Bonnem, "Good Marketing Helps a Hospital Grow," in same issue, 70–73.
22. Bureau of the Census, *Statistical Abstract of the United States, 1976* (Washington, D.C.: Government Printing Office, 1976), p. 427.
23. Navarro, *Medicine Under Capitalism,* pp. 148–49.
24. Marianna O. Lewis, ed. *The Foundation Directory,* 6th ed. (New York: Foundation Center, 1977), pp. xiii, xxi.
25. See, for example, G. William Domhoff, *Who Rules America?* (Englewood Cliffs, N.J.: Prentice-Hall, 1967); and Domhoff, *The Higher Circles.*
26. Vicente Navarro, "National Health Insurance and the Strategy for Change," *Health and Society, Milbank Memorial Fund Quarterly,* 51 (Spring 1973), 236–37.
27. See, for example, David Mechanic, *Public Expectations and Health Care* (New York: Wiley-Interscience, 1972), p. 27.
28. Eliot Marshall, "What's Bad for General Motors," *New Republic,* March 12, 1977, pp. 22–23.
29. Gibson and Fisher, "National Health Expenditures."
30. From the voluminous literature on HMOs, some useful favorable articles are: Cambridge Research Institute, *Trends,* pp. 221–60; Ernest W. Saward and Merwyn R. Greenlick, "Health Policy and the HMO," *Milbank Memorial Fund Quarterly,* 50 (April 1972, pt. 2), 147–76; Ira G. Greenberg and Michael L. Rodburg, "The Role of Prepaid Group Practice in Relieving the Medical Care Crisis," *Harvard Law Review,* 84 (1971), 887–1001. The business point of view, also very favorable, is represented by Committee for Economic Development, *Building a National Health Care System* (New York: Committee for Economic Development, 1973); Michael B. Rothfield, "Sensible Surgery for Swelling Medical Costs," *Fortune,* (April 1973), 110–19; and "Containing the Cost of Employee Health Plans," *Business Week,* May 30, 1977, pp. 74–76. Some good critical articles on HMOs include Howard B. Waitzkin and Barbara Waterman, *The Exploitation of Illness in Capitalist Society* (Indianapolis, Ind.: Bobbs-Merrill, 1974), pp. 89–107; Thomas Bodenheimer, Elizabeth Harding, and Steve Cummings, *Billions for Band-Aids* (San Francisco: Medical Committee for Human Rights, 1972), pp. 75–98; and Judy Carnoy et al., "The Kaiser Plan," *Health PAC Bulletin,* no. 55, Nov. 1973, pp. 1–18. The enabling and funding legislation is the Health Maintenance Organization Act of 1973 (P.L. 93–222).
31. *JAMA,* 227 (1974), 1171.
32. See, for example, Bruce C. Vladeck, "Interest-Group Representation and the HSAs: Health Planning and Political Theory," *American Journal of Public Health,* 67 (1977), 23–39.
33. Committee for Economic Development, *Building a National Health Care System.*

34. Lewis, *Foundation Directory*, p. xxi; and David E. Rogers, "The President's Statement," *Robert Wood Johnson Foundation Annual Report, 1973* (Princeton, N.J.: Robert Wood Johnson Foundation, 1973).

35. Alford, *Health Care Politics*, pp. 190–217.

36. Falk, "Medical Care in the U.S.A.," 29–30 (emphasis added).

37. Recent legislative efforts to control rising hospital costs led to conflicts among hospitals, which were concerned mainly with limitations on their revenues, and investment bankers and medical equipment manufacturers, who were upset with limitations on capital expenditures that would reduce hospital construction and purchase of major equipment such as CAT scanners. See "Bankers and Manufacturers Meet to Discuss Opposition to Hospital Cost Containment," *Washington Report on Medicine and Health,* 31 (Aug. 29, 1977), 2.

38. Alford, *Health Care Politics*, p. 193.

39. *Health United States, 1975* (Rockville, Md.: National Center for Health Statistics, 1976), pp. 405, 409; Lu Ann Aday, "The Impact of Health Policy on Access to Medical Care," *Health and Society, Milbank Memorial Fund Quarterly,* 54 (Spring 1976), 215–33; Ronald Andersen, Joanna Kravits, and Odin W. Anderson, *Equity in Health Services: Empirical Analyses in Social Policy* (Cambridge, Mass.: Ballinger Publishing Co., 1975), p. 178; Adele D. Hofmann, "Health Care of Inner-City Adolescents," *Clinical Pediatrics,* 13 (1974), 570–73; A. F. Brunswick and E. Josephson, "Adolescent Health in Harlem," *American Journal of Public Health,* 62 (1972, suppl.), 1–62; K. D. Rogers and G. Reese, "Health Studies—Presumably Normal High School Students," *American Journal of Diseases of Children,* 108 (1964), 572–600; and *Health Attitudes and Behaviors of Youths 12–17 Years: Demographic and Socioeconomic Factors,* Vital and Health Statistics, series 11, no. 153 (Washington, D.C.: National Center for Health Statistics, 1975).

40. *San Francisco Chronicle,* July 14, 1977.

41. Lois C. Gray, "The Geographic and Functional Distribution of Black Physicians: Some Research and Policy Considerations," *American Journal of Public Health,* 67 (1977), 519–26. See also Eva J. Salber et al., "Access to Health Care in a Southern Rural Community," *Medical Care,* 14 (1976), 971–86.

42. Cambridge Research Institute, *Trends,* p. 128.

43. Marjorie Smith Mueller, "Private Health Insurance in 1973: A Review of Coverage, Enrollment, and Financial Experience," *Social Security Bulletin,* 38 (Feb. 1975), 21–40.

44. Gibson and Fisher, "National Health Expenditures."

45. Quoted in L. Frederick, "How Much Unnecessary Surgery?" *Medical World News,* 17 (1976), 50–66.

46. John P. Bunker, "Surgical Manpower: A Comparison of Operations and Surgeons in the United States and in England and Wales," *New England Journal of Medicine,* 282 (1970), 135–44.

47. House Committee on Interstate and Foreign Commerce, *Cost and Quality of Health Care: Unnecessary Surgery* (Washington, D.C.: Government Printing Office, 1976).

48. R. D. Lyons, "Surgery on Poor Is Found Higher," *New York Times,* Sept. 1, 1977.

49. Cambridge Research Institute, *Trends,* p. 366.

50. Ibid., pp. 357–66.

51. On the commodification of health services, see Navarro, *Medicine Under Capitalism,* pp. 183–228; and Rodberg and Stevenson, "Health Care Industry."

52. See, for example, Harry Schwartz, *The Case for American Medicine* (New

York: David McKay, 1972); and his article, "A Half Century of Health Progress," *Ohio State Medical Journal,* 71 (1975), 58–59.

53. T. McKeown, "A Conceptual Background for Research and Development in Medicine," *International Journal of Health Services,* 3 (1971), 17–28; and McKeown, *Medicine in Modern Society* (London: Allen & Unwin, 1965).

54. Warren Winkelstein and Fern E. French, "The Role of Ecology in the Design of a Health Care System," *California Medicine,* 113 (1970), 7–12.

55. John Powles, "On the Limitations of Modern Medicine," *Science, Medicine, and Man,* 1 (1973), 6. For similar data, analysis, and conclusions applied to the United States, see John B. McKinlay and Sonja M. McKinlay, "The Questionable Contribution of Medical Measures to the Decline of Mortality in the United States in the Twentieth Century," *Health and Society/Milbank Memorial Fund Quarterly* (Summer 1977) 405–28.

56. René Dubos, *Mirage of Health—Utopias, Progress, and Biological Change* (Garden City, N.Y.: Anchor Books, 1959), pp. 30–31.

57. George Rosen, *A History of Public Health* (New York: M D Publications, 1958), pp. 192–275; and Dubos, *Mirage of Health,* pp. 139–40.

58. *Health United States, 1975,* pp. 227, 358–59.

59. C. L. Erhardt and J. E. Berlin, eds., *Mortality and Morbidity in the United States* (Cambridge, Mass.: Harvard University Press, 1974), p. 174; and *Health United States, 1975,* pp. 338–47, 371.

60. Barbara Starfield, *Health Needs of Children,* Harvard Child Health Series Project Reports, vol. 2 (Cambridge, Mass.: Harvard University Press, 1976); and Erhardt and Berlin, *Mortality and Morbidity,* pp. 28–29.

61. Harold S. Luft, "The Probability of Disability: The Influence of Age, Race, Sex, Education, and Income," Paper presented at Annual Meeting of the American Public Health Association, Chicago, November 17, 1975; and "Socioeconomic Differentials in Morbidity," *Metropolitan Life Insurance Company Statistics Bulletin,* 53 (June 1972), 10–12.

62. S. Leonard Syme and Lisa F. Berkman, "Social Class, Susceptibility, and Sickness," *American Journal of Epidemiology,* 104 (1976), 1–8; M. H. Nagi and E. G. Stockwell, "Socioeconomic Differentials in Mortality by Cause of Death," *Health Services Reports,* 88 (1973), 449–56; A. Antonovsky, "Social Class, Life Expectancy, and Overall Mortality," *Milbank Memorial Fund Quarterly,* 45 (1967), 31–73; Stephanie J. Ventura et al., "Selected Vital and Health Statistics in Poverty and Nonpoverty Areas of 19 Large Cities, United States, 1969–71," *Vital and Health Statistics,* series 21, no. 26 (Rockville, Md.: National Center for Health Statistics, 1975).

63. Warren Winkelstein, "Epidemiological Considerations Underlying the Allocation of Health and Disease Care Resources," *International Journal of Epidemiology,* 1 (1972), 69–74.

64. Winkelstein and French, "The Role of Ecology"; and G. A. Lillington, "Health Effects from Air Pollution," in W. D. McKee, ed., *Environmental Problems in Medicine* (Springfield, Ill.: Charles C. Thomas, 1974), pp. 314–24.

65. See *Forward Plan for Health,* [Fiscal Year] 1978–82 (Washington, D.C.: Public Health Service, 1976), p. 77; Daniel M. Berman, *Death on the Job* (forthcoming from Monthly Review Press), chap. 2; J. A. Page and M. O'Brien, *Bitter Wages* (New York: Grossman, 1973); and P. Brodeur, *Expendable Americans* (New York: Viking Press, 1974).

66. Blue Cross Association *Consumer Report,* March 1976, p. 1.

67. J. Eyer, "Hypertension as a Disease of Modern Society," *International Journal of Health Services,* 5 (1975), 539–58; S. L. Syme, T. Oakes, and G. Friedman,

"Social Class and Racial Differences in Blood Pressure," *American Journal of Public Health,* 64 (1974), 619–20; S. L. Syme, M. M. Hyman, and P. E. Enterline, "Cultural Mobility and the Occurrence of Coronary Heart Disease," *Journal of Health and Human Behavior,* 6 (1965), 178–90; M. Friedman, R. Rosenman, and V. Carroll, "Changes in Serum Cholesterol and Blood Clotting Time in Men Subjected to Cyclic Variation of Occupation Stress," *Circulation,* 17 (1958), 852–61; H. Russek and B. Zohman, "Relative Significance of Heredity, Diet, and Occupational Stress in Coronary Heart Disease of Young Adults," *American Journal of Medical Science,* 235 (1958), 266–77; M. Friedman and R. Rosenman, *Type A Behavior and Your Heart* (New York: Knopf, 1974); and S. Kasl and S. Cobb, "Blood Pressure Changes in Men Undergoing Job Loss: A Preliminary Report," *Psychosomatic Medicine,* 32 (1970), 19–38.

68. Erhardt and Berlin, *Mortality and Morbidity,* pp. 28–29.

69. Special Task Force to the Secretary of Health, Education, and Welfare, *Work in America* (Cambridge, Mass.: MIT Press, 1973), pp. 77–79.

70. Robert J. Haggerty, "Session III—Present Strengths and Weaknesses in Current Systems of Comprehensive Health Services for Children and Youth," *American Journal of Public Health,* 60 (1970), 74–98.

71. Walsh McDermott, Kurt W. Deuschle, and Clifford R. Barnett, "Health Care Experiment at Many Farms," *Science,* 175 (1972), 23–31.

72. Joel Alpert et al., "Delivery of Health Care for Children: Report of an Experiment," *Pediatrics,* 57 (1976), 917–30.

73. Paul Starr, "Who Needs Medicine? The Politics of Therapeutic Nihilism," *Working Papers for a New Society,* 4 (Summer 1976), 48–55.

74. U.S. Congress, Office of Technology Assessment, *Development of Medical Technology—Opportunities for Assessment* (Washington, D.C.: Government Printing Office, 1976), pp. 14–15.

75. David M. Kessner et al., *Infant Death: An Analysis by Maternal Risk and Health Care* (Washington, D.C.: Institute of Medicine, National Academy of Sciences, 1973), pp. 1–18.

76. Naomi M. Morris et al., "Shifting Age-Parity Distribution of Births and the Decrease in Infant Mortality." *American Journal of Public Health,* 65 (1975), 359–62.

77. Shryock, *American Medical Research,* pp. 96–97; and *General Education Board Annual Report, 1940,* pp. 191–96.

78. Shryock, *American Medical Research,* pp. 277, 289.

79. *Basic Data Relating to the National Institutes of Health,* 1974 and 1977 eds.; S. P. Strickland, "Integration of Medical Research and Health Policies," *Science,* 173 (1971), 1093; Strickland, *Science, Politics, and Dread Disease* (Cambridge, Mass.: Harvard University Press, 1972); and NIH Study Committee, *Biomedical Science and Its Administration, A Study of the National Institutes of Health* (Washington, D.C.: The White House, 1965).

80. American Foundation, *Medical Research: A Midcentury Survey,* vol. 1 (Boston: Little, Brown and Co., 1955), 144, 147; and David E. Rogers, "Medical Academe and the Problems of Primary Care," *Journal of Medical Education,* 50 (Dec. 1975, pt. 2), 171–80. In 1967–68, federal support equaled 53 percent of U.S. medical schools' operating income, state and local government support totaled another 15 percent, while tuition and fees came to only 4 percent and endowment income to only 3 percent; see Ray E. Brown, "Financing Medical Education," in William G. Anlyan et al., eds., *The Future of Medical Education* (Durham, N.C.: Duke University Press, 1973), p. 180.

81. Rogers, "Medical Academe"; Herman M. Somers and Anne R. Somers,

Doctors, Patients, and Health Insurance (Washington, D.C.: Brookings Institution, 1961), p. 42; and James W. Begun, "Refining Physician Manpower Data," *Medical Care,* 15 (1977), 780–86.

82. See Barbara Ehrenreich and John Ehrenreich, *The American Health Empire: Power, Profits, and Politics* (New York: A Health-PAC Book, Vintage Books, 1971); and Cecil G. Sheps and Conrad Seipp, "The Medical School, Its Products and Its Problems," *Annals of the American Academy of Political and Social Science,* 399 (Jan. 1972), 38–49.

83. Hans Zinsser, "The Perils of Magnanimity: A Problem in American Education," *Atlantic Monthly,* 159 (1927), 246–50; see also the short article by the director of the National Science Foundation, William D. McElroy, "The Making of Science Policy," *Proceedings of the Federation of American Societies for Experimental Biology,* 31 (1972), 1553–55.

84. *JAMA,* 37 (1901), 200–01, warned, "Rich men may injure the cause of medical education" unless their giving is guided by the private practice medical profession.

85. *Basic Data Relating to the National Institutes of Health,* 1977 ed.

86. American Foundation, *Medical Research,* vol. I, 11, 108–10, 132.

87. *Basic Data Relating to the National Institutes of Health,* 1974 and 1977 eds.

88. *Forward Plan for Health, FY 1978–82,* p. 97; Daniel S. Greenberg, " 'New Broom' at the Cancer Institute?" *New England Journal of Medicine,* 297 (1977), 679–80; Samuel S. Epstein, "Environmental Determinants of Human Cancer," *Cancer Research,* 34 (1974), 2425–35; and *Los Angeles Times,* Sept. 12, 1978.

89. Greenberg, " 'New Broom' "; and Greenberg, "The 'War on Cancer': Official Fictions and Harsh Facts," *Science and Government Report,* 4 (Dec. 1, 1974), 1–3. See also *Forward Plan for Health, FY 1978–82,* p. 97. Other researchers have concluded that some of the improvements in cancer survival rates with most kinds of therapy are due to deficient tumor registry methods: Ralph D. Reynolds et al., "Survival in Lung Cancer," *Western Journal of Medicine,* 127 (1977), 190–94. There have been some notable improvements in detection and treatment of cancer (particularly for Hodgkin's disease and childhood leukemia), but these have had very little impact on overall cancer mortality and, of course, no impact on the incidence of cancer.

90. *Forward Plan for Health, FY 1978–82,* p. 96; and Vicente Navarro, "The Underdevelopment of Health in Working America: Causes, Consequences, and Possible Solutions," *American Journal of Public Health,* 66 (1976), 538–47.

91. Zachary Y. Dyckman, *A Study of Physicians' Fees* (Washington, D.C.: President's Council on Wage and Price Stability, 1978), pp. 74–75.

92. Office of Technology Assessment, *Development of Medical Technology,* pp. 80–87; *Basic Data Relating to the National Institutes of Health,* 1977 ed.

93. Office of Technology Assessment, *Development of Medical Technology,* pp. 80–81 and 85; see also Milton Silverman and Philip R. Lee, *Pills, Profits, and Politics* (Berkeley: University of California Press, 1974).

94. Office of Technology Assessment, *Development of Medical Technology,* pp. 11, 27.

95. Ibid., pp. 11–13, 20, 27. See also James L. Goddard, "The Medical Business," in *Scientific American,* eds., *Life and Death and Medicine* (San Francisco: W. H. Freeman and Co., 1973), pp. 120–25; David A. Loehwing, "Biomedical Technology—All Systems Are Go," *Barron's,* Nov. 5, 1973; and Loehwing, "Biomedicine Abounds in Risks as Well as Rewards," *Barron's,* Nov. 12, 1973; and Eliot Marshall, "Rendezvous with a Machine," *New Republic,* March 19, 1977, pp. 16–19.

96. David E. Rogers, "On Technologic Restraint," *Archives of Internal Medicine,* 135 (1975), 1393–97.

97. Anne R. Somers, "Health Care and the Political System: The Sorcerer's Apprentice Revisited," in *Technology and Health Care Systems in the 1980s* (Rockville, Md.: National Center for Health Services Research and Development, 1973), p. 39.

98. *Basic Data Relating to the National Institutes of Health,* 1974 and 1977 eds.

99. Victor R. Fuchs, "The Growing Demand for Medical Care," *New England Journal of Medicine,* 279 (1968), 190–95.

100. Dubos, *Mirage of Health.*

101. Ivan Illich, *Medical Nemesis: The Expropriation of Health* (New York: Pantheon, 1976).

102. Marc Lalonde, *A New Perspective on the Health of Canadians* (Ottawa: Government of Canada, 1974).

103. On the limits of modern medicine, in addition to Illich, see A. L. Cochrane, *Effectiveness and Efficiency: Random Reflections on Health Services* (London: Nuffield Provincial Hospital Trust, 1972); Rick J. Carlson, *The End of Medicine* (New York: John Wiley, 1975); Victor Fuchs, *Who Shall Live? Health, Economics, and Social Choice* (New York: Basic Books, 1974); McKeown, "Conceptual Background"; McKeown, *Medicine in Modern Society;* and Powles, "On the Limitations of Modern Medicine." On medicine as social control, in addition to Illich, see Barbara Ehrenreich and John Ehrenreich, "Medicine and Social Control," and Irving Kenneth Zola, "Medicine as an Institution of Social Control," both reprinted in John Ehrenreich, ed., *The Cultural Crisis of Modern Medicine* (New York: Monthly Review Press, 1978), pp. 39–79 and 80–100, respectively; Waitzkin and Waterman, *Exploitation of Illness,* pp. 16–65. See also the classic works of Talcott Parsons, *The Social System* (New York: Free Press, 1951), and "Definitions of Health and Illness in the Light of American Values and Social Structure," in E. G. Jaco, ed., *Patients, Physicians, and Illness,* 2nd ed. (New York: Free Press, 1972), pp. 107–127; and of Thomas Szasz, *The Myth of Mental Illness* (New York: Harper and Row, 1961).

104. Nedra B. Belloc and Lester Breslow, "Relationship of Physical Health Status and Health Practices," *Preventive Medicine,* 1 (1972), 409–21.

105. Fuchs, *Who Shall Live?* p. 46. For some epidemiological evidence to the contrary, see discussion earlier in this chapter (pp. 219–23) and accompanying references.

106. For critical reviews of this literature, see Robert Crawford, "You Are Dangerous to Your Health: The Ideology and Politics of Victim Blaming," *International Journal of Health Services,* 7 (1977), 663–80; Navarro, *Medicine Under Capitalism,* pp. 103–31; and Howard S. Berliner, "Emerging Ideologies in Medicine," *Review of Radical Political Economics,* 9 (Spring 1977), 116–24.

107. J. W. Meigs, "Can Occupational Health Concepts Help Us Deal with Childhood Lead Poisoning?" *American Journal of Public Health,* 62 (1972), 1483–85.

108. Pranab Chatterjee and Judith H. Gettman, "Lead Poisoning: Subculture as a Facilitating Agent?" *American Journal of Clinical Nutrition,* 25 (1972), 324–30.

109. *Conference on Future Directions in Health Care: The Dimensions of Medicine,* Sponsored by Blue Cross Association, Rockefeller Foundation, and University of California (San Francisco) Health Policy Program, New York, Dec. 1975, pp. 4–5.

110. Ibid., pp. 2–3.

111. Fuchs, *Who Shall Live?* p. 27.

112. Leon R. Kass, "Regarding the End of Medicine and the Pursuit of Health," *Public Interest*, no. 40 (Summer 1975), 39, 42.

113. See, for example, E. A. Suchman, "Social Patterns of Illness and Medical Care," in E. G. Jaco, ed., *Patients, Physicians, and Illness*, pp. 262–79; S. S. Kegeles et al., "Survey of Beliefs About Cancer Detection and Taking Papanicolaou Test," *Public Health Reports*, 80 (1965), 815–24; and W. A. Wingert et al., "Effectiveness and Efficiency of Indigenous Health Aids in a Pediatric Outpatient Department," *American Journal of Public Health, $a65 (1975), 849–57.

114. M. R. Greenlick et al., "Comparing the Use of Medical Care Services by a Medically Indigent and a General Membership Population in a Comprehensive Prepaid Group Practice Program," *Medical Care*, 10 (1972), 187–200; Alpert et al., "Delivery of Health Care for Children"; R. J. Haggerty, K. J. Roghmann, and I. B. Pless, *Child Health and the Community* (New York: John Wiley, 1975); and C. H. Goodrich, M. Olendzki, and G. Reader, *Welfare Medical Care: An Experiment* (Cambridge, Mass.: Harvard University Press, 1970). See also C. K. Reissman, "The Use of Health Services by the Poor," *Social Policy*, 5 (May–June 1974), 41–49; and John B. McKinlay and Diana B. Dutton, "Social-Psychological Factors Affecting Health Service Utilization," in S. J. Mushkin, ed., *Consumer Incentives for Health Care* (New York: Prodist, 1974), pp. 251–303, for reviews of the issue and the literature. The myths about why patients break medical appointments are corrected in Philip Hertz and Paula L. Stamps, "Appointment-Keeping Behavior Re-Evaluated," *American Journal of Public Health*, 67 (1977), 1033–36.

115. For an example of such a program, see the article by California Governor Ronald Reagan's head of the state's Health and Welfare Agency, Earl W. Brian, "Government Control of Hospital Utilization—A California Experience," *New England Journal of Medicine*, 286 (1972), 1340–44.

116. C. Arden Miller, "Societal Change and Public Health: A Rediscovery," *American Journal of Public Health*, 66 (1976), 54–60.

117. See Crawford, "You Are Dangerous to Your Health," pp. 673–74, especially quote from former UAW president Leonard Woodcock. For another example of such a program, see report on the Department of Labor's "Employee Health Program," an alcohol treatment program designed to "stabilize work behavior," in C. J. Schramm, "Measuring the Return on Program Costs: Evaluation of a Multi-Employer Alcoholism Treatment Program," *American Journal of Public Health*, 67 (1977), 50–51.

118. E. Richard Brown and Glen E. Margo, "Health Education: Can the Reformers Be Reformed?" *International Journal of Health Services*, 8 (1978), 3–26.

Index

hiring A. Flexner, 144
medical profession interests and,
152–53
role in Carnegie Foundation, 53, 58–59
role in medical education reform, 189
Professional-managerial stratum
development, 9, 14, 51, 58–59, 192
philanthropy and, 51, 186
rationalization of medical care and,
204, 208
Progressive movement and party, 49, 117,
126, 131, 132, 168, 169, 174, 191,
200, 201
Public health programs, 47–48, 103,
115–17, 124
Public health school, first in U.S., 103,
129
Public Health Service, United States, 225
Pusey, Robert, 79

Railroads, 15–16
Rauscher, Frank J., Jr., 229–30
Rationalization
in industry, 51
in medical care, 6–9, 193–96, 199–203,
204–12, 237, 239–41
defined, 6, 8
full-time plan and, 175
private practitioners and, 191
Reader, W. J., 85
Reductionism in medicine, 10, 75,
119–22, 127–30, 133, 228–31
see also Scientific medicine; Technology in medicine
Reed, Charles A. L., 84, 90, 137
Religion, 31–40 *passim,* 64, 105, 121,
122–25, 127
Rensselaer Polytechnic Institute, 27, 29
Roberts, John B., 125
Robert Wood Johnson Foundation, 206,
210
Rockefeller, David, 187
Rockefeller, John D.
attacks on, 49, 168–70, 182
attitude toward science, 110–11
Baptist church and, 32–33, 34, 123
Commission on Industrial Relations
and, 170
contrasted with his son and Gates, 42
Gates and, 34–37, 41, 43, 54
gifts to
General Education Board, 46, 49,

50, 165, 176–77, 179
Rockefeller Foundation, 49
Rockefeller Institute, 104, 105, 108
University of Chicago, 56
growth of fortune, 15–16
homeopathy and, 109–11
innovations in industry, 52
philanthropy and, 9, 18, 32–33, 35–36,
52
Pocantico Hills estate, 20
politics and, 19
poor health, 35
Rockefeller Institute and, 49, 105–09
role in Rockefeller philanthropies,
41–42, 50–51, 111
and his son, 41–42, 56
Standard Oil Co. and, 35
University of Chicago and, 34–35,
56–57, 180
views on wealth and poverty, 33, 43
Rockefeller, John D., Jr., 52, 56
Commission on Industrial Relations
and, 170
contrasted with his father and Gates, 42
corporate liberalism and, 54–55, 187
and his father, 41–42, 56
first public health school in U.S. and,
129
Gates and, 41–42, 54–55
on Gates' role in General Education
Board, 48, 111
origins of General Education Board
and, 46, 49
professional-managerial stratum and,
52
role in Rockefeller philanthropies,
41–42, 51, 54, 56, 111
in Rockefeller Institute, 107–09
in Rockefeller Sanitary Commission,
116
on philanthropy, 52
Southern education movement and, 44,
46
on state universities, 184, 186
Rockefeller Foundation, 195, 206
attacks on, 169–70
charter problems, 169
full-time plan and, 173, 176, 227
gifts from Rockefeller, 49
grants to medical schools, 189
political uses of medicine, 122, 124,
129

medical research and, 76–77, 225–232, 234

medical technology and, 218

national health insurance and, 217–18

rationalization of medical care and, 200–03, 207–12, 218

role in medicine, 8, 9, 12, 195, 205, 239–40

State universities, 11, 47, 53–54, 177–87

Stevens, Rosemary, 99, 162, 193

Stevens Institute, 27

Stiles, Charles Wardell, 115–16, 129–30

Stokes, Anson Phelps, 171, 174

Surgery, 92, 214

Sweden, 221

Tarbell, Ida, 49, 168

Taylor, Frederick W., 126

Technological determinism, 2–4, 126
Marxist critique of, 3

Technology in medicine, 3, 239–40
corporate class and, 4, 228–31
costs, 233–34
decline in support, 234–38
health work force and, 6
impact on health status, 223–25
medical technology industry, 204–05, 231–33, 239
physicians incomes and, 6, 232
role in medical system, 198, 215

Topping, John, 115

Tuberculosis, 220, 223, 225

Tucker, William Jewett, 32

Tulane University, 27

Tuskegee Institute, 44, 45

Universities. *See* Higher education; State universities; *specific universities by name*

University of Chicago, 34–35, 56–57, 179
full-time plan and, 165, 175
Rush medical college and, 107, 109

University of Cincinnati, 183

University of Colorado, 183

University of Georgia, 183

University of Iowa, 177, 183, 184

University of Michigan, 153

University of Oregon, 183

University of Pennsylvania, 27, 61, 72–73

Van Rensselaer, Stephen, 27

Vanderbilt family, 20

Vanderbilt University, 27, 165, 175

Vaughan, Victor C., 150, 161

Villermé, Louis René, 127

Vincent, George, 124, 171, 184

Virchow, Rudolf, 72, 127

Wall, Joseph F., 52

Walsh, Frank, 170

Wanamaker, John, 44

Warner, Amos, 22

Washington, Booker T., 45, 247*n*69

Washington University at St. Louis, 165, 175

Watson, Tom, 18

Welch, William H., 86, 111, 112, 145, 156, 157
AMA and, 191
career, 102–04
desire for career in research, 81–82, 159
on economic benefits of medicine, 118
first pathology laboratory in U.S., 72
first public health school in U.S. and, 103, 129
full-time plan and, 164–65
Gates and, 103
on private practitioners, 191
Rockefeller medical philanthropies and, 103–04, 108

Wharton, Joseph, 27

Wilbur, Ray Lyman, 264*n*4

Wilensky, Harold, 68–69

Wiley, Harvey, 251*n*40

Williams, William Appleman, 58

Wilson, Charles, 240

Wilson, President Woodrow, 170

Winkelstein, Warren, 222

Women in medicine, 88, 96, 149, 154

Workers
conditions, 16–17, 23, 114–16, 220
development of industrial work force, 16
Gates on workers, 130–32
health status, 113, 116–19, 220, 222–23, 230, 231, 238
occupational cancer, 229
see also Labor unrest and organizing

Yale Scientific School, 26

Yale University, 26, 72–73

Yale University medical school, 165, 175

Zinsser, Hans, 227